The Agony of the Russian Idea

The Agony of the Russian Idea

Tim McDaniel

PRINCETON UNIVERSITY PRESS

PRINCETON, NEW JERSEY

Library of Congress Cataloging-in-Publication Data

McDaniel, Tim.
The Agony of the Russian idea / Tim McDaniel.
p.   cm.
Includes bibliographical references and index.
ISBN 0-691-02786-2
ISBN 0-691-00248-7 (pbk.)
1. Russia (Federation)—Civilization. 2. Post-communism—
Russia (Federation) 3. Political culture—Russia (Federation)—
History. 4. Russia (Federation)—Politics and government.
5. Russia (Federation)—Social conditions. 6. Soviet Union—
Social conditions. 7. Communism—Soviet Union.
8. Russia (Federation)—Civilization—Public opinion.
9. Public opinion—Russia (Federation) I. Title.
DK510.762.M4 1996
947.08—dc20   95-53191

This book has been composed in Baskerville

Third printing, and first paperback printing, 1998

http://pup.princeton.edu

Printed in the United States of America
10   9   8   7   6   5   4   3

For Marina Kozlova, Vladimir Kozlov,
Alexander Krotov, and Mikhail Puchkov

With great affection

Contents

Acknowledgments

From the fall of 1991 to the summer of 1993 I was director of the University of California program in St. Petersburg. I received so much help during that time that I do not know where to begin my acknowledgments. Aside from the four people to whom this book is dedicated, who know that I have no words to express my gratitude, I would like to begin by thanking the people at the central University of California Education Abroad Program, including the director John Marcum and especially Rodney Sangster, whose advice, support, and humor in very difficult times were indispensable to me. My successor as director in Russia, Arch Getty, freely gave of his vast store of experience when it was very much needed.

I should also mention many of my California students in Russia, especially, in no particular order, Jennifer Flaim, Hilary Stockton, Mark Paskowitz, Judy Chase, Lisa Buckley, Donna Tsifrin, Bill Herkelrath, Chris Dargis, Darren Hartzler (who was my *starosta*), Glenn Davenport, John Kenyon, Dan Ahern, and Matt McClure. I am sure I have left out someone that I should not have.

Over the years I have given many talks on Russian themes to public groups in San Diego. I would particularly like to thank the La Jolla Rotary Club for their hospitality and intelligent questions on several occasions. Provost Pat Ledden's Muir College faculty seminars got me thinking about these themes in a much more systematic way. Peter Kenez, from the Santa Cruz campus of the University of California, kindly invited me to participate in a conference comparing contemporary Russia and Weimar Germany. The discussions and comments on my paper helped sharpen the arguments in the final chapter.

On the Russian side I would like to thank at least the following people, among the dozens whom I ideally should mention: Vera P. Puchkova, Gennady Bordiugov, Boris Marushevsky, Valentina Frolova, Natalya Slepokurova, Natalya Fyodorova, Irina Lysakova, Leonid Gordon, Yuri Puchkov, Viktor Danilenko, Galina Volosova, Boris Andreyev, Alexander Etkind, Vil Bakirov, and Sergei Agapanov.

Among my friends and colleagues, I would like to thank Victoria Bonnell, Harvey Goldman, Andy Scull, Ramon Gutierrez, Ali Gheissari, Dan Levy, Jeff Haydu, Rick Biernacki, Jerry Doppelt, Peter Gourevitch, and Steve Cox for their continuing support and friendship. Some took the trouble to read the entire manuscript. Their collective comments and encouragement much improved it. It was Steve Cox who convinced me that I might be able to write the kind of book that is now before you. Barbara Stewart and Trisha Stewart (no relation) read much of the manuscript and gave their sensitive impressions. They have also helped in countless other ways, almost always being patient with a boss (me) who had too many things to do at the same time. Vladimir Oboronko gave me very beneficial research assistance during the writing of this book, and he and his wife Julia tried to make sure that I wasn't responsible for too many "cranberries," as the Russians say when someone has gotten something all wrong about their country.

Neil Smelser has been a source of personal and professional inspiration to me, as for all sociologists who want to study large-scale social change. Stanley Holwitz gave much needed advice and guidance from the very inception of this book. Professors Abbott Gleason of Brown and Daniel Chirot of the University of Washington read the manuscript for the press. Their comments were a model of careful criticism, and the book is far better for their efforts. I am pleased to express my gratitude to them.

Anita O'Brien made excellent editorial suggestions. Michelle McKenna at Princeton University Press worked with me on the manuscript with humor and efficiency. Peter Dougherty, social science and public affairs publisher at Princeton University Press, knows everything about how to publish a scholarly book. I am glad that this book could count on his stewardship.

The Agony of the Russian Idea

Cycles of Breakdown in Russia

FOR MANY DECADES young minds in the Soviet Union were taught to think in terms of "historical necessity." The worldwide crisis, and then collapse, of capitalism, followed by the triumph of the purer principles of Communism, was "necessary" both scientifically (in terms of the laws of history) and morally (in terms of the realization of human needs). It took Communist rulers many decades to recognize officially that their capitalist rivals seemed likely to survive for the foreseeable future and so had to be reckoned with in a system of "peaceful coexistence." Even later, it was one of the many ideological innovations of the Gorbachev period to recognize that there were shared values between the Communist and capitalist systems (previously the idea of convergence had been anathema) and that the Soviet Union actually had much to learn from the capitalist West.

The collapse of Communism in its Soviet and East European heartland, together with its disarray in Cuba and China, seems to give force to another vision of historical necessity: the inevitable collapse of any type of society other than liberal capitalist democracy. Twenty years ago such a postulate would have been greeted with widespread incredulity. For the common wisdom during the years of détente held that Communism, and Soviet Communism in particular, embodied the logic of a viable alternative form of modern society. Whereas the capitalist West—so went the common wisdom—was based upon private property, the market, and the large corporation, modern Communism was based upon state control and initiative. Although both systems had their various flaws, it was widely held that modern capitalism and Communism had alike developed reasonable solutions to the problems of political order and economic progress.

Although both Marxist and contemporary Western concepts of historical necessity are rooted in the idea of progress, there is in fact no necessary connection between a deterministic theory of history and the notion that history has a moral meaning and an upward trajectory. From Ibn Khaldun in medieval Islamic thought to Chinese theories of dynastic decay to Spenglerian or Toynbeeian visions of historical cycles, there have been innumerable nonlinear visions of historical change. According to these views the collapse of a particular system does not imply that it was somehow out of step with history, or that the succeeding regime or system will somehow embody a higher set of principles.

But with the near universal collapse of Communist systems, it is tempting indeed to impute both scientific and moral meaning to these great events. For if Communism fails not just in one case or two, but everywhere, regardless of cultural differences or variations in economic performance, the explanation sought may be of broad and lawlike significance. And from here it is a short step to full-fledged espousal of the idea of progress, perhaps the most tenacious and ineradicable social and political assumption of the modern age.

It was almost inevitable that the assumptions underlying the idea of progress would be applied to the collapse of worldwide Communism. Perhaps coteries of scholars can discipline themselves to separate "fact" and "value" radically, thus refusing to conflate scientific analysis and moral vision. But for the public at large, and among them many scholars as well, the demise of Communism was due to its failure as a type of modern society. Not the ineptitude of particular leaders or the chance conjunction of unforeseen events lay behind Communism's collapse, but the cardinal fact that it was out of step with "progress." It smothered economic innovation, violated individual rights, impeded the development of science, frustrated the aspirations of the educated sectors of society: such is the indictment of modern Communism in the court of "progress."

The assumption of progress thus implies that certain ideas and practices, certain groups and individuals, are being stifled, artificially held back. In the next stage—for all theories of progress postulate a series of vertical stages—these new sources of creativity will be able to operate in greater freedom. For despite Communism's inability to come to terms with the requirements of modernity, advocates of the Western version of progress often maintain that Communism inadvertently gave rise to creative new forces, including a professional middle class and a cosmopolitan cultural elite, that would be the foundation for movement forward. Just as it could be said that the germs of a modern capitalist class and state bureaucracy had developed within the framework of feudal society in Europe, so optimists discerned the integument of a truly "mature" form of modern society within Communism. If one instinctively believed in progress, if one felt that there was a necessary logic of modern society, the collapse of Communism could not merely be decay. There had to be something there to replace it, for otherwise it could not have collapsed. Social change, after all, takes place in stages, one system replacing another according to the logic of progress.

For reasons that should become increasingly clear throughout this book, from this point on I will write of Russia and the Soviet Union rather than Communism in general. For I do not believe that there has been a grand historical logic in the collapse of Communism, nor do I think that the transition to some other social and political condition follows some innate laws of historical development. Half a decade has passed since Soviet Communism faded into oblivion, and it is time to put to rest some comforting illusions. Russia is not moving along the path of Western progress. Soviet Communism has not been succeeded by some kind of higher stage. No social groups or political forces committed to economic and political Westernization or able to carry out such a project ever matured within the Communist system, nor do they exist now. Instead of imposing our own wishful assumptions about progress, we need to understand the kind of society that did exist, why it exhausted itself, and the reasons that it did not engender any short- or medium-term alternatives.

Russia has been in turmoil for a longer period than our own Civil War, and if one counts the heady years of Gorbachev, for a longer time period than even the Russian Revolution and civil war from 1917 to 1924. Unbelievable price increases and currency devaluations have destroyed lifetime savings (in the fall of 1991, when I arrived in St. Petersburg a few days after the coup, there were roughly 30 rubles to the dollar; now the figure is approximately 4,500 to the dollar) and drastically undermined the position of virtually all salaried government workers. Crime, both random street violence and organized criminal activity, has led Muscovites and Petersburgers to compare their cities to Chicago in the 1920s. The president, who enjoys almost no public confidence, has dissolved the Supreme Court and ordered an attack on the Parliament. A humiliating and bloody war has been waged against tiny Chechnya in the northern Caucasus.

Yet, outside appearances to the contrary, the turmoil of Russia in the 1990s has seldom been dramatic, even if often violent. Rather, it has been accompanied by a deadening sense of fatality, for hope and optimism about the future are rare. I well recall the utter indifference with which the public greeted the escalating tension between President Yeltsin and the Russian Parliament throughout 1992 and 1993, events that from the outside seemed fascinating and dramatic. Nor is there a sense of lost historical opportunities for positive social change (even though these certainly existed), but a crushing sensation of the absence of possibilities.

Apathy born of hopelessness characterized the public mood in Russia even in the aftermath of the collapse of the Communist system, widely touted in the West as a democratic revolution. I arrived in St. Petersburg three days after the August "revolution" and was immediately struck by the absence of euphoria. I knew well that the collapse of the Russian monarchy in February 1917 had given birth to a short-lived, but real, period of jubilation and heightened hopes. Yet it was premature disenchantment that I sensed almost everywhere in the fall of 1991.

The unexpectedly somber mood of the city was especially palpable at "Democracy Wall." One of the innovations of the perestroika period in Moscow and Leningrad (as St. Petersburg was still officially named until the time of the defeated coup) was the appearance of public places where people gathered in passionate debate, where notices of upcoming meetings and events were posted, and where announcements and declarations were displayed prominently. In St. Petersburg this place was a large wall near Gostinnyi Dvor, the old merchant quarters in the center of the city that had also served as the main department store during the Communist period. For a short time it was named, according to the Chinese example, "Democracy Wall." Subsequently sellers of soft drinks and souvenirs and peddlers of nationalist propaganda would vie for this spot. I was surprised and dismayed by the bitter and hopeless tone of many of the signs that appeared at this shrine of glasnost every day. Here is a "declaration to the Russian people" that I took down in early October 1991:

> You really think that you got rid of the party, which oppressed you for so many years. In fact, the party threw you out when it saw there was nothing more to take from you. It fled, stealing what it could. Poor slaves, you won't be able to find another master. In the twentieth century, slaves are of no use to anyone. It's better to be a farmer in Texas than president of this country.

Here is bitter testimony that the victory of "democracy" was often interpreted as the abandonment of the people.

My subsequent two years in Russia did nothing to disconfirm my initial impressions of a reigning mood of cynicism and apathy. During this period, I managed to visit more of Russia than I had ever been able to see during my many previous trips and stays. Travel restrictions had been largely lifted, though there remained the truly vexing problems of tickets and places to stay. Through friends I was able to go to previously forbidden areas like the southern Urals, closed because of the huge number of military bases and research centers in the region. I did not see, or try to see, any of these bases, but I did visit some decaying old centers of the Soviet metallurgical industry, where I talked, as everywhere, with a wide variety of people, many of whom warmly received me into their homes. Some of the people I stayed with possessed geiger counters, fearful of the ever-present risk of nuclear mishaps and aware that the atmosphere was frequently radioactive to an unhealthy degree. Almost all of the people I met and stayed with spoke with disarming frankness.

I also made trips to western Siberia, a large number of other Russian cities, and numerous Russian villages in different parts of the country. Within the cities, particularly Moscow and St. Petersburg, where I have close friends, I visited factories, sports establishments, public schools, theological seminaries, fire and police stations, academic institutions of every description, the offices of political parties and social organizations, and several weddings and funerals: in short, everywhere I could go. Almost everywhere I went I found similar sentiments of bewilderment, powerlessness, and betrayal. Hope was by no means absent, but it was expressed against a general background of despair about the past of the country and a poignant questioning of its future. Even the minority of people profiting from the new opportunities opened up by the collapse of the old system were often highly pessimistic about the future.

Let me share some representative examples. I remember my conversations with a retired chief engineer at a leading shipbuilding plant in St. Petersburg, a man who now felt that his life's work had come to naught because of the general disorganization in the country and the disheartening state of the factory that he had worked all his life to help build. This bitter old man, once an enthusiast of socialist construction, told me that the great majority of intelligent Russians would support the only conceivable positive outcome for their country: that it should become a colony of the United States.

A movie director friend of mine, whom I have known for many years, analyzed the situation in late 1991 as follows: Before, he said, we were like animals in the zoo. They fed us, cleaned up our messes, fed us again. Now they've opened the cages and told us that we're free. But we, helpless animals that we are, don't know how to take care of ourselves and only soil ourselves and each other.

Numerous times I was told, including by one of the country's most prominent psychiatrists, that the fundamental problem in the country was the destruction, throughout the years of Communist rule, of all the intelligence of the country, leaving a depleted gene pool. I also know of an internationally known biological scientist who holds this view, and I have a published interview with a prominent figure of the intelligentsia who stated the same scientifically questionable opinion.

Perhaps most vivid in my memory is a conversation with an old man of peasant background, who, as the son and brother of so-called rich peasants murdered in the Stalin period by the government, suffered greatly throughout the Soviet regime. After the murder of his family, he was blacklisted from work for many years and had to use his wits to survive. He had fought in the defense of Moscow in World War II. He now lives in a largely rural area several hours by train from St. Petersburg, where he has used his great talent and energy to build a house incorporating all kinds of his own inventions. After a long recount of his incredibly painful and rich life experiences, he looked at me and said: the worse thing is that we have nothing to give to the young, and to future generations. What is the benefit from all this? We worked all our lives, and we can give nothing. But perhaps what we can give is a lesson: that this was all senseless, and that these socialist ideas go nowhere. Otherwise unable to see how this worthless past would provide a bridge to the future, he looked upon the country's prospects with trepidation.

My reference to his participation in the war brings to mind another poignant reminiscence. Close friends of mine told me that their father, decorated during the war for his sacrifices, was unwilling to wear his medals to his grandson's wedding. (Those who visited the Soviet Union before the perestroika period will recall with what pride veterans, both men and women, displayed their chestfuls of medals.) He was aware that young people only thought him foolish for having fought for Stalin. In this connection I was often told that young people look with condescension at the older generation, whom they regard as little more than dupes of history, willing accomplices in a past that must be completely rejected.

Our optimistic believer in progress might attempt to explain away the bleak mood pervading the country through the following line of argument. Such forebodings are inevitable during transition periods, but the predictable and entirely natural difficulties should not be allowed to obscure the overall course of events. In 1917, after Russia had been exhausted by several years of war, Communist leaders took power in Russia and initiated a catastrophic experiment that led the country, after seven decades, to a moral, political, and economic dead end. At the first breath of real freedom, during the perestroika period, people became aware of the historical catastrophe imposed upon them by the Communist regime and began to understand what kind of alternative society they should seek. There was then revealed and there remains today broad public support for Western-style capitalism and democracy. In the meantime, there will be a painful transitional period when the new and the old struggle against each other. But because Russia can no longer depart from the overall course of world civilization and because social modernization has created the necessary prerequisites, especially an educated middle class, the new society will eventually emerge. Meanwhile, during the transition period there will be great ugliness, inevitable because of the distortions of the Communist regime. It will be parallel to the process that Marx called the "primitive accumulation of capital" in pre-nineteenth-century Europe: the nascent capitalist class used every form of violence and deception to accumulate property, which later became the basis for capitalist modernization. Russia, too, for the time being must undergo such a trial by fire, partly in payment for the historical errors of past generations.

I heard this interpretation of contemporary events innumerable times in the two years that I lived in Russia. My reactions to it were always complicated, for it is both repellent and comforting. It is repellent because it can be, and I have heard it, used to justify any form of inequality or despoilment as the necessary part of an eventually favorable transition. Because of this logic, lamented an article published in *Komsomolskaia pravda*, one of the largest-circulation newspapers in the country, emphasis on important moral qualities like honesty has disappeared from public discussion in contemporary Russia. After all, what can be done when the country is only on the threshold of civilized society?[1] Similarly, in factories that I visited I heard the presumed rigors of the transitional period used to justify breeches of industrial safety or horrendous pollution of the environment: now is not the time, I was told, to address these secondary issues.

On the other hand, the image is comforting, in the same way as the Stalinist assurance that after a generation or two of socialist construction temporary deprivations would end and a society of abundance would be created. In this sense, it is one of many contemporary ideas reminiscent of the logic of the Bolsheviks. Another is the idea frequent among radical democrats that the worthless traits of the old system must be completely negated in order to build the new. No matter how paltry the moral vision embodied in the model of the cruel, but passing, transition period, it is certainly true that contemporary Russians need some set of goals to believe in.

And yet the faith that Russia will eventually return to the folds of world civilization threatens to obscure under the cover of a false universalism the most truly pressing contemporary question: why, as compared with the other post-Communist countries, have the positive results and achievements of post-1991 Russia thus far been so negligible? For surely five years is sufficient time to permit us to render a harsh indictment of the new Russia. How, after such a significant period, can there still be no authoritative political parties, institutions, or leaders, none that garner even a marginally respectable degree of support? In the economic realm, how can the country continue to live by international trade in primary materials, contraband, and speculation rather than by production? Why is it that so many people, from all walks of life, continue to wonder whether the country has any future? "Will the Russians not repeat the fate of the Assyrians, the Huns, the Mongols? Starting already from the next century will they not exist in the form of dispersed fragments, a pale shadow of a once great people?"[2]

"Whither goes Russia?": this is the title of the 1994 book from which this quotation is taken. It echoes, no doubt consciously, the famous peroration at the end of Nikolai Gogol's *Dead Souls*, that monument of Russian cultural self-definition:

> Whither art thou soaring away to, then, Russia? Give me thy answer! But Russia gives none. With a wondrous ring does the jingle-bell trill; the air, rent to shreds, thunders and turns to wind; all things on earth fly past and, eyeing it askance, all the other peoples and nations stand aside and give it the right of way.[3]

This question of Russia's historic destiny as a nation among "all the other peoples and nations" has been a central preoccupation of Russian social and literary thought for the last two centuries. Beginning with Peter the Great's Westernizing reforms, which, in the words of the philosopher Georgy Fedotov, "succeeded in sundering Russia for centuries,"[4] Russian writers and thinkers have posed the same searching questions with unparalleled intensity. What is distinctive about Russians as a people? Where does the country fit into the scheme of world civilization? Are its culture and institutions a precious legacy to the rest of the world, a potential model for the future of mankind, or should what is distinctively Russian be abandoned in the name of a higher vision of progress?

With remarkable continuity and consistency the responses to these questions have given shape to two warring camps. Slavophiles in the early part of the nineteenth century, many revolutionary populists in its latter half, and neo-Slavophile dissidents of the Brezhnev period, including Alexander Solzhenitsyn, passionately insisted on the uniqueness and superiority of Russia. Whether they emphasized institutions such as the paternalistic state or the peasant commune, or cultural traits such as religiosity, capacity for suffering, or cultural unity, these advocates of Russian national superiority contrasted Russia's brighter future with the decay and despair of the West. For Dostoyevsky, an ardent exponent of such ideas, "the future of Europe belongs to Russia" because of the social harmony reigning in this land of popular satisfaction.[5]

For such defenders of Russian tradition, the evil comes from without—from the West and from those Russian rulers and intellectuals, foreign to the people, who would recast Russian institutions in the West's image. Peter the Great and the Communists, the latter seen as representatives of Western rationalistic ideology, are the great villains of Russian history. For the famous twentieth-century émigré philosopher Ivan Ilyin, for example, the sin of the Bolsheviks was that they understood nothing about Russia and did not see its particularities and "national tasks." They decided "to rape it politically" according to European schemas.[6]

In the broadest sense, this is the meaning of "the Russian idea": the conviction that Russia has its own independent, self-sufficient, and eminently worthy cultural and historical tradition that both sets it apart from the West and guarantees its future flourishing. Characteristically contrasting Europe and Russia, the influential Slavophile Khomiakov declared that while Europe must reject its own unfortunate past and construct on the basis of entirely new principles if it is to prosper in the future, Russia had the advantage of a rich and fruitful heritage. This heritage of beliefs, centered on Orthodox Christianity, and of institutions, primarily the peasant commune and a powerful all-protecting state, only had to be brought back to consciousness and then to life among the people for Russia to prosper.[7] Quite opposite to what actually occurred historically, proponents of the Russian idea believed that Europe would be the arena of social rupture and revolution in the near future, whereas Russia would be blessed by harmony and continuity.

The specific tenets of the Russian idea will be more fully elaborated in the next chapter. Here I need only specify that this broad usage encompasses much more than the meaning given to the phrase by the renowned Russian philosopher Nikolai Berdyaev in his influential book *The Russian Idea*. Seeking to uncover the cultural connections between Bolshevism and earlier Russian religious and ideological traditions, Berdyaev argued that there was a specifically Russian eschatological and messianic idea of the ethical transformation of society. This Russian idea, "the vocation of the Russian people," was inherently religious and maximalist, leading Russians to seek to establish purer forms of community. "The Russian people, in accordance with its eternal Idea, has no love for the ordering of this earthly city and struggles toward a city that is to come, towards the new Jerusalem."[8]

Although my broader usage of the term may be confusing to those who identify the concept with Berdyaev's work, it corresponds to the meaning current in Russia. In present-day discussion of the historical destiny of Russia, Berdyaev is only one among a great many exponents of the Russian idea. For example, in recent years there have appeared two major anthologies entitled *The Russian Idea*, one of them devoted to classical writings, the other a two-volume compilation of specifically émigré works. In addition, the philosopher Arsenii Gulyga has recently published a study, *The Russian Idea and Its Creators*,[9] that gives brief sketches of the ideas of thirteen leading Russian thinkers in this tradition, from Dostoyevsky and Vladimir Solovyev to Berdyaev and Ilyin. Although these works admirably demonstrate the diversity of conceptions of the Russian idea, some of them close to Berdyaev's usage, some quite distant, it is fair to say that all these thinkers insist on the specificities of Russian culture and history and posit for Russia a separate and potentially higher form of modernity.

Since the middle decades of the 1830s, opponents of the idea of a separate and higher Russian historical destiny have been called Westernizers. Perhaps the first locus classicus of their views (which are also marked by diversity) is Vissarion Belinsky's "Letter to N. V. Gogol," in which the great writer is excoriated for his defense of serfdom and autocracy and his celebration of the religious purity of the Russian people. But, writes Belinsky, "you have failed to notice that Russia sees her salvation, not in mysticism, asceticism, or pietism, but in the advances of civilization, enlightenment, and humanism."[10]

The early Westernizers and their spiritual heirs, from the prerevolutionary liberal political movement and Marxist reformist Mensheviks to dissident opponents of Solzhenitsyn, have counterposed science, individual rights, and the rule of law both to the moral vision of the Russian idea and to those social institutions, such as the autocratic state, the peasant commune, or the Orthodox Church, that were held to embody its values. For such enlighteners, Peter the Great did not go far enough in his adoption of Western culture. And their indictment of Communism is not that it was based upon Western rationalism and atheism, but that it too quickly succumbed to Russian traditions of despotism and obscurantism. Thus, for such Westernizers, behind Stalin's collectivization of agriculture lay not Marxism "but the social and moral-psychological tradition of serfdom and the ancient communality of the 'mir.'"[11]

More broadly, a leading Russian dissident of the 1970s held that the weakness in Russia of such characteristic Western virtues as "common sense, responsibility, [and] discretion in the weighing of choices"

> does not mean, as Russians have flattered themselves for centuries, that we possess a moral nature of our own that is different from Western culture but just as valuable. On the contrary, it signifies formlessness, spiritual sloth, a dead-end existence—not mysticism, but an all-destroying mediocrity of the soul.[12]

Instead of their opponents' stress on Russian tradition, with its idealism, community, and continuity, Westernizers emphasize the emptiness and hypocrisy of the claim to a separate historical identity. The passions aroused by these debates, whether the Belinsky–Gogol or the Sakharov–Solzhenitsyn controversies, have by no means been extinguished. I attended a small conference in Moscow in late 1991, the main attraction of which was the attendance of the editors of two rival journals—one "Slavophile" and the other "Westernizer." The Slavophile editor had a long beard and a solemn and weighty presence. By appearance, his counterpart could have worked at *The New Yorker*. They could hardly bring themselves to speak to each other.

Who can deny that there has indeed been a very specific and tragic Russian historical destiny in the modern world? In his famous "Letter to Soviet Leaders," Alexander Solzhenitsyn put forth the plausible claim that the Russian nation has suffered more than any other in the twentieth century. But neither Slavophile nor Westernizer interpretation of Russian history holds the key to the tragedies of social breakdown, revolution, and civil war that have afflicted modern Russia. The Slavophiles blame the West, both for its ideas themselves and for their influence on the domestic fifth column. By contrast, the Westernizers attack the native ideas and practices that the Slavophiles celebrate, finding in them the sources of Russia's historical backwardness and breakdowns.

Paradoxically, both camps rest their case on the uniqueness of Russia. They both would agree with the first great analyst of Russian historical development, Pyotr Chaadaev, that "we never went together with other peoples."[13] But surely these claims to uniqueness, as formulated by the warring sides, are untenable as proposed. With respect to advocates of the Russian idea, it is inescapably clear that many countries have had cultural traditions and institutions similar to those they celebrate. Imperial Germany was alleged to have had a special path, more communal, imbued with belief, and regulated by a solicitous state than England or France. Theorists of Islamic or African socialism, and even Catholic corporatism, have also stressed, with some justice, the more communally oriented social patterns prevailing in their societies. The Russian idea sounds suspiciously like the German, Islamic, African ujaama, or Catholic "idea." All alike are cognate responses to the challenges of the English and American models of modern society.

Nor is Russia unique in its "lacks," as judged by the measuring rods of Western capitalist democracies. Especially in the 1960s and 1970s, armies of American scholars gave countless studies of how third world peoples lacked an ethic of achievement, a civic culture, a constitution of liberty, universalistic social patterns, and the like. In this regard it is by no means uncommon for contemporary Russians to state that their country, in its departures from the Western model, has deep resemblances to third world countries.[14]

Regarded from the standpoint of either rival camp, Russian historical change becomes both more routine and more easily comprehensible. Russia is either a "traditional" society ravaged by an alien process of modernization or a country unable to overcome its historic deficiencies and reach maturity.

As opposed to the attempt to fit Russia in general categories, I do agree with Chaadaev and the Slavophiles that there is a tragic distinctiveness about social change in Russia in the modern period. But the roots of the repeated turmoil and breakdown can be perceived only if we leave aside the polar and polemical explanations suggested by these rival camps.

Rather, what is unique about social change in Russia over the past two centuries is the yoking together of three elements that could never be assimilated to each other: the Russian idea, the despotic state, and the commitment to rapid modernization. Both the tsarist and Communist states embraced many elements of the Russian idea in order to claim a higher form of legitimacy than in the capitalist West. Similarly, many of the cultural values and institutions celebrated in the Russian idea were given prolonged, though distorted, life in the official value systems of tsarist and Communist dictatorships: equality, the primacy of community, the emphasis on belief and harmony, and the like. Finally, whatever the particular character of individual regimes, modernization in Russia and the Soviet Union was always held to conform to a higher model, thus avoiding the moral pitfalls of the Western pattern.

Thus, crucial dimensions of an alternative system of values were utilized for many decades as an ideological tool of socioeconomic modernization. And no matter how great the lack of fit between professed ideology and social practice, elements of these ideas penetrated the society, working their way into institutions and also into the consciousness of broad sectors of the population. Successive Russian rulers promoted the idea that their regimes embodied some or all of these values, and they claimed that the social, economic, and political practices stemming from them provided a model of modern society both more just and more effective than that offered by Western society.

There were periods in the last hundred years when it seemed that this synthesis of the Russian idea, modernization, and state power might indeed triumph. Particularly in the Communist period, the regime, with some successes to its credit, was able to persuade people far beyond the borders of the Soviet Union that a superior model of modernity had been discovered. But in fact, as I will argue in subsequent chapters, the state's attempt to modernize incorporating elements of this higher set of values contradicted crucial imperatives of modernization as well as the regimes' own practices. Consequently, both in the late tsarist period and the late Communist period a whole set of distortions revealed themselves: word did not correspond to deed, professed belief to actual practice. Society acquired surreal qualities; every word and act had to be interpreted, not according to face value, but in terms of the hidden meaning of events. The official hypocrisy provided no guide to the actual conduct of social affairs. Thus, elites and institutions, despite their apparent power, gave off an eerie scent of decay and had much less legitimacy than their august facades sought to convey. The society was much less solid, the political regime less stable than they seemed to be. The social world was constructed on a foundation of mendacity. Herein lies one of the fundamental sources of repeated crisis and breakdown in modern Russia.

The contradictory path of state-led modernization envisioned and justified partly through elements of the Russian idea eventuated in breakdown in both 1917 and 1991. It would be an exaggeration to argue that this uneasy synthesis of modernization and traditional elements of Russian culture, which embodied a fundamental contradiction between practice and ideas, and which also stood in tension with basic necessities of modernization, was the only cause of collapse. International events obviously played their role—for the 1917 revolution, World War I looms large; in the 1980s, the arms race and economic competition with the United States. So did the ineptness of political leaders at crucial times. If Nicholas II had been a wiser ruler willing to accept the reforms necessary for the survival of his regime, the Bolsheviks might never have taken power. If Alexei Kosygin and not Leonid Brezhnev had been general secretary of the Communist Party after the fall of Khrushchev in the late 1960s, reforms of the rigid Communist system might have given more scope for initiative, and thus more dynamism in the society.

I do not want to press my point too far: the yoking of elements of the Russian idea with state-induced modernization was not the only determinant of political crisis in both periods. Yet if we do not understand how the moral and ideological underpinnings of society were undermined through their abuse in the periods of modernization, we cannot explain the widespread sense of moral vacuum that fatefully undermined the regimes' own efforts.

The last point bears additional emphasis. What has been most important in periods of social breakdown in Russia, whether in 1917 or in 1991, has been the widespread sense of moral decay. It is this same sense of decay that has impeded attempts to reconstruct society along more humane lines. Although it is true that at one time Soviet Communism truly generated an overarching social morality, thus giving meaning and stability to social practices, in the long run the pattern of despotic modernization presented partly as an embodiment of many traditional Russian values exploded the moral foundations of the regime. People stopped believing in the system and its claims long before it fell. This erosion of belief in large part explains why this seemingly imposing political edifice collapsed with so little drama. It had almost no real defenders.

This central argument, to be fleshed out in the historical chapters of the book, has a number of controversial implications. First, from this standpoint, as compared with many more economically or politically oriented interpretations, which correspond more closely to the false universalism of the idea of progress, problems of moral vision and the experience of injustice are guiding forces of social change. Tsar Nicholas II, captive of an outmoded moral vision, was unable to perceive the new forms of social relations emerging around him. Unable to comprehend their logic, he violated the sense of justice of the new social groups created through autocratic modernization. Even more explicitly moralistic, the Communist regime was able to create a powerful new synthesis of meaning for many decades. But it was never able to reconcile the contradictions between its exalted moral claims and the practices to which they were in principle linked.

Communism, this great effort to give meaning to the everyday world, perhaps comparable in its ambition only to Protestantism in the modern era, ended by depriving both itself and quotidian activities such as work of any ethical dimension. Without a moral warrant, practices and institutions were less solid and substantial, and so more vulnerable. The effects of moral decay may be less immediately tangible than poor economic performance or political tyranny, but its corrosive effect is far more potent.

There are also several implications more specifically pertinent to the question of Russia's historical destiny. I propose that there is a central unifying theme of modern Russian history, and I argue that the same fundamental dilemmas underlay the collapse of the tsarist regime and the crisis and demise of Communism, and also that their legacy shapes the extraordinary difficulties of post-Communist reconstruction.

I also maintain that these dilemmas, born of the attempt to marry the despotic state, modernization, and the Russian idea, were unsolvable. Although the late tsarist regime and post-Stalin Communism were rich in proposals for reform, some of them of quite remarkable scope, they all failed. Obviously, if this is the case the blame cannot be ascribed solely to individual people such as Nicholas II, Count Witte, Khrushchev, or Gorbachev. Rather, a fundamental set of dilemmas, born of insurmountable contradictions, dictated that attempts at reform would always threaten the system with collapse. Until Gorbachev, Russian rulers always balked at the sight of this abyss.

Tragically, neither the late tsarist system nor late Communism was able to generate a viable alternative society in embryo, one with a new social logic and potentially authoritative new leaders, to replace the old system. In both cases, the replacement of the old regime has been twisted and painful beyond expectations. The reasons for this sterility are complex, but surely the pervasive impact of the overall moral decay must be singled out for attention. Also significant is a general paradox of tyranny: while in general it is impotent to solve the fundamental problems of a modern society, it is yet highly effective in weakening and discrediting potential alternative leadership.

The aforementioned traits give to Russian history a distinctive rhythm: a pattern of repeated social breakdown, with little capacity to build upon past failures.

It is a depressing conclusion, but one very much in line with assessments offered by some eminent contemporary Russian scholars. Yuri Lotman, a recently deceased semiotician and cultural historian, developed, together with colleagues, a particularly powerful perspective on the causes of Russian historical breakdowns. In his various books, including his last work, *Kultura i vzryv* (Culture and explosion), he argues that Russian culture, unlike the culture of the West, embodies an underlying binary logic of opposition. Without necessarily being aware of these patterns, individuals and groups conceptualize social life in terms of sets of absolute alternatives that admit of no compromise. There is no neutral ground: either one or the other must be chosen, and in this choice either one or the other must be absolutely victorious. In terms of human values, Lotman gives the following sets of polar oppositions: charity versus justice; love versus the law; personal morality versus state law; holiness versus politics. As we know from ancient literatures, particularly Greek, the Russians were not the first to perceive the tensions among these qualities. But in Russia, argues Lotman, the tendency is to present the opposition starkly: either one or the other.

A fateful corollary of binary thinking, according to Lotman, is that the victor, after utterly defeating an opponent, always tries to radically annihilate the past. The past is regarded not as the foundation of organic growth, but as the source of error that must be completely destroyed. Total destruction must precede creation, and so creation takes place in a void. Means and ends are thus separate, as the longed-for new world can only be constructed on the utter ruins of the old, which was wholly corrupt.

In his last work Lotman derives moral and political lessons from this history of tragic and ultimately self-defeating negations: Russians, and especially their political leaders, need to acquire an authentically *evolutionary* consciousness and to leave behind the past based on polarization, maximalism, and "explosions." True forward movement requires coming to terms with, and not simply rejecting, the past, for absolute rejection leads only to fruitless cycles of negation.[15]

Beyond such heartfelt appeals, Lotman is unable to explain how reversals of deep-seated cultural models can come about. Surely they are among the least tractable elements of human experience, especially since they are often hidden from awareness. Yet such cultural patterns as binary consciousness or the Russian idea may well shape social and political transitions as decisively as macroeconomic policy or international relations strategies, which get far more attention from "transitologists." If Russians and their foreign mentors do not confront these cultural and moral questions but continue to insist that the reform of Russia is primarily a technical and economic question, it is all the more likely that capitalism will continue to be wild and immoral, and that formal democracy will have a profoundly antidemocratic content.

Unfortunately, an awareness of these moral and cultural dimensions does not necessarily increase our optimism. For whatever new possibilities were opened up by the failure of the Communist attempt to create a specifically Russian path to modernity, in its wake it also left a profound skepticism about many of the traditional values of Russian life. The result is a profound sense of disorientation, palpable throughout the society.

I remember my conversation with a group of fire fighters at their firehouse in Chelyabinsk, a major city in the southern Urals. We are living in a "dark forest," they told me, and at great length they explained to me that they had a hard time accepting what was happening to them. But because they also did not understand the new situation engulfing them, they did not know what to do. The same sense of moral uncertainty led the labor activists and journalists with whom I met at the St. Petersburg offices of the labor newspaper *Solidarnost* to raise with me the question of whether Russia had a future. The same doubts pervade a moving article published shortly after the failed coup of August 1991 in one of the country's major newspapers. We need to rediscover our place in today's world, the author opined. We can no longer see ourselves as a chosen nation—we now know too much about the rest of the world. But this has meant that we have lost our national identity. We are becoming more like the third world, and society is becoming more and more polarized. We no longer have any faith.[16]

Another disheartening response to the present climate of moral vacuum is to grab whatever opportunities are currently available, without any thought of moral constraints or long-term consequences. Anyone who has spent any significant amount of time in contemporary Russia is well aware of the depressing results of such an attitude. It is especially prevalent among the younger generation, who have grown up under conditions of uncertainty and risk. I know personally a promising young artist, himself the son of a respected artist, who is now serving a jail sentence for mafia violence. I also know an extraordinarily intelligent and kind young woman, at the top of her class in a prestigious institute, who supports her aged parents through prostitution.

In the long term, escape from this atmosphere of moral confusion will require the return of a sense of national dignity. At the present time this process of collective healing is hindered by the perceived imperatives of historical inevitability mentioned earlier. The syllogism has the following structure: The West is best; we are unable to become like it; therefore our culture has no value. However, without a sense of a worthy and valid national identity, there can be no belief in a stable future. And without such a belief, people will not act in fruitful and constructive ways. Whatever its flaws, for several decades Soviet Communism did succeed in making the future seem pregnant with possibilities. What hope can there be in the nightmare of a failed Americanization?

Fortunately, of course, this sense of a worthy national cultural identity has not completely disappeared. It sometimes takes aggressive forms, which can only repeat the self-defeating logic analyzed by Lotman. But it also makes it appearance in less bombastic ways, and even if somewhat defensive, it reflects the important truth of the authentic pluralism and diversity of humanity. I very much like the following disjointed reflections of Alexander Panchenko, a leading literary scholar from St. Petersburg, member of the Academy of Sciences, and frequent commentator on Russian cultural history on television. These musings come from a newspaper interview with him in March 1993, entitled "The Left-handed Civilization."[17] (The title was inspired by a well-known story by the late-nineteenth-century writer Nikolai Leskov.)

The left-hander, Panchenko reflects, is a national hero in Russia. This is why, he explains. We left the countryside, which, in its modesty and goodness, gave us our only really satisfactory life. In the city we have always been left-handers. Our real talent has not been to create a viable urban civilization. Instead, we're a literary civilization: this is what we've done best of all.

Now we're looking for some new Viking invaders to save us. We want supermarkets and the like. But I don't want to live like a Westerner, for that kind of life is extremely boring and we don't need it. Our contemporary Calvinists [reformers of a Westernizing cast of mind] look at a person only as producer and consumer. But where is contemplation? I look at how they write in the West. They always describe how their characters dress and eat. What superficiality! This is pure Protestantism—which tempts us now because of our poverty.

They think that everything depends on the economy. Well, it does for them, but for us it's the reverse. Nothing whatsoever depends on the economy, and everything depends on the soul, on consciousness. According to European pragmatic civilization, Russia is a developing society. Peter the Great and Marx tried to force it along. But in general we Russians fear civilization, and rightly so. It's not at all clear whether it's good or bad, and for us it wasn't necessary because we have such great space and wealth. And now we've destroyed rural civilization, and this is the reason that we're perishing. It's humiliating, of course, that such a great power fell apart. I know why: no one wants to be a Russian anymore.

I have met people who, in the spirit of Panchenko, relish the carnivalistic elements of Russian life. There's always something unexpected to impart surprise and wonder, and very often despair. In such an atmosphere, such people can almost be heard to say, the disenchantment of the world, the sense that the world runs in a predictable course that constrains the spirit, is not felt with such pathos. Russia is like a theater of the absurd, and the theater has its own allure.

For some, there is the added consolation that Russians have always gotten along somehow, even if as "left-handers." Such awareness may, more than all the Calvinist preachings about economic reform, help to encourage people to want to reaffirm their Russianness. An air of stoic resignation can easily be combined with a half-proud recognition that "we Russians are just like this," perhaps citing Nikolai Gogol or Mikhail Saltykov-Shchedrin as the most authentic portraitists of the Russian soul.

Especially often have I heard Saltykov-Shchedrin, the nineteenth-century Russian satirist hardly known in the West, referred to as the most trenchant guide to the Russian character, especially in its present incarnation. His *History of a City*, the latter with a name roughly translatable as Stupidville, together with other works such as *Pompadours and Pompadouresses* and *The Diary of a Provincial in St. Petersburg*, present a rogues' gallery of corrupt Russian officialdom and swindling traders and capitalist businessmen. Dishonest and reprobate as they obviously are, such literary parallels to the present decay nonetheless provide some assurance that the country will somehow survive, not just physically but also in terms of its cultural distinctiveness. They also suggest that part of its salvation will be its people's ability to cut corners, to use their wits, and somehow to save the situation. In the words of the nineteenth-century writer and revolutionary Alexander Herzen, "disorder saves Russia."[18]

I am not advocating disorder as a solution to Russia's problems, for in the late twentieth century Russia does need a new source of order appropriate for a complex modern society. Further, in the past this famous Russian chaos always generated visions of oppressive state control, many of them imbued with the idea of historical inevitability. These often utopian models were out of tune with the basic rhythms of Russian life, which they tried to regiment or negate. The Calvinism (as Panchenko calls it) of Yeltsin's government in its early years finds numerous parallels in Germanic models of reform favored by ambitious leaders, from Peter the Great to Stalin.[19] The great question now is whether, after the terrible mistakes of Yeltsin's regime, there can still emerge a new form of order, one that will be a pragmatic vision in accord with Russian culture and institutions. Or will order once again take the form of a model imposed from above in the name of historical inevitability? Only the former choice, in the spirit of both Lotman and Panchenko, will save Russia from yet another tragic repetition of the logic of explosion.

CHAPTER ONE

The Russian Idea

> It must be said, however, that it is not as easy as some may think to understand and formulate the basic principles which underlie the Russian style of life.
>
> —Ivan Kireevsky[1]

THE IDEA that Russian society forms a world apart, that it departs from all other nations, cannot be absolutely true. There are universal traits shared by all societies, as well as more specific traits shared by different categories of societies. Yet the idea that Russian society and history are somehow distinctive is supported by a number of historical "firsts." Russia was the first "backward" country, that is, the first country whose leaders so defined it with respect to Europe. Their sense that Russia lagged behind, not just in the military or technological sense, but in the social and cultural spheres as well, led them to attempt to recast Russia partially along foreign models. Russia, especially with the advent of Peter the Great around the turn of the eighteenth century, became the pioneer society of forced modernization.

Russia was also the first relatively industrialized country to witness a social revolution: Marx's predictions that capitalist industrialization would culminate in revolution were not borne out in Europe, but in Russia a radical proletarian movement played an absolutely central role in the 1917 revolution. The process of industrialization, with all of its underlying contradictions in autocratic Russia, was one of the main underlying catalysts of the Bolshevik revolution. Nowhere else have the rigors of early capitalist industrialization been so central to the revolutionary process.

Equally significant, Russia, now no longer the Russian Empire but the Soviet Union, was the first country to embark on the project of creating a socialist society. It claimed to be pioneering a universal model on the basis of a general theory of human social development, but in fact much of the logic of modern Communist societies was rooted in Russian particularities and imposed elsewhere.

Finally, with the initiation of perestroika in 1985 and its culmination in the collapse of the old system, the Soviet Union was the first industrial country ever to self-destruct in such a dramatic way. Perhaps the closest historical parallel is Weimar Germany.

This list of historical "firsts," which together make Russian history so fascinating for outsiders and so painful for the country's inhabitants, is intimately connected with the centuries-old efforts to delineate a separate Russian path to the modern world. Brief reflection on the vast differences between early-nineteenth-century tsarist Russia and Stalin's Soviet Union should be enough to dispel any simple sense of the uniformity of these efforts. Nonetheless, the repeated attempts to follow a different path from Europe's, to create a society, economy, and government felt to be more in tune with the country's own character, all involved the uneasy combination of despotic state power, rapid modernization, and the propagation of a model of society quite different from, and in many ways hostile to, the West.

Although the Russian vision of modernity was widely believed to embody higher moral principles than those of the West, the attempt to modernize partly on the basis of the "Russian idea" was the source of innumerable tensions and dilemmas in the society. Whether sincere or insincere, the official propagation of an alternative vision, and its partial embodiment in actual practices and institutions, conflicted with many of the fundamental imperatives of modern society. And it is the contradictions inherent in these efforts that largely explain why, as the Russian philosopher Georges Florovsky observed, "the history of Russian culture is all made up of interruptions, of paroxysms, of denials or enthusiasms, of disappointments, betrayals, ruptures."[2] In broad scope, this is the story that will be told throughout the following chapters. With the collapse of the Communist regime, a whole set of perspectives and values at the heart of Russian life for centuries has come into question as never before in Russian history, leaving in its wake a sense of profound moral crisis.

Many books have been written on Russia using a fundamentally different approach. Instead of trying to identify the distinctive positive values and institutions upon which many tried to construct an alternative kind of society, writers have often focused only on what Russia *lacked*: for example, a developed sense of legal consciousness or a strongly rooted middle class. They have failed to see the other side of the picture, that there was in fact a well-elaborated set of alternatives. Unfortunately, an appreciation of the values upon which an alternative Russian path to modernity was to be built does not diminish our sense of the tragedies of modern Russian history, for this alternative vision has always been inconsistent with crucial imperatives of modern large-scale societies.

The very phrase "the Russian idea" is in some senses misleading; indeed, all three of the words that compose it, even the article "the," will need to be interpreted and qualified. But whatever its limitations, the phrase cannot be avoided, since for over a hundred years this has been the formulation in use by Russian writers preoccupied with these problems. It was first introduced in a systematic way by Russian philosopher Vladimir Solovyev, in an article originally published in French, based on a talk given in Paris in 1889; the article first appeared in Russian after Solovyev's death, in 1909. The dual use of the term to encompass, first, what is seen to be most distinctive about Russian culture and institutions, and second, the ideal model of society based on and extrapolated from these elements, continues to the present time. There is an inevitable tension between the first use as an abstract historical model and the second use as a cultural ideal, as the competing perspectives in the two large anthologies mentioned in the introduction clearly demonstrate.

Yet the two meanings are inseparable, for the ideal model was held to be based on an interpretation of Russian history and institutions; and the latter, in turn, were often seen to embody the ideal model of society. The resulting ambiguity will also find expression in the following analysis. For although "the Russian idea" *is* a set of ideals, it is not only a phenomenon of culture. As the meaning given to, at times imposed upon, practices, institutions, and historical change, it was also made flesh in economics, politics, and society.

The tension between these two aspects of the Russian idea does not pertain only to the world of concepts. For the very friction between the ideal and the real, between the pristine vision of society and its embodiment in history, led people to judge society's deficiencies in the light of proclaimed, but unrealized, values. Ultimately, the lack of correspondence between ideal and reality led to their mutual discrediting: "really existing socialism" undermined the ideal, just as the ideal called into judgment the system.

Toward a Conceptualization: Three Negations

Negation One

The "Russian" idea is not entirely or exclusively Russian. It is not entirely Russian, because many of its elements were in fact borrowed from European social thought. The rejection of egotistic utilitarianism; the desire for community; the suspicion of private property; the hatred of formalism in social relations, especially as concerns law; the desire for a state that will protect the subject against social elites; indeed, the very idea of a distinctive national essence: these key themes of the "Russian" idea can be found in various currents of European thought of the early industrial period, especially romantic conservatism. Indeed, the first really visible current of thinkers to propose a fairly consistent version of the Russian idea were the Slavophiles of the mid-1800s. Some of their leading figures had in fact traveled or lived in Europe, studying with some of the leading lights of German philosophy, such as Hegel or Schelling, from whom they absorbed many of their ideas. Thus, when writers like Ivan Kireevsky or Alexei Khomiakov interpreted Russian history, they did so not as careful students of the Russian past who wanted to visualize the social world of pre-Petrine Russia, but as philosophically sophisticated opponents of the new order that was being created in Europe. From its early flowering, then, the Russian idea will in part be a kind of antibody to modernity, incubated in Europe but grown much more potent in its Russian environment.

But the Russian idea was not just an imitation of European romantic conservatism as reinvented for patriarchal and peasant Russia by a group of nativist ideologues. It was not simply an ideological construction. For indeed, Russia was very different from the West, perhaps more so by the middle of the nineteenth century than it had been for two centuries. Russian society *was* in many ways more communal, less individualistic, than was Germany or England; legal consciousness and the attachment to private property were truly less rooted in the population than among the inheritors of Roman tradition; and religious and political institutions had a different logic and history. When the Slavophiles, revolutionary populists, or official ideologists of autocracy proclaimed Russia's separateness from the "West," which they tended to regard as singular and homogeneous, and announced that Russia had a superior path to modernity, they pioneered a set of ideas that would become widespread outside of European civilization throughout the late nineteenth and twentieth centuries. Every part of the non-European world was either threatened with or came under European political, economic, or cultural dominance. Intellectuals everywhere searched their societies' heritages and analyzed their institutions in order to create the same kind of hybrid national ideas.

Everywhere these ideas, represented as "traditional" and embodying the essence of the nation, also bore the imprint of their origins as a reaction to European civilization. It is not surprising, then, that they often bear family resemblances to each other. Islamic religious ideologies, like the Russian idea, emphasize the communal nature of Islam and counterpose it to the conflictual, individualistic West. The Japanese ideology of *kokutai* in the late nineteenth century proposed a familial model of society that sought to validate the paternal authority of the government. Japanese social relations were held to be at heart communal and not based on individual interests. Socialist ideas in Africa and Latin America were also based on claims of a more communal and harmonious social order than existed in the decaying, individualistic West. In China at the turn of the nineteenth century the political leader and thinker Kang Youwei attempted to create a Chinese version of progress based upon a modified Confucian world view. Is the Russian idea simply the pioneer version of a more general ideological revolt against the West that had its apogee in the anticolonial struggles of the early and mid-twentieth century, but has now waned as a result of the further consolidation of an international economic and political order?

Not entirely. While it is true that the Russian idea bears obvious similarities to the responses of elites in non-Western countries to the Western threat, there are vital differences that should be stressed at the outset. First, it would be difficult to find a complex of values that are more hostile to the logic of Western institutions among other leading civilizations. For example, Islamic values embody much more respect for individual enterprise and private property than does the Russian idea. Even more significant, the sanctity of contracts and law is central to the Islamic tradition. As in Russia, communal values are given great weight in Islam, but not in opposition to law, as in Russia, where the law was seen to be a cold and external force that undermined community. Similarly, the Confucian tradition gives great positive value to this-worldly activity, as well as to the ethical norms that should regulate it. The extreme dualism between the present world of everyday life, given little positive value, and the world of the spirit, oriented toward higher values and the future, is not characteristic of Confucian ethics. In addition, both Japanese and Chinese civilizations are based on hierarchical values that help legitimize social elites. There is little of that egalitarianism, at times bordering on social anarchism, characteristic of the Russian idea. As compared with both China and Japan, social elites in Russia have always been regarded as legitimate only to the degree that they served the general goals of the state and not their own private interests: this is not a promising cultural foundation for modern capitalism.

The above comparisons indicate a deeper and more profound distinction. In Russia, the role of religion and the ancient values based upon it is posed in an entirely different way from Islamic or Far Eastern societies. For peculiar historical reasons, the Russian idea could not be mainly a "nativist" rejection of Western values on the basis of an independent cultural tradition. Similarly, its main formulators were not members of a traditional religious elite whose position was threatened by social and cultural modernization, but an educated, secular intelligentsia. There never was, and probably could not have been, a figure similar to the Ayatollah Khomeini in Iran or Kang Youwei in China, who based their revolutionary goals on a great indigenous cultural tradition.

Russian thinkers from Chaadaev to Fedotov have meditated upon this profound difference. The Christian religion in Russia, borrowed from the Greeks, did not furnish the country with the same kind of independent cultural heritage to oppose to Western ideas. In the words of G. P. Fedotov, whose authority on such questions is unsurpassed, "the countries of the East were the homelands not only of great religions and artistic cultures, but also deep thought. They were not 'speechless' as was Ancient Rus. They had something to oppose to European reason, and they are prepared to begin their conquest of it."[3]

The relative poverty of Russian tradition helps us understand Kireevsky's remark that it is unusually difficult to formulate "the basic principles which underlie the Russian style of life." His friend and opponent in debate Alexander Herzen traced this difficulty to the "mistake of the Slavophiles . . . in their thinking that Russia once had an individual culture. Russia never had this culture and never could have had it."[4] Similarly, the great nineteenth-century publicist Belinsky not only was skeptical of the life-giving power of Russian tradition but even argued that old Russia consisted of nothing but deformation. His consolation was: even though Russian culture was degraded by Byzantium and the Tartars, the fact that these faults were acquired and not endemic also meant that they could be cast off. The great merit of Peter, for Belinsky, was to begin this work and to attempt to bring Russia into the civilized world.

As significant as this perceived cultural poverty is another cardinal distinction of Russian society: well before the threat of the West was felt in such acute form elsewhere in the world, the Russian state began an attack on Russian tradition in the name of progress. Holding old Muscovite ways in contempt, Peter the Great, with all his enormous energy, sought to break the hold of Muscovite religion on his subjects, especially the elite, and inculcate new cultural values based on Western pragmatism. His was the first "cultural revolution" from above in modern history. His efforts were the source of one of the great schisms that afflict Russian history. State and people; educated classes and the peasantry; adherents of the old and new cultural systems: these were some of the gaps that were opened up by Peter's reform.

The consequences for the Russian idea were of incalculable importance. From the start it was not an organic reaction of the leaders of a traditional culture against Western values on the basis of that culture but was itself largely a rejection of Western values. Of course, national self-definition always has both a positive and a negative pole. The definition of what one is necessarily implies an image of what one is not. But because of the relative weakness of an independent national cultural tradition and because modernization was identified with Europe and the state, ideas of national identity had a distinctively "anti" character in Russia. According to this logic, if Europe is based on the individual, then we do (empirically) and should (ideally) emphasize the collective. If Europe respects law, then how fortunate that we honor only the higher truth of justice!

In so rejecting Europe, many formulators of Russian identity and advocates of national distinctiveness imported antimodern ideals and practices into Russian life as well. For example, both Dostoyevsky and Nicholas II perceived Russian political life in terms of the following primitive logic. They believed that European civilization was composed of "societies," in the specific sense of mere agglomerations of conflicting and egotistical social groups with no common purpose. By contrast, for them Russia was not and should not be a "society," but a united people. Catastrophically, they identified the real with their ideal and so were blinded to the changes taking place around them.

Because of its origins in opposition to perceived European maladies, this rejectionism was based not on a fair and balanced view of Western culture, but on a schematized view of the West fully in accord with the logic of binary opposition. From the beginning, then, the Russian idea was more ideology than "culture." Further, the rigidity characteristic of ideology was reinforced by the paranoid sense that Russia was held in contempt by the West. Dostoyevsky, for example, refers to "that permanent, general animosity of Europe toward us . . . a disgust for us as for something repugnant."[5] For him, domestic Westernizers were even more malignant, considering it "a crime to think of our own independence."[6] Thus, proponents of Russian particularism displayed a strong note of defensiveness together with their rejectionism.

For these reasons, the Russian idea could not be based on synthesis, on that process of compromise that Yuri Lotman found so absent in Russian cultural history. If Kang Youwei could attempt to incorporate elements of modern values into a synthesis with Confucian tradition, or if Japanese intellectual leaders could accept much of Western pragmatism secure in the belief that the heart of their culture was not at risk, the same was not true of the early proponents of the Russian idea. From the very beginning, from the time of Yuri Krizhanich's defense of Slavic civilization in the late seventeenth century, to Nikolai Danilevsky's pan-Slavist attacks on Western civilization in the late nineteenth century, to the relatively casual comments of Alexander Panchenko to a newspaper reporter in 1993, the dilemma is the same: Russianness was always defined *in opposition* to something else.

Consequently, the parallels to the Russian idea noted earlier, though valid, are also superficial. For although the Russian idea is not utterly distinct from similar cultural trends in much of the rest of the non-Western world, it is more fundamentally oriented toward a negative self-definition than elsewhere. Herein, too, lies much of the tragedy of modern

Russian history: the attempt to delineate a separate Russian path according to these prescriptions would create multiple dead ends in Russian historical development. In rejecting the West, advocates of a separate Russian path would seek to construct on the basis of semimythical values, ones that were unable to substitute for the organic cultural foundations undermined by Peter and his successors. The Russian idea was a result of schism; and, when incorporated into government modernization policy, it was also the source of further schism in the society.

Negation Two

"The" Russian idea is not the only Russian idea, nor is it a unified perspective. Indeed, precisely because it was not based on tradition, and thus on a shared cultural substratum, as was Confucianism in China or Islam in the Arab world, it was always hotly contested in terms of its accuracy as a typological model of Russian life *and* as an ideal. For example, Vissarion Belinsky both denied that the Russian people were united in their Orthodox piety *and* rejected the idea that Russian society should be based on a shared religious value system. Interestingly, Marxists did not break so radically with the Russian idea. Although they disputed the claim that Russians at that time formed a united people, they believed that the transcendence of class society would create future harmony.

And so the Russian idea was only one among many cultural tendencies struggling for influence in Russian life. One type of rejection of the Russian idea was denial of a shared cultural tradition in Russian life at all. The Russian idea was seen as merely a myth adopted by a certain sector of the intelligentsia. For example, for Chaadaev, Russia did not have a real history, which implies unity. The Russian past was just a collection of facts, whereas real historical existence as a nation implies, for him, a chain of events connected and penetrated by an idea. All individual facts and events express this underlying idea, as was the case, Chaadaev asserts, in medieval Europe.[7] He explicitly disputed the Slavophiles' attempts to conjure up a pure Russian tradition prior to and opposed to Peter's reforms. And until the creation of a real history based on an "idea," to which Chaadaev called his people, Russia would continue to contribute nothing of significance to world culture.

Denial of the claim that there was a specific Russian cultural essence that represented the genius and destiny of the country easily led into the espousal of rival cultural models. A plethora of competing visions vied for dominance in nineteenth-century Russia, as they do today in the country's post-Communist moral disarray. The Westernizers disputed the claims of the Slavophiles point by point, both empirically and ethically. How, they asked, could the Slavophiles celebrate the communal traditions of Russian life when these were based on serfdom? Further, they questioned whether the homogeneous peasant community could be the foundation of a modern society. Similarly, under the Soviet regime dissidents empirically challenged the ideological claims of the Soviet regime: for example, that it was more egalitarian than Western societies. They also attacked excessive egalitarianism as an ethical ideal.

Parallel debates took place within government circles both in the late tsarist period and under Soviet Communism. Although Nicholas II and many of his leading officials believed that the autocracy embodied a special Russian path that would ensure justice, community, equality, and shared values, many high political actors favored more representation of interest groups, the development of capitalist social and economic relations, and a relaxation of imposed cultural harmony. Similar debates agitated both prerevolutionary Marxism and the Communist regime, as some socialist leaders were more willing than others to countenance markets, cultural pluralism, and diverse political inputs. (The Mensheviks, Bukharin, and many Communist reformers of the 1960s are good examples of this latter tendency. For Bukharin and the 1960s reformers, see Moshe Lewin's *Political Undercurrents in Soviet Economic Debates.*)[8]

Why, then, do I emphasize the Russian idea rather than any of these competing tendencies? Moshe Lewin's phrase "undercurrents" signals the answer. For no matter how complex and plural the cultural and political undercurrents of tsarist Russia and the Soviet Union, until Gorbachev the victory was always to those who advocated a special Russian path oriented around a separate set of values and founded on a different pattern of institutions. These claims may have been empirically false or ethically deficient, but they nonetheless shaped social change decisively.

A related observation: *the* Russian idea is also not an entirely appropriate term because it can be taken to imply more unity of perspective among advocates of a separate Russian path than is in fact the case. The very large selection of documents gathered together in the recent one-volume Russian compilation *The Russian Idea* gives us fair warning of this diversity. Any such selection of documents would have to include, as this one does, both Alexander Herzen, famous as the first major advocate of an indigenous Russian version of socialism based on the village commune, and Nikolai Gogol, whose apologetic for serfdom and the tsarist regime in his *Selected Passages from a Correspondence with Friends* shocked much of the educated public in the 1840s. Similarly, *The Russian Idea* includes a piece by K. N. Leontev, who hated Europe for its corrosive effect on Russia, and one by Vladimir Solovyev, who held that Christian universalism had to be the foundation of any ethical system, and who rejected any narrow sense of national superiority. These fundamental differences in perspective, belonging together as do a set of musical themes and variations in different keys, suggest that the internal tension among elements is just as much a part of "the" Russian idea as is any kind of unity. The state, the intelligentsia, and various strata of the population at large will seize upon different, at times conflicting, versions of the Russian idea to further their own purposes.

Nonetheless, whatever the differences, there is also this very important source of unity: the insistence that the Western path can and should be avoided in the name of a harmonious and egalitarian Russian society based on a higher form of belief.

Negation Three

Not only is the Russian idea not uniquely Russian nor unambiguously dominant in Russian cultural history nor uniform in content; it is also really much more than an idea. In tracing the fate of the Russian idea in modern Russia, I am not writing intellectual history or arguing for a cultural determinism to turn materialistic conceptions on their head. The Russian idea is not some transhistorical essence that inserts itself into social life pure and untouched, a kind of demiurge of change—or, in this case, a demiurge of social breakdown. My conclusion cannot be reduced to some anodyne formula such as "ideas truly matter."

What, then, is the Russian idea, if not an idea? Here I need only repeat what has already been emphasized. It is an interweaving of social practices, ideological interpretations of these social practices, and transformative activity with respect to these practices based partly on the ideas that they helped generate. Social practice, interpretation, and action together formed a complex of distinctive traits that were associated with each other and then identified as part of a certain general view of Russian society and social change. This general view generated polar opposition to it, which in turn helped give coherence to the loose configuration of elements.

Undoubtedly the three key institutional features associated with the Russian idea were the Orthodox Church, the tsarist state, and the peasant commune. Any one of these could be chosen to clarify my meaning, but let us for the moment take the example of the peasant commune. The peasant commune, in which land was not owned individually but periodically redistributed on the basis of family need and size, served as an empirical basis for ideological interpretations of the communal nature of Russian society, superior in its principles to Western individualism. The commune, egalitarian in essence, was held to ensure a superior moral climate in Russian society, one based on the harmonious relationship of the individual to society. The commune, it was frequently asserted, avoided the war of all against all characteristic of Western society.

This ideological interpretation, generated in large degree by opposition to Western institutions as much as by a real knowledge of the workings of peasant villages, cannot help but strike us by its moral blindness, at least as applied to the period until 1861. Until that year the majority of these harmonious peasant communes existed under serfdom. Further, after the 1861 emancipation the ideologists of the peasant commune chose not to notice how these closed communities could foster the exploitation of the weak by the powerful. They also underestimated the anger of the village toward the rest of society.

Whatever its inaccuracies, the myth of the idyllic peasant commune became dear to the hearts of many landowners and government officials, who came to believe that the maintenance of the peasant commune at any cost was vital to the stability of the country; in it were anchored the immemorial values of the peasant. The support of the commune, and even the extension of its powers over its individual members, became a key note in government policy until the eve of World War I, when the futility and artificiality of this policy were recognized by some government officials. Nonetheless, the state had succeeded in linking itself and its policy to an important institutional bulwark of the Russian idea. It was also embraced by many revolutionary populists, who refused to understand the social conflicts dividing the peasantry and believed that these self-enclosed little worlds might form the building blocks of a complex modern society.

Thus, the Russian idea is also the logic and principles underlying such combinations of social practice, ideological interpretation, and social policy, all of which influence and transform each other. When I write of the values of the Russian idea, then, I am really referring to these values partly as inherent in practice, partly as ideologically interpreted, and partly as acted upon in order to consolidate and strengthen them. The key elements of the Russian idea are thus not some kind of abstract ideological essences, but principles discernible in both thought and social action. It was precisely the partial correspondence between the ideological formulations of the Russian idea and the social practices from which they abstracted that gave credibility to the larger idea of a separate and superior Russian path to modernity.

FURTHER CLARIFICATIONS: FOUR AFFIRMATIONS

Affirmation One: A Society Based on Ultimate Values

The religious historian and philosopher G. P. Fedotov, writing in 1938, looked with horror upon the spectacle of a materialistic and utilitarian Soviet Union, armed to the teeth. Russia was becoming like America, losing its soul to the machine and the promise of prosperity. "The accumulation of wealth in socialist forms is no more honorable than the pursuit of bourgeois wealth," he declared.[9] This was the meaning of the Russian Revolution for Fedotov: the triumph of American-style materialism over the previous spiritual wealth of Russia. "Civilization" was triumphing over culture in a country that before the revolution was giving the world an entirely different treasure. "During the recent materialistic slumber of the West it [Russia] burned with a fire of astonishing spirituality. It was Christ's chosen [*zvana khristovoi*]. It was among the great nations—Greece, France, Germany—to whom in succession belonged the spiritual hegemony of mankind."[10] But now, wrote Fedotov, having risen so high, it has fallen so low. Rupture, loss of belief: this was what Communism meant to Holy Russia.

Fedotov was wrong. Russian Communism was not some kind of Americanoid technologistic nightmare. It was a nightmare of another kind, one in which a materialist belief in the means of production as the driving force of history was strangely married to a new faith in the advent of a social utopia. Huge numbers of Russian people still burned with hope and enthusiasm, now baptized in a new faith that replaced religion. Holy Russia was succeeded by a new bearer of "the spiritual hegemony of mankind." More than elsewhere, people were still guided more by an ultimate goal than by calculation and interest.

This view of Russian culture as centered around some vision of final goals, whether religious or socialist, has always been at the heart of the Russian idea. Such an assertion is both an interpretation of Russian reality and the declaration of an ideal that should guide it. As individuals, it is claimed, Russians have more need of a set of ultimate values to orient their lives. The routines of daily life are not enough to satisfy their larger spiritual cravings. Only a government and society based on such a deeper vision can be truly legitimate in the eyes of the Russian people.

On the ethical plane, the good individual is motivated by belief, not happiness or self-interest. The following passage from the memoirs of the émigré writer Mikhail Osorgin, who suffered heavily for his beliefs, illustrates the meaning of such a choice. The goal of life, he wrote,

> is the breadth and nobility of spiritual strivings, the possibility to develop them and live by them. Maybe we were wrong [when we lived according to belief as revolutionaries], but then what a beautiful error! It's worth repeating it again and again, it's worth dying without betraying it.[11]

Quite characteristically, Osorgin asserts that action in pursuit of the "beautiful error" may lead to suffering, but that suffering is redemptive. It is redemptive for the individual, since it will lead to humility and purification. And it will also cleanse society in preparation for collective renewal. For only from the depths of societal humiliation and degradation can resurrection take place.

This theme of redemption through suffering is absolutely fundamental to Russian culture, and central to a great many views of Russian distinctiveness. For Dostoyevsky, "the main and most fundamental spiritual quest of the Russian people is their craving for suffering."[12] Alexander Solzhenitsyn's essays in *From under the Rubble* exemplify the same judgment. More recently, and empirically, the Russian scholar Ksenya Kasianova has used proverbs and religious beliefs to claim that the values of patience, humility, and suffering are the foundations of Russian cultural distinctiveness.[13] On the social level, Iosif Gessen, among many others, affirms the connection among collective fall, suffering, and ultimate redemption in Russian history, expressing his faith that the same sequence will lead to the demise of Bolshevism.[14] Such examples could be multiplied endlessly.

The expressions of this uniquely Russian emphasis on higher truth are held to be observable everywhere in Russian culture. Russian religion is at heart eschatological, interested in the complete and final transformation of human life rather than the ethical dimensions of religion. Russian philosophy is characterized by its orientation toward *logos*, cosmic rationality, rather than by an interest in system or logic.[15] Russian literature, as we know from Panchenko, is concerned, not with how people dress and eat, but with the values that they live by.

Finally, with respect to art, these are the judgments of Ilya Kabakov, an artist currently residing in the West. In the West, he claims, the artist must contribute something novel in the context of an already existing cultural environment. The significance of the artist's work is judged within this system of signs, this pluralism of voices that constitutes a kind of dialogue. The Russian artist, he claims, does not feel part of such a known cultural context, within which one seeks to be heard and understood. Instead, each artist claims to speak the final truth to the spectator, completely in isolation from others. Thus, form is important in the West; the enunciation of a truth is the characteristic of Russian/Soviet art.[16]

We are already familiar with the underlying logic of such assertions, so ubiquitous in the self-perception of Russians: they are based on self-definition through polar opposition. Thus, as Russia's "other" the West is materialist, present-oriented, rationalistic, concerned only with means, legalistic, and the like. Characteristic in this regard was Ivan Kireevsky's view of the United States, whose literature showed "an obvious disrespect for all moral principles, such that at the basis of all this mental activity lies the most petty life, cut off from everything that lifts the heart above personal interest."[17] Not essentially different, notes Gleason, was the socialist Maxim Gorky's excoriation of America, which had an enormous influence on Soviet views of the United States. Both were based on the contrary image of Russia and the Soviet Union as realms of higher values.

Of more interest to us than the question of the validity of such judgments is the sociological issue: what happens if such a moral vision becomes part of a people's conception of itself, embedded in social institutions, and acted upon by the state? Catastrophe.

Truth is unitary and compulsory: this is the terrible political principle implicit in the Russian idea. Individuals and groups will have a legitimate place and voice in the country to the extent to which they conform to this truth, whether it be Orthodoxy or Communism. The community must also be unitary. Opposition and diversity is falsehood and therefore deserves no hearing. Government must be an expression and protector of this community based on a uniform commitment to truth. Unfortunately, much of government policy under both the tsars and the Communists can be understood in terms of these assumptions. And repeating the worst lessons of the past, both present-day "democrats" and their "national-patriot" opponents often act according to the same logic. Black and white judgments, leading to categorical opposition; the search for scapegoats; the inability to compromise: these traditional tragic themes of Russian politics continue to pervade contemporary perceptions and events.

The consequences for ethics are as troubling as for politics. A Russian friend showed me a newspaper article published in *Nezavisimaia gazeta* by Vladimir Lefevr, who now lives in the West (in the United States, I believe). My friend, an extremely well-educated and perceptive observer of Russian life, was in complete agreement with the analysis. According to Lefevr, there are two fundamental types of ethical systems: the first, which is based on the search for compromise, refuses to accept that good ends can be achieved through evil means. This kind of ethical system, says Lefevr, predominates in the United States. The logic of the second type is the opposite: bad means can be used to pursue a good end, because only the end is significant; the purpose of action is the complete victory of this good end over its rivals. Confrontation rather than compromise is the norm. The second kind of ethics is characteristic of Russian social life, he holds.[18]

This example is interesting because it comes from a recent newspaper commentary, but the shortcomings of an ethics based on ultimate ends have long been noted by critics of Russian culture. Indeed, this kind of dissection of Russian ethical norms has become part of the self-criticism of the Russia intelligentsia, from the time of the important collection of essays *Landmarks*, published in the aftermath of the 1905 revolution, to our own time.

Human practices simply cannot be judged *sub specie aeternitatis* if society is to function. The constant comparison of social practices, leaders, and institutions with the ideal version of them will discredit them all and will ultimately corrode the values as well. Here are some examples of this logic. The Russian Orthodox Church that exists at present is not the real church, Russians have been told since long before the Communist regime. It is not the "true Universal Church, founded by Christ" (in the words of Vladimir Solovyev), and therefore it has no authority. The law is too formal, it does not embody authentic justice; truth is more important than rules. Therefore, laws do not need to be obeyed. The government has departed from the correct path; it no longer follows Truth. Therefore, it is no government at all. It's necessary to have a revolution and start all over again! By this logic, all institutions are only shadow institutions, deprived of legitimacy, even of reality. They are only temporary pretenders, awaiting their inevitable replacement by the true embodiments of the ideal. It is for these reasons that, as Kasianova remarks in her recently published study *On the Russian National Character*, Russians "in general exclude formal relations from the 'human sphere' in our consciousness." From ancient times, she claims, Russians have seen the government as something foreign and hostile, and so no moral criteria apply to it.[19]

In the voice of a contemporary Russian philosopher:

> We are people who have not found and do not value relative truth. . . . Common sense is not enough for us. If we find truth necessary, then only the last and final truth—therefore we will always live in a lie; if freedom is necessary, then only absolute freedom; and if good, then only real sainthood—and therefore we will always live in evil. This is our paradigm, and from this comes our inability to compromise, to have dialogue. We are not suited for moderation and measure, which are the marks of rationality.[20]

In a society in which such cultural assumptions are pervasive, human motivation is also conceived in a very special way. On the empirical level, rationalistic self-interest is seen to have less motivational force for Russians. For example, I was told by an eminent social scientist, then rector of one of Moscow's leading research institutes, that Russians are fundamentally nonrational, and so foreigners cannot possibly understand the country. Look at what happened at the time of the 1917 revolution, he exclaimed. The Russian people were deeply religious, but they passively stood by as the Bolsheviks destroyed their churches. In this regard, recall Panchenko's assertion that in Russia economics counts for nothing. Similarly, an influential social thinker claimed that Russia's whole thousand-year cultural history shaped a people who are unable to define, differentiate, and pursue their own interests.[21]

It is not, of course, that people do not have preferences or aspirations that they ardently pursue. But an "interest" is more than this: like an opinion, it is explicit, conscious, the result of deliberation, and a spur to action. Because of the higher value given to belief in Russia, desires and preferences are less frequently transformed into explicit interests; nor do they occupy such a central role in human motivation as in the rationalist West—so it is widely believed in Russia.

In addition to such empirical assertions, throughout Russian history proponents of the idea of Russian distinctiveness have urged that people *should not* act according to mere self-interest. Such an attitude explains the doubtful legitimacy of the capitalist class in the waning years of imperial Russia, as well as the palpable hostility to the private cooperatives under Gorbachev and to the new businesspeople at the present time. They are all swindlers! So I have been told countless times.

Such attitudes can easily be found among intellectuals. The literary scholar Boris Tarasov admits that there is nothing disgraceful about one's trying to advance in one's career, but only if one is following a higher ideal and with the goal of becoming a better person. Otherwise one will become trapped within the logic of consumerism, attempting to quench all sorts of unnecessary thirsts that arise in the "civilized" person. The destructive effect of such consumerism on the consciousness of people is self-evident: life becomes ruled by the logic of unquenchable pride and excess self-esteem.[22] (Recall here the characteristic emphasis on humility and self-limitation in much of Russian ethics.)

All of this is not to deny contrary tendencies in Russian culture. Russia, after all, was the birthplace of Pavlov and the incubator of the revolutionary advocates of self-interested egotism, as portrayed by Turgenev and Dostoyevsky. Furthermore, Leninism was a ruthlessly materialistic interpretation of Marxism, stripping it of much of its Hegelian ethical underpinnings. Thus, in stressing the centrality of belief in the Russian idea, I do not deny the existence of all kinds of contrary currents. Nor do I think that Russians always act according to higher values. Nonetheless, this cultural and social paradigm has had enormous currency, with immense political effects. For example, it was incorporated into the Stalinist modernization drive, which stressed belief and enthusiasm over mere calculating rationality.

Belief and enthusiasm, it is widely held, can perform miracles. Such miracles more than compensate for the routine, rationalized action characteristic of the West. Here are some reflections typifying this kind of judgment published almost forty years ago in *Novyi mir*, at that time the main intellectual forum of the country. The construction of Magnitogorsk, the giant Soviet metallurgical plant that is now in the throes of economic crisis, was a "miracle." It was built from nothing, and with almost nothing. We had to invite American advisers, so that we could then surpass our teachers. There were many quarrels with them—they did not believe that we could do it so quickly. "Yes, they did not believe. But this was completely natural. They judged like technicians, and not as knowers of the psychology of a people who have become masters of their fate." They could not understand "the soul of our people."[23]

This soul, held writer Ilya Ehrenburg, was quite different from that in the United States, where there is "a different approach to life, a cult of prosperity, a fear of heroism, of sacrifice, of the unknown."[24]

Or here is a recent journal article about a provincial pianist whose motivation was to become like the great Horowitz. Such unobtrusive articles, found everywhere, provide better evidence for the pervasiveness of such attitudes than do noisy ideological or philosophical pronouncements. After gushes of admiration about the young pianist's talent, the author writes: "This is Russia! This is character! He grew up here. He acquired his inimitable traits here, in his motherland. And note—not with any ulterior motive, not for money, did this young musician act this way! He did this for himself. And there are a multitude of such examples."[25]

According to some reflections published in *Nezavisimaia gazeta*, these differences can be traced in a comparison of American and Russian folklore. American folktales are imbued with the rational spirit; there is not such a gap between dream and reality. Heroes do not just wait for help from above, and they don't spend endless hours in contemplation, but they constantly work and struggle. Paul Bunyan, for example, is direct, straightforward, and full of initiative. He is not miserly, but careful and precise. In Russian folklore, by contrast, work is an unpredictable burst of activity. Heroes can perform miracles, and "for us there are no limitations either on sea or on land."[26]

These observations are echoed in Osorgin's memoirs, which include his reflections on his émigré life in France. This European country seemed to him narrow, bourgeois, and confined by its "putrid history," a country in miniature inhabited by petty cretins. But Russians were "naked heroes" who thrived on disorder and expanse. "This Russia will go by separate routes and to other goals" because of its people's greater faith and enthusiasm.[27]

I myself have felt the power and beauty in Russia of life lived according to belief and enthusiasm. Such an orientation toward the world gives rise to a kind of freedom from constraint whose parallel is hard to find in the much more organized world of Western societies. The authority of institutions and social structures is not so binding in Russia—they are, after all, really only phantoms of their true essences. The person is left to himself or herself to discover the truth that lies completely apart from them. People depend on their wits and their friends much more than on fixed procedures and routines. There is little authority in the formal authorities of the world, for Russia is a literary world where appearances seldom correspond to reality. Everyone knows that appearances always lie, and people are constantly engaged in a process of interpretation and decoding. It is partly for this reason, I believe, that Russians so much more attentively scrutinize each other's faces. What, they are asking, is really behind the words? What does the person really mean? It is as if they are Platonic dualists by birth, in this country where a deeper logos is held to transcend the world of appearances. Perhaps Panchenko was right: Russians are not Protestants, they are poles apart. For Protestants are convinced of the deep meaning and seriousness of the everyday world, whether in the realms of work or in personal relations. All of it is an arena upon which the moral drama of salvation is played out. Daily life is to be lived according to binding ethical norms; every action is a decision.

In Russia, the world is not so "disenchanted" (in the famous term that Max Weber used with respect to modern Western societies). Miracles and mystery still inhere in daily life. Everyone who has lived with Russians will have heard remarkable statements that seem to come out of ancient mystery cults. Magic formulas or herbs or berries, or a fish caught from a certain lake, can heal dreadful diseases. A recent guest of mine informed me that whenever she is sick she sleeps with her dog, for the dog will draw the illness out of her body. I myself, in the company of Russians, made pilgrimages to magic wells deep in the forest, away from all roads, that could cure the ills of old age. I will not forget this beautiful example: I was told with deep conviction by a young Siberian man that not far away there was a holy spring with healing powers, which had burst forth at the site of the murder of priests by the Communists. Now it has become a site of pilgrimage.

Whatever its aesthetic qualities for personal life, the reliance on belief and enthusiasm for motivation in a large-scale modern society has obvious limitations. Not that there was ever a complete dethroning of interest and organized routine. As we will see, debates and shifts on these issues characterize the whole history of Soviet Russia, as the advantages of material incentives for personal motivation were repeatedly recognized. It bears repeating that social institutions and practices were never some kind of direct translation of the Russian idea into reality. Nonetheless, the belief in consciousness, will, and values over interests, incentives, and abstract rules has been an enduring trait of modern Russian society. This formulation indicates part of the problem: belief versus incentive; ideology versus interest; enthusiasm versus economic constraints. The whole issue is phrased in terms of binary oppositions that create false choices and real dilemmas. In this sense, the Russian idea as a counterreaction to Western rationality throws up enormous obstacles to economic and social rationalization. With resignation we may be forced to agree with writer Andrei Platonov, who wrote decades ago in his notebook that it is "the petit bourgeois rather than the hero who carries history forward."[28] Yet we also recall the exclamation of Alexander Herzen: "Petite bourgeoisie is incompatible with the Russian character—and thank God for it!"[29]

Affirmation Two: A Higher Form of Community

> Western Christians have no knowledge of that sort of community which belongs to the Russians.
>
> —Nikolai Berdyaev[30]

The superior aptitude of the Russian people for community life runs through all versions of the Russian idea. Human relations are held to be warmer and deeper in Russia, to have quasi-familial overtones of shared kinship. Abstract, formal relations based on contract or interest were always held to be inferior to the more embracing emotional relations of Russian society, based on a strong sense of shared participation in the *rod*, which can be translated as kin or clan, although the word has much richer associations than either of these translations. Fedotov explains its meaning as "the eternal kinship-community,"[31] which unites the individual to ancestors, to future generations, and to the larger society.

Examples of some related words may give a sense of the richness of connotation of this fundamental concept: *rodit'* means "to give birth"; *rozhdenie* means "birth"; *roditeli* is the word for "parents"; a *rodstvennik* is a relative; *rodina* can be roughly translated as "motherland" or "homeland"; *rodnoi* is an adjective that refers to something familiar, close, deeply connected to oneself (as opposed to what is *chuzoi*—foreign, alien): these are just some examples of the associative richness of the word *rod*. (In Dal's dictionary, first published in the late nineteenth century, examples of words related to *rod* occupy almost three large, double-columned pages.) Taken together, they suggest a fundamental continuity among the life of the individual, the extended family, and the larger society, all of them conceptualized in terms of the *rod*.

As Berdyaev's remarkable statement above implies, the sense of community based on membership in the *rod* was held to have religious roots, some in Russian paganism and some in Eastern Orthodoxy. Western Christianity, by contrast, was seen to be based on separation and opposition: the individual, the family, the church, and the society in the West had all become highly differentiated from each other, a process that had even been given juridical recognition. By contrast, many nineteenth-century social thinkers and religious philosophers held Russian Orthodoxy as characterized by *sobornost*: a symphonic unity among individual, family, and society, in which all elements contributed to the development of each other.

As with all the other elements of the Russian idea, this claim to a highly developed capacity for communal life was hardly confined to Russian social thought. For example, German thinkers reflecting on the changes brought about by industrialization and the emergence of mass politics in nineteenth-century Europe developed a cardinal distinction between "community" (*gemeinschaft*) and "society" (*gesellschaft*). "Community," in which Germany was still held to excel in comparison with its more modernized rivals, was based on shared belief and richer social relations. "Society" was abstract, formal, and heartless. The mechanical social relations based on interest impoverished the emotional life of the individual. The deficiencies of "society" were most fully expressed in the modern city, that nightmare of impersonality and superficiality. Human life was at its richest in the countryside, where human relations could still acquire depths of meaning. Such ideas became the basis of antimodernist ideologies insisting on the need to maintain the purity of national cultures against the impact of soulless modernization. The German nation should protect itself against the leveling effects of bourgeois society, which turns all relations into expressions of interest.

Such ideas also became standard responses of non-Western countries to the threat of Western cultural and political domination. For example, Japanese political elites seeking to modernize their countries also insisted upon the distinctiveness of Japanese communal traditions. Japan, it was said, was also like one huge family, headed by the paternal figure of the emperor. According to their different traditions, Islamic and African thinkers and leaders also emphasized the communal bases of their societies, proposing that the fundamental principles underlying their collective life were in fact ultimately superior to those of the West. Virtually everywhere, intellectual and social movements arose claiming that, whereas in the West the individual might be freer and the state stronger, the intermediate term—the community—was in fact more developed in their own cultures. All, then, would have agreed with Berdyaev that the West was tragically deprived of one of the most fundamental of human experiences.

Was there anything distinct in the vision of community embodied in the Russian idea? I believe so, although I do not want to push my argument about the uniqueness of this second key dimension of the Russian idea too far—there certainly were common elements also found in other countries. Nonetheless, certain traits of Russian society did give rise to a very specific historical experience of community, as well as a distinctive intellectual interpretation of the nature of that community. Community was experienced in Russia primarily in very local contexts. It did not tend to be generalized to larger worlds, in large part because the logic on which it was based excluded such extension. It was also very narrow sociologically: that is, community was seen to include only those groups very similar in social makeup. People from different backgrounds, either class, ethnic, or religious, were not *rodnoi*—that is, not part of the extended family concept that was the basis of the experience of community in Russia. Thus, to an unusual degree, the sense of community in Russia was always *in opposition to* some other group. Such an orientation toward the larger world, which culminated in the sharp division of society between those who were and those who were not *rodnoi*, inhibited the creation of broader and more general social ties.

Many of the key sources of this tendency toward a dual experience of the world in terms of "we" versus "they" can be found in the nature of Russian peasant society. If the local peasant community was experienced by its members in a quasi-familial way, social ties outside the village and between the peasants and other social groups were unusually weak. Crucial to this relative isolation of Russian peasant society from the larger world was the role of the large landowner in Russian society. Russian rural society was at the other end of the spectrum from the English countryside, so dominated by the presence of a landed elite. In Russia the landowner, who was also a serfowner until 1861, typically lived in the city and left the management of his estate to stewards. Not until roughly the turn of the twentieth century did there begin to develop a distinctive and politically significant society of the nobility in the Russian provinces, one that could leave a real imprint on Russian rural life. The nobility received work and payments from the peasantry, but otherwise their role in peasant affairs was quite limited. Even when the landowners lived on their estates and were not, as in so many cases, absentee, they often had little to do with key decisions connected with their peasantry. The great majority of local affairs were left in the hands of the peasants themselves.

Based largely on this very different social role of the nobility in the countryside, rural Russia was not nearly as socially differentiated and complex as rural England, or, for that matter, rural China or Japan. The provincial society of the nobility was not rich or developed enough to give rise to as highly complex a division of labor in the countryside. Nor could the Russian countryside support the kind of provincial educated class, composed of lawyers, doctors, and other educated groups, that played such an important role in European societies in the eighteenth and nineteenth centuries.

This rather monochrome social topography of rural Russia also weakened the links between city and country: there were not nearly as many paths through which city culture could extend its influence throughout the country's vast rural hinterlands. Cities were weak, not merely in the numerical sense as percentage of the population, but also in their capacity to spread urban values and life-styles elsewhere. Indeed, even at the present time it is easy to feel that cities like Moscow and Petersburg are isolated outposts of urban life in a vast rural expanse largely indifferent to them. Similarly, there is still an almost impassable divide beteen the peasant village and the outside world. Even today, rural Russians treat Muscovites "with an illogical mixture of mistrust, servility and ill will. Their attitude toward foreigners is similar."[32] In support of this view, Brezhneva recounts the fate of the sophisticated Moscow woman whose dacha was anonymously burned down by the villagers, in much the same way that the peasants' ancestors ejected noble intruders under the tsars when they could.

Peasant villages were of course not completely cut off from the outside world. Peasant youths served in the army. Many peasants left the villages in order to find work in the cities, often returning either seasonally or for good. Even before the revolution literacy was spreading rapidly throughout the countryside. I do not want to portray a countryside of pristine isolation from the effects of modernization. Nonetheless, what struck observers then and social historians now was the depth of the division, the width of the gap, between peasant Russia and the rest of the country.

And it was in peasant Russia that the quasi-familial model of community was so strongly rooted, for the village community was in many ways like a large extended family. Everyone shared the same religious beliefs, celebrated the same holidays, and was subject to the same social norms, heavily based on tradition. The extended family household was the key economic and social unit; authority within it was vested in the male head of the household, chosen on the basis of age and experience. The village assembly, called the *mir*, was composed of these heads of households. It met periodically to make crucial decisions relevant to the affairs of the village community, including decisions about land use and rights, apportionment and collection of taxes, the observation of religious rites, and family feuds: in short, just about every issue, major and very often minor, affecting the lives of its members.

This common life, based on face-to-face interaction, a shared culture, and economic interdependence, created a strong sense of belonging together, even if we should be careful to avoid any idylls of communal harmony. But the other side of this strong sense of familial group identity was a pronounced sense of isolation from the rest of the society, which found expression both economically and politically. Economically, every time the peasant commune was allowed the chance, it turned in upon itself and took on the traits of a natural economy based on the local production and exchange of goods. (The crisis of recent years has also led to a considerable naturalization of the rural economy, as once again villages find it unprofitable to exchange with the cities.) The prerevolutionary Russian village showed the same tendency politically: peasants almost always showed utter indifference to big-city parties and ideologies.

The relative weakness of urban influences; a limited division of labor in the countryside; the absence of a flourishing noble provincial culture; considerable peasant autonomy in the administration of their own affairs; great social and cultural homogeneity: these were the social factors underlying a sense of communal identity based upon the *rod*. This collective way of life excluded outsiders just as firmly as it forcibly embraced insiders. In both senses it contradicted basic traits and requirements of modernity, which favors both more individual autonomy and more standardization of social relations. Modern economics and politics simply cannot be based upon the model of self-enclosed quasi-familial micro worlds exercising enormous powers of control over their members.

Whatever its limitations as a model of community in modern society, the example of the peasant commune inspired several generations of Russian intellectuals, from Slavophiles to populists. On its basis—or rather, on what they knew of it, for their image was as much mythology as sociology—they constructed an imaginary alternative historical path for the country. Peasant practices became transformed and incorporated into abstract ideologies of Russian superiority. In this process, the Russian idea of community was once again created through the logic of rejection and opposition. Just as the peasant opposed the world of the village to the larger world outside, with nothing to mediate between them, so the Russian intellectual assimilated the communal experience of Russian peasants with a whole series of other oppositions: Russia versus the West; tradition versus modernization; Orthodoxy versus Western Christendom; the community versus individualism; personal relations versus the abstractions of rules and law; and other misleading polarities.

The consequences for the ability of Russian social and political thought to understand and confront the dilemmas of modernity were catastrophic. Moral values appropriate for life in the village, suitable for rich and many-sided relations based on personal acquaintance, were mechanically transferred to the whole society. Rules and law, for example, were seen to inhibit the deeper forms of community life. But social relations in a complex society require fixed norms. The adequate functioning of large-scale social organizations is simply impossible without rules; they cannot depend purely on the quality of personal relations. In small-scale communities people may be able to trust each other based on personal knowledge, but in complex societies trust depends upon shared recognition of and adherence to rules.

Similarly, society cannot be conceived as the collective search for salvation, as Slavophiles such as Khomiakov conceived of it. The necessity of the recognition of cultural diversity is not just a politically correct slogan rooted in modern American life, but a vital moral imperative in any complex modern society. Finally, in modern society the state cannot simply embody some mythical will of the community, for the community is always multifaceted. Any ideology that advocates this goal will begin by a normative bifurcation of the social world, separating what is pure and impure, permitted and proscribed. The ideal of quasi-familial community life spells disaster when transferred to the arena of modern politics.

And yet this kind of moral stance toward society still pervades a great deal of social discourse in contemporary Russia. Loyalty to the collective and collective salvation, in the sense of creating a just society, are praised in opposition to the pursuit of egotistic self interest. Self-interest has no warrant in morality; material gain, a purely quantitative individual good, excludes the qualitative dimensions of life centered around service to the community. The identification of truth with a presupposed moral vision and identifiable community is used to exclude authentic pluralism. Personal conscience and righteousness are opposed to law. The highest goal of "mere" law, it is said, is to transform the open war of all against all into juridical battles based on malicious litigation. Such a form of law is particularly important in the United States, where rootless people use it to substitute for the lack of trust among them. "From the point of view of natural community the most developed legal consciousness is to conscience as a horse's hoof is to human fingers."[33]

Community *as opposed to* law, abstract associations, formal organization, and mutual interest: this was the vision of the Russian idea. It was an "idea" elaborated by intellectuals, and so truly an element of "culture", but it was partly rooted in the practices of the Russian countryside, where private property and individual initiative were weak. It was further brought down to earth from the heady reaches of abstract thought by government policy, in both the late tsarist and the Soviet periods. Like the intellectuals, many political leaders opposed Russia to the West and sought a separate Russian path based partly on the logic of communal associations. After the liberation of the serfs in 1861, the tsarist government not only preserved, but even extended, the rights of the commune over its members. Major changes, forced upon the government by the economic and political weaknesses of the countryside, were initiated only on the eve of World War I and never became fully instituted. Later, the Soviet government used elements of a communal, antibourgeois vision of society to strengthen the role of all kinds of "collectives," even after it had destroyed the peasant communes in the proper sense.

We will see what this uneasy synthesis of a fundamentally antimodern communal idea and modernization meant for the population of the country. It would have been better for everyone concerned if the Russian idea of community had remained an element of abstract culture, to be furiously debated in the country's heady intellectual life. When it came down to earth, it did its part to prepare the ground for tragedy.

Affirmation Three: Equality

> Of the great revolutionary principles sowed in the Russian earth, the shoots of freedom were soon smothered, but equality of rewards and in slavery soon ripened.
>
> —Mikhail Osorgin[34]

Equality has long been seen as one of the key virtues of Russian society, and one of the sources of its superiority over the West. Two related empirical claims have repeatedly been made. First, Russian culture is seen to give more positive weight to equality than do Western societies, particularly in opposition to such other possible cultural values as freedom or individualism. Second, Russian society has frequently been judged to be highly egalitarian. Also pervasive are the ethical belief that the good society should be fundamentally egalitarian and the political conclusion that the state should ensure the equality of its subjects.

Here is Krizhanich's seventeenth-century statement of the theme, characteristic also for its explicit contrast of Russia with the West: whereas in the West, the upper class rolls in luxury while the landless workers "drink nothing but clear water and live on insufficient bread alone," in Russia, "all people, by the kindness of God, the richest as well as the poorest, eat rye bread, fish and meat and drink kvas, even if they lack beer."[35] From the Slavophiles to the Communists, the same claim has repeatedly been made in modern Russian history: because of such factors as the lack of private property, the weakness of feudalism, or the strength of government solicitude, Russian society has managed to avoid the inequalities of bourgeois society in the West.

Although proponents of the Russian idea may not always have been precise in endorsing the value of equality, we must be clear on the different meanings of this vague concept. Clearly, the Russian emphasis on equality does *not* mean equality of opportunity. A society based on equal opportunity openly embraces differences in individual talent and initiative; very unequal results are perfectly consistent with equal opportunities. Indeed, the cultural underpinning of equality of opportunity is a belief in individual autonomy, the desirability of individual persons to advance themselves free from social constraints. The person who wins the race has full rights to the fruits of his or her talents and efforts. The concept of equality, then, refers to means and procedures—the *rules* of the race—and not to outcomes.

It should not surprise us to find that for the Russian advocate of equality such a vision will be too narrow. It conflicts with both of the previous values that we have already discussed: it violates the emphasis on final results as opposed to procedural formalism, and it elevates the interests of the individual over those of the group. Accordingly, what we find characteristic of the Russian idea is a strong emphasis on equality of outcomes, a belief that material conditions in society should not vary too greatly among individuals and classes. Such a commitment to equality of conditions can be found, in different forms, in the egalitarian reflexes of the peasant village as well as in the ideological reflections of the intelligentsia and the levelling policies of the state.

Equality of material conditions, and not of other aspects of social status, was the primary area of concern. The peasant village was not noted for its tolerance of Jews, foreigners, or people of other faiths. Non-married individuals were looked upon as only partly human. Women had their defined and subordinate place in peasant society, and age was also an extremely important marker of status hierarchy. The intelligentsia, too, were far from consistently egalitarian by contemporary standards. Women played a secondary role in the revolutionary movement, although there were famous female revolutionary heroes. And many populist and Marxist ideologists harbored grave doubts that the people were worth listening to in their own right.

Thus, it was the kind of equality that Krizhanich found so appealing in the Russian style of life that always loomed so large in the Russian idea. Upon the desirability of equality of material conditions illiterate peasant and populist theorist could agree, even if their emphases were necessarily different. For the peasant this kind of egalitarianism flowed naturally from the whole form of life of rural Russia. The culture of individualism was not at all developed, and so it is hard to see where a belief in unequal reward for unequal merit might come from. There was relatively small scope for the expression of individual talent, even different aptitudes for work, in these very patriarchal and community-oriented miniature worlds. Even when, as was inevitable, there emerged relative extremes of wealth or poverty within the peasant community, "these extreme groups abandoned the commune and departed for the city, industry, trade, and the army because they found it difficult to get along inside the commune. By expelling 'social rejects' and making access difficult for outsiders, for a long time the commune was able to preserve its socioeconomic homogeneity."[36] Without such a strong degree of material homogeneity, it would have been extremely difficult to preserve the quasi-familial tone of village social relations.

All of this is not to say that the peasant village was absolutely egalitarian. There were always rich peasants, not all of them "expelled" through a process of natural selection. But such deviants always aroused the resentment of their neighbors, for their greater prosperity was not seen as a legitimate result of their harder work or greater abilities. And given that it was not seen to be connected to merit, it was dangerous, because it aroused envy. It was for this reason that even such a populist revolutionary as the poet Nikolai Ogarev could look upon the peasant commune as the equality of universal slavery: for him it was "the expression of envy of all against the individual."[37] Ogarev, like his friend Herzen, still favored the commune, but only a reformed version that would liberate the individual from its forceful control.

If Russian peasants rejected excess wealth within the confines of the village, they were positively Jacobin in their attitude toward the outside world. Basic to peasant psychology was the idea that land belonged to God, and so to the community as a whole, and therefore could not be appropriated by private landowners. Private ownership was an act of usurpation. Landowners had no legitimacy in the eyes of the peasant, particularly as they were regarded as outside parasites who played no productive role in the village. Relations between the peasantry and the nobility were thus based on a fundamental discord that could not be healed, but only exacerbated, by reform. Villagers never accepted the social hierarchy that they felt had been unjustly imposed upon them. The landowner's status was little different from that of a foreigner occupier. The landowner was not *rodnoi*, did not fit in with the texture of life of the peasant *rod*. In peasant Russia one was either part of the community of equals or utterly foreign and illegitimate. Community and equality were inseparable in the life of the village. The emphasis on equality thus emerged naturally from the polarized social experience of the Russian peasantry, where all social relations were defined strictly in terms of a "we versus they" opposition.

The roots of egalitarianism among the Russian intelligentsia, both prerevolutionary and contemporary, are more complex. Partly it was based on knowledge and appreciation of Russian social practices, which were in some ways more egalitarian than those in the West. But equally, appeals to equality typically bore the marks of an ideological opposition to the West and an isolation from the people that gave them a strident and abstract tone. The imprint of binary opposition to anything Western is easily observable in the creation of a whole series of overstated oppositions: equality versus freedom; equality versus private property; equality versus individualism; equality versus formal democracy; and the like. In short, equality, like community, was seen as an alternative to the injustice of bourgeois society and so became defined in terms of abstract oppositions. The peasant commune itself became conceptualized in terms of such polarities, and its complexity thereby distorted.

Also distorted through this process of ideological filtering was the concept of the people, in Russian the *narod*. The word is in some ways untranslatable, for as compared with the English word people it has strong normative overtones. Particularly in the eyes of the intelligentsia, the narod was a moral category: it was the common people, unsullied by the usurpation of land or by bourgeois contamination. The "bourgeoisie," which came to be a blanket term for anyone who did not belong to the "people," was corrupt, the people pure and blameless. The "people" were relatively homogeneous, living a life free of materialist grasping and the pursuit of inequality.

This characterization may sound exaggerated, but it is not difficult to encounter such an undifferentiated conception of the "people" in contemporary discourse. For example, in a book published in 1989, Valentin Rasputin, one of the country's most eminent writers and now an advocate of right-wing views, lamented the increasing stratification of the population as a result of the changes under Gorbachev. At the present time, he said, "it is difficult to speak about the people as an entity united by a shared goal." We are now a population composed of individuals trying to show their differences, whether based on culture, age, nationality, or profession. Perhaps we didn't always follow our principles before, but "previously we knew what was good and what was bad, but now these concepts are confused and mixed up."[38]

Equality, then, is held to be inherent in the Russian people. The threat to brotherhood came from alien forces introducing concepts and practices foreign to the narod, united in its belief and not split apart by any major sources of social differentiation. A sense of community, commitment to a common set of values, a homogeneous people not broken up by social inequality: these same elements of the Russian idea have been ardently advocated by the bulk of the Russian intelligentsia over the past two centuries. They dovetail nicely with the popular conceptions of equality and morality rooted in the way of life of the peasant village discussed above, which also identified social elites and any processes generating inequality with what was foreign and alien.

The conceptions and practices of the Russian autocratic state and, needless to say, the Communist regime were also in part rooted in a certain commitment to social equality. Despotic regimes always fear the emergence of social elites that might limit their independence. From Ivan the Terrible's attacks on the boyars, the old Muscovite social elite whose ability to challenge his rule he feared, to the cautious and skeptical stance of the tsars in the nineteenth century toward the emergence of a capitalist elite, to the Communist leaders' attacks, in word and at times in murderous practice, on the developing party autocracy, Russian despotism has always embodied a strong anti-elite sentiment. Throughout many centuries it has also claimed to transcend any particular social class, and to be acting in the interests of the people as a whole. It proclaimed itself to be the protector of the poor and downtrodden and always claimed to listen to the grievances of the lower classes against their oppressors.

If Russian people have almost never had the right to choose their leaders, there have always been mechanisms through which they could directly appeal to their rulers for protection—personal petitions to the tsar, denunciations to party leaders. As the first head of the tsarist secret police, Count Benckendorff, expressed the mission of his agency to his subordinates: "Every man will see in you an official who through my agency can bring the voice of suffering mankind to the throne of the Tsars, who can instantly place the defenseless and voiceless citizen under the protection of the Sovereign Emperor."[39] The encouragement of such practices fit in with the rulers' own desire to keep social and political elites firmly under their own control.

Further, in its denunciations of capitalist exploitation, the Communist regime was only following in the footsteps of its tsarist predecessors, who were also suspicious of the market and the bourgeoisie. Only with reluctance did they allow market forces to penetrate the countryside, and capitalist industrialization, no matter how necessary for the country's development, was looked upon with suspicion and considerable hostility. High government officials themselves attacked the capitalists for their exploitation of the workers, and there were always threats, seldom carried out, to expropriate factories or expel foreign industrialists. From this standpoint, the increased inequality brought about by capitalism might undermine the loyalty of the lower classes to the regime, part of whose legitimacy was rooted in the popular image of the tsar as father and protector of the people. Similar principles, in a much exaggerated form, were at the heart of the claim to legitimacy of the Communist leaders. But the tsars and party leaders alike had to face the following evident dilemma: unequal rewards are indispensable in any policy of economic modernization, whether capitalist or socialist. It was for this reason that even Stalin could attack egalitarianism as a petit bourgeois delusion inimical to the imperatives of socialism.

Affirmation Four: The Good State

It is inevitable that all these elements of the Russian idea find their expression in a distinctive conception of the role of the state in society. Just as an emphasis on procedures, pluralism, abstract social relations, individualism, and equality of opportunity can only be consistent with a political system centered on representation, arbitration, and compromise, so the Russian idea logically entails a paternalistic conception of government. The Russian people are interested not in politics, but in truth, say proponents of the Russian idea. Democracy has no power to inspire people; it is petty and mean-spirited. Let an authentically Russian government rule in accord with truth so that the population can live according to pure spiritual values. This was the political message of the Slavophiles, and it has echoed throughout Russian political culture, embracing advocates of both monarchism and Communism.

The antidemocratic implications of the Russian idea are clear. But many puzzling questions remain. The Russian people are held to be indifferent to politics, passive in the face of a government that promises to protect them. How, then, do we explain the turbulent course of Russian history, with its countless popular rebellions, political breakdowns, and revolutions? Russians are said to be prone to grant legitimacy to whatever regime is in power. How, then, do we explain the rapid disappearance of the government's legitimacy? The tsar-father is quickly transformed into a German agent; the Communist rulers come to be identified as traitors to the people. We were taught, a friend of mine told me, that the capitalists were our enemies, but our enemies turned out to be the Communists. One popular singer, Igor Talkov, the object of a cult of martyrdom after his murder, wrote songs portraying the Communists as a satanic force responsible for the moral corruption of the people. How do such polar transformations occur, on the basis of what principles of political culture? On the one hand, Russians can identify the values associated with *gosudarstvennost*—statehood or the state system— as vital to the people's national life; on the other, they can portray themselves, as the writer Maxim Gorky did, as an anarchic people, to whom government had to be brought in from outside—by the Vikings, Tartars, or Baltic Germans, for example. How do we explain such contradictory self-interpretations?

To explain such paradoxes, let us look more closely at the political implications of the Russian idea. They are admirably summarized in the work of a school of thinkers called the Eurasianists, who flourished in the Russian emigration after the Communist revolution. In the spirit of the Slavophiles, they sought to pinpoint what was distinctive about the Russian conception of government, and to argue its superiority over Western forms of rule. Although writing in exile and prohibited in the Soviet Union for many decades, their ideas have found contemporary adherents, such as the enormously popular thinker Lev Gumilev, the recently deceased son of the poet Anna Akhmatova. His well-received books in the Eurasianist spirit are among the few serious intellectual works that can compete with the flood of mass consumption imports from the West. In addition, a summary and selection of the work of the Eurasianists has recently been published in the volume *Puti Evrazii*.[40] This volume is the source of my following remarks.

The true Russian conception of politics, they argued, was founded on the idea of a "Government of Truth," whose tasks were threefold: to protect Orthodoxy; to return truth to the Earth; and to oppose the predominance of materialistic values among the people. The Government of Truth was to be strictly distinguished from the government of law favored in the West. "Heroes" ruled in the Government of Truth, not just average people; and they ruled on the basis of religious zeal, not materialistic strivings. For this it was necessary for them to act on the basis of a "ruling idea," based on religion, that would give a moral foundation to political life and inspire people with belief. The life of the people would be guided according to this "ruling idea" generated by political heroes. Truth, the community, and the government would form an organic whole all united by adherence to these principles.

This is an extreme vision, of course. But I have chosen it because its very radicalism brings into relief assumptions about politics that were pervasive in Russian political culture and practice in both the tsarist and Communist periods. It also allows us to perceive the weaknesses of such a political vision. First, a government that claims to be the protector of the truth sets impossibly high tasks for itself. No human institution can justify itself purely on the basis of an ethical vision, governments least of all. One of the functions of an emphasis on rules, procedures, and pluralism is to substitute for this impossible claim of ethical purity. If the tsar or the party has to be all-knowing and wise, any perceived fallibility will have a catastrophic effect on legitimacy. This political vision will also create a psychology of dual consciousness, according to which public beliefs and statements must conform to the ideal image of the Government of Truth, which in their private lives people know has not been realized. Further, and equally important, the government cannot act to safeguard the truth of a community united around it, for such a uniform and cohesive community exists only in ideological visions, not in reality. Any concrete government will take measures that will be favored by some groups and opposed by others. If politics is interpreted in terms of conceptions of absolute truth, then any government action will create *raskol*, a fundamental split, in some part of society—for part of the society will always interpret any action as evil.

For these reasons, the political vision of the Russian idea is inevitably connected to schism and extreme polarization. The very claim to rule the whole community on the basis of truth leads some groups to the conviction that the government is acting on the basis of falsehood. This was particularly the case in Russian history, where tsarist and Communist regimes sought to transform society on the basis of some set of goals foreign to and not understood by the people. Peter the Great was widely regarded in his time as either a German or the anti-Christ. Communism is now widely regarded as a German plot, or the evil work of non-Russian nationalities, particularly Jews and Georgians, who imposed these non-Russian ideas upon the innocent Russian people.

In addition to its ethical deficiencies, the Russian idea of politics also makes poor political sociology. For contrary to the hopes of rulers, the claim to represent and the effort to impose truth will always fail. Under the tsars, the exercise of autocratic power inevitably created semi-oligarchic elite camarillas engaged in self-protection. In society at large, workers and peasants managed to create self-enclosed micro worlds quite impermeable to autocratic control.

Stalin battled against these same mechanisms of self-defense against centralized authority. But his successors, unwilling to engage in mass purges, had to confront the reality of closed elite groups subverting party intentions, as well as of popular sectors living their lives in only formal and external conformity to official norms. In this regard, too, the Russian idea of politics, celebrating truth and harmony over the diversity of modern society, inevitably gives rise to processes that subvert it.

We can thus begin to understand the paradoxes listed above. As long as the Russian people are willing to accept that their rulers represent some higher values that give them legitimacy, they tend to be passive and apolitical. But this very claim to legitimacy engenders polar opposition, because it is impossible to sustain in any complex and changing society. This opposition will not be constructive, but will be based on scapegoating, demonization, the avoidance of shared responsibility, and an inability to perceive the fundamental nature of the issues involved. The cycle of continued breakdown and negation described by Lotman will begin again, repeating the errors of the past in different forms. The conception of politics inherent in the Russian idea is not a viable answer to the fundamental issues of modern politics.

CONCLUDING REMARKS

In his philosophical letters written at the time of Nicholas I, Pyotr Chaadaev cast a despairing glance at the cultural emptiness of Russia: it seemed to him that Providence had "given no thought to our destiny. . . . [E]ras and generations succeed each other without leaving us anything of value. . . . We are alone in the world, we have given nothing to the world, we have taught it nothing."[41] After the publication of the first letter, Chaadaev was declared mad by the government and prohibited from publishing in Russia. Shortly afterward he published a famous essay, "Apology of a Madman," in which he presented a somewhat more hopeful forecast of Russia's future. Russia's very cultural emptiness, he said, could turn out to be an advantage, for the country was not obstructed by so many fixed prejudices and egotistic interests. Not being so constrained by its past, it could be more open to reason and will. The experiences of other countries could be surveyed and analyzed, and what was just and useful could be brought to Russia through strong political leadership. If Russia did not create its own independent tradition, it could nonetheless find its place in the world of nations through its ability to synthesize, a capacity that stemmed from its very cultural backwardness. And so Russia will have a "great future," for it is "called upon to resolve a large part of the problems of social order . . . to answer the most important questions which occupy humanity."[42]

Many other eminent Russian thinkers, including Dostoyevsky, have praised Russia's ability to absorb the contributions of other countries and have argued that its culture is more universal. But whatever these hopes, the Russian idea did not develop through synthesis, incorporating reason and the experience of other nations to solve the social and cultural problems that they themselves had been unable to manage. Rather, although it was in some ways based upon authentic traits of Russian society and culture, it was given ideological shape through dogmatic opposition to what was regarded as Western. Defined in this way, it was inevitably characterized by a series of overblown oppositions that, through the centuries, acted as antibodies working against the absorption of many fundamental traits of modernity. Put in another way: the Russian idea was certainly not synthetic, nor was it an outgrowth of Russian tradition; it was from the beginning defined largely negatively, as a rejection of the West.

The incorporation of the Russian idea of belief, community, equality, and politics into state policy had especially harmful effects on the country's transition to modernity. Government sponsorship of an orthodox system of beliefs, and its censorship of alternatives, had the effect of reinforcing the idea that truth is unitary, and that institutions and governments should be judged by its standards. Through this policy, both tsars and Communists reproduced and reinforced schism in the society: we versus they; friends versus enemies; pure and impure—the permutations based on an identical logic were endless. Rulers therefore undermined the cultural bases of their own authority, partly through the intransigent opposition they created, and partly because they themselves could never live up to the moral standards they constantly advocated. Neither, it is important to stress, could any other kind of regime, since, fortunately for all of us, there is no such thing as a Government of Truth.

CHAPTER TWO

The Dilemmas of Tsarist Modernization

EVEN AFTER almost eighty years it is difficult to take the measure of the end of the tsarist regime in 1917 and its replacement by a Communist government. Indeed, it is probably more difficult now than it was ten years ago to weigh the significance of these events in the context of the larger sweep of modern history. When the Communist regime was still in power, and social relations and political life in Russia seemed to have more or less settled into a separate Soviet system of modern society, the meaning of the end of imperial Russia and the victory of Bolshevism seemed clear, for they could be judged and interpreted in terms of a fixed outcome. For although few Western scholars felt that the Soviet regime was without contradictions, and many wrote perceptive analyses of the pressures for change in the Soviet Union, even fewer were bold enough to predict the immanent collapse of socialism.

The apparent existence of an objective outcome of the Russian Revolution made it seem easier for scholars to study late imperial Russian history. It was felt that the relative permanence of the Soviet Union gave the necessary historical distance and perspective. Historians often rightly pride themselves on their refusal to judge events until their larger meaning has become clear after the passage of time. Without some degree of historical closure, it is difficult to separate the minor ripples from the deeper current of change. The historical profession has always been somewhat suspicious of the study of "contemporary history," a term that to many is internally contradictory—what is contemporary cannot yet be interpreted on the basis of any historical perspective.

In a certain sense, therefore, the late tsarist period of Russian history has now once again become contemporary. It is easy to draw parallels between the tsarist regime's inability to reform itself in the decade before World War I and the political paralysis of the Communist leadership in the perestroika period. Both periods also witnessed heightened political polarization, a sense of moral crisis, and the widespread belief that the country had lost its moorings. Complaints about rising criminality, the loss of respect for elders, the harshening tone of interpersonal relations: all of these pervade accounts of both periods. But the late tsarist period has become contemporary in another sense as well. Whereas before, from the perspective of a seemingly stable Soviet social order, the destruction of the old regime in 1917 clearly marked both an end and a new beginning, now it is easier to regard the extraordinary drama of social change in twentieth-century Russia as having a single plot: the failure of the attempt to create a special Russian path to modern society. From this vantage point the same questions faced the country in 1994 as in the last decades of tsarist rule. The history of the collapse of the tsarist regime in this sense is still contemporary history.

I well remember when things looked so different. I was never present in Moscow for the anniversary of the November 1917 revolution, the month that, after ninth months of rising political conflict, saw the Bolsheviks come to power. But I did witness the holiday in Leningrad, and I will never forget the power and beauty of the celebration. The vast columns of people, organized by school or workplace, all with red flags and banners, weaving their way by different routes to the Palace Square in the heart of the city; the streets lined with soldiers, standing virtually arm to arm for countless miles, making sure that no one paused even for as long as to tie one's shoelaces (as I tried to do, getting pushed to my feet for my mistake); the glittering torches placed along the bridges and the great thoroughfares in order to light up the frosty night; and the magnificent display of fireworks over the Neva River, brilliantly illuminating the boats and ships brought in to the center of the city to mark the historic events. Anyone seeing this extraordinary spectacle instantly came to believe in the solidity and permanence of the world to which the revolution had given birth. The meaning of the revolution was then just as clear as were the bridges and boats dramatically outlined by the fireworks: an old order had ended in 1917, replaced by the world's first socialist society.

The 1917 revolution validated a new sense of historical time and an ideology of progress based upon it. Everything now could clearly be divided into past and future, bad and good. This new vision of history, consecrated by the ideology of the victors, did not entirely exclude romanticization of the Russian past, but this was almost always experienced as a kind of romantic escapism. Who could have imagined that the Romanov claimant to the Russian throne might return to his ecstatic people from France in 1992, shortly before his death? Did any sane person in Stalin's Russia in the 1930s believe that the nobility might once again attempt to organize themselves to participate as an active force in Russian politics?

Such utterly unexpected events naturally compel us to question the meaning of the end of the tsarist regime all over again. In the post-Communist period, as in 1917, the statues and monuments of leaders have been mercilessly destroyed, and so has the equally firm mold of historical interpretation been completely overturned, especially in Russia itself. The 1917 revolution was not a new beginning, it was only an interruption, goes the chorus of opinion now. It was an unnatural and artificial break with the authentic foundations of progress in modern society: democracy, capitalism, integration into world politics and society. Russia before 1917 was headed in this direction; now it can resume its path. The *real* revolution will be 1991, for just as the French Revolution can be seen to have swept away the feudal obstacles to economic and political modernization, so the end of Communism will lead to upward progress, this time defined through the prism of liberalism.

Obviously, this new view of the 1917 revolution as an unnatural interruption of Russia's rise toward Western civilization has even less grounding than its predecessor in long-term historical perspective. So far there is dismayingly little evidence that a capitalist, democratic society will emerge in Russia, thus casting the 1917 revolution and Soviet socialism into the shadows of history. Even more importantly, this optimistic view, which can be found much more frequently in journalism than in serious scholarship, rests upon the following dubious interpretation of the potentials of Russian society under the last tsars: that Russia had every possibility of joining the brotherhood of successful capitalist nations able to combine economic progress with growing democratization.

Those who argue that before World War I Russia was well on its way toward Europeanization, especially in its German variant, can point to much powerful evidence on behalf of their argument. Industrial growth and the development of technology were advancing apace, especially in the period immediately preceding the outbreak of World War I. Much of this industrial growth was spearheaded by native capitalists, who appeared to be transforming themselves into a powerful new elite able to carry its weight in Russian politics. Literacy was rapidly increasing, higher education met international standards, and cultural life was in flower. The tsarist government, in responding to the revolutionary crisis of 1905–1906, had undertaken some important social and political reforms, including the legalization of trade unions, the encouragement of individual peasant landholding, and the creation of a representative assembly, the Duma, based upon popular election, even if unfairly weighted. Proponents of the Westernization and rationalization of old peasant Russia seemed to have every reason to be optimistic.

Yet how much of this "progress" was appearance, how much reality? Seventy years earlier, the Marquis de Custine had called Russia a country of facades, where the surface of things always concealed an entirely different inner essence. There were in early twentieth-century Russia all kinds of signs suggesting that progress was at least in part illusory, that in its foundations social and political life was frail and vulnerable. One danger came from violent challenges to the nascent representative political system. These were years of political terrorism, when leading political figures feared for their lives, and when many were assassinated, including Pyotr Stolypin, the forceful prime minister who was spearheading rural reform. Plots, conspiracies, and rumors of a violent upheaval pervaded the country's two great cities, leading many high officials to expect the outbreak of revolution at any moment. The very threat of revolution brought with it the equally great danger of reaction.

In cultural life, decadent cultural and artistic movements experimented with avant-garde cultural forms and prophesied the end of the world. In a certain sense, they were following European fashions, especially those of the French symbolists, but Russian symbolists were more messianic and apocalyptic, more certain that the corrupt old world was soon to be replaced by a radiant new order. Drawing upon many themes from the Russian idea, such as the conviction that government should be based on truth and that society should be founded on harmony, their works helped accustom educated people to the idea that their world might soon collapse. Other cultural currents cast equally strong doubt on the permanence of the status quo. Theosophy, mysticism, and religious occultism vied for attention with advocacy of total sexual liberation among cultural visionaries.

All of these new cultural tendencies further separated the tiny and Europeanized cultural elite from the rest of the population, leading many writers to question whether there were any values uniting the nation at all. Rather, the society seemed to be based on schism: the people, "a hundred and fifty million on the one hand," and the intelligentsia, "a few hundred thousand on the other"—"unable to understand each other in the most fundamental things."[1]

Nor did the unbridgeable rift between the intelligentsia and the state seem to be narrowing. Certainly no comfort could be found in the atmosphere reigning in high government circles and the court. The government was unable to understand, much less solve, the most obvious and pressing political problems of the time, especially the land question, the labor question, and the issue of political reform. The court was the scene of political intrigues mixed with religious charlatanism. Grigory Rasputin, the decadent monk from Siberia who believed that human beings must sin in order to become humble, and through this route achieve salvation, attained the heights of political power through his influence on the royal couple. He was preceded at court by a whole series of other dubious characters with outlandish religious credentials, including the "God's fool" Papus and the barefoot religious wanderer Vasya Tkachenko.

Was it possible to believe that such a society was on the verge of modern enlightenment and rationality, that its drive toward capitalism and its halting steps toward political liberalization could continue for long?

Were not the fundamental divisions in the society growing more pronounced with the modernization of the country? In their profound sense of social dislocation, in their unyielding efforts to penetrate behind the world of facades, in their prophetic denunciations of the hypocrisies of their contradictory society, the symbolists and religious visionaries frequently saw more deeply than did the confident apostles of progress. They perceived much more clearly that there was little to hold the society together, that the world around them had lost its coherence.

Fundamental to this lack of coherence was a profound contradiction between the logic of the emerging new world and a set of older values that had already become rigidly antimodern in their centuries-long confrontation with change. Forming much of the basis for government policy, for the action of revolutionaries, and for the orientations of social movements, these elements of "the Russian idea" were at war with many of the very changes that the leaders imbued with them themselves wanted to promote. It was almost as if the cultural unconscious of society was taking revenge against the overly conscious efforts to remake society in the image of an unattainable other. If the logic of the new society demanded government based upon the representation of interests, both government and opposition continued to want to impose truths in the name of social harmony. If the development of capitalist economic relations required the breakup of previous forms of community and the acceptance of inequality, social movements rejected social stratification and sought to isolate themselves from the impact of the division of labor. They still saw themselves as organic and undifferentiated communities that had a right to expect protection from the ruler who embodied their own values.

What, then, was political representation if the tsar himself had no conception of society, looking upon his country as an organic people united in devotion to himself? What was a parliament if the government remained autocratic? What was capitalism if workers did not accept the market determination of wages? Where was permanence and stability if virtually all social groups rejected law in favor of the realization of their own higher values? Words and things were disconnected from each other, appearances gave the lie to the underlying realities. Social practices and institutions thus lost their objective grounding in a web of shared expectations based on predictable outcomes. People could not conceptualize the changes that were occurring around them, much less accept their justice and legitimacy. Old standards of justice were used to condemn new practices that had not yet been assimilated in moral experience. Given the right opportunity, huge sectors of the population were ready to reject social elites and overthrow their rulers. Defenders of the status quo turned out to be amazingly impotent, having undermined the cultural foundations of their own legitimacy.

The contradictions between the Russian idea and key aspects of the logic of modern society were nowhere more apparent than in the fate of the monarchy in Russia. By 1917 no one, least of all the tsar himself, understood how his role in society should be defined. Caught between ancient images of himself as the embodiment of his people's values and his modern role as the source of progress, he was able neither to relinquish his autocratic power nor to keep its integrity intact. The very institution that was held to be the foundation of order in society turned out to be its main engine of destruction.

The Russian Revolution of 1917, then, was not a historical accident precipitated circumstantially by war and German treachery. But neither was it ordained, as Marxists would have it, by the inevitable development of capitalism. It was not primarily economic contradictions, though Russia indeed abounded with these, but political dilemmas that gave birth to the Russian Revolution. Fundamentally, the political assumptions inherent in the Russian idea prevented the emergence of modern representative political institutions. Meanwhile, social and economic changes, promoted by the autocracy for the sake of its own survival, either undermined the older conceptions of tsarist rule or helped turn these conceptions against the tsar himself. Autocracy and modernization turned out to be incompatible with each other. After the downfall of the tsarist government in February 1917, in essence the battle was between those who rejected the Russian idea in favor of a Westernized conception of politics and those who sought to revitalize the Russian idea in search of a more consistent model of a Russian path to modern society. In a certain sense, then, when the Bolsheviks consolidated power after October 1917, their victory also marked the triumph of a new version of Russian traditionalism.

NATURE AND DILEMMAS OF RUSSIAN AUTOCRACY

On January 9, 1905, a day forever after known as Bloody Sunday, troops of the tsar fired upon thousands of St. Petersburg workers marching to the Winter Palace to ask the tsar to grant them rights and justice. The shooting down of nearly 1,000 peaceful petitioners, with about 150 killed, was the opening act of the 1905 revolution. By late January worker strikes had spread throughout the country, paralyzing much of industry. Spurred on by the workers, virtually all other sectors of Russian society soon began to express their social and political grievances. Students fought for civil rights and academic freedom in the universities.

Educated middle-class groups, including doctors and lawyers, voiced their demands for a constitutional regime. Even sectors of the industrialist class, never before displaying any touches of political radicalism, called for political reforms of various kinds. Radicalism swept the countryside, as peasants demanded land and political rights. The revolutionary intelligentsia participated fully in these struggles, seeking to radicalize demands and coordinate the vast movements of social protest.

The revolution reached its apex in the fall, particularly with the great October strikes and the ever more clamorous demands for a constitution. It is only a slight exaggeration to state that, throughout this year of radicalism, the outcome depended on the decisions of one man, Nicholas II, tsar of all the Russias. It was his decision whether to abrogate the principles of autocracy. He had the power to grant or withhold a constitution. He could authorize a legislature and define its powers and how it would be elected. Throughout the months of discussion and debate at the highest reaches of Russian government, it was always understood, even by such a formidable figure as Count Witte, who stood far above Nicholas in energy and intelligence, that the crucial decisions were his alone. Witte also knew that his own political career depended entirely upon the tsar's favor, for there were no organized constituencies or political parties to give a degree of independence to the tsar's top ministers.

This was the exercise of autocratic power at its most dramatic. But autocracy also meant that the tsar was authorized to make minute decisions about the lives of his tens of millions of subjects on the basis of his own discretion. He received vast quantities of petitions and requests from his humble subjects, touching upon subjects as diverse as exemptions from military service, complaints against economic exploitation, requests for divorce, and the pardoning of crimes. The tsar obviously did not personally review all such matters, but he was always the court of last resort, and officials could never know for sure what would reach him. Complaints about air ventilation in a Urals factory might indeed be acted upon by order of the tsar.

Autocracy means precisely this autonomous exercise of power from the highest to the lowest levels of society. But we are not referring to a ruthlessly efficient totalitarian police state. We must understand both "autonomy" and "power" in relative terms. The tsar could not entirely disregard the law, unsystematically compiled in massive tomes over countless decades, though he could make exceptions, give exemptions, and not infrequently break codified law (which was neither well-known nor well-defended by an organized legal profession). As the example of the 1905 revolution shows, he could not completely ignore the voice of his own people, no matter how distasteful it might have been to him. Similarly, even though he hated the Petersburg bureaucracy—the machinery of his own government—he could hardly do without bureaucratic politics and decision making in his vast empire.

If his autonomy was always limited, his power was perhaps even more so. Paradoxically, the very institution of autocracy impeded the ruler's ability to achieve his goals. The weakness of law and the predominance of personal ties over fixed procedures inherent in autocracy made administration inchoate and unpredictable in its results. The personal dependence of officials on the favor of the autocrat made them fearful to take initiative and deeply committed to political intrigues. Surrounded by a vacuum of organizations, which might have expressed the interests and desires of different sectors of the population, the tsar had no base in society for the changes he might want to promote. Laws hung in the air, indifferently acted upon by the administration and almost completely disconnected from social interests. In these respects, the political leaders of more legalistic and organized societies like France, Germany, or England had more actual power. In his capacity to shape society, the autocratic tsar often seemed close to impotence, able only to watch helplessly as his initiatives were subverted or otherwise came to nothing.

By 1900 the Russian autocracy was one of the few surviving members of a vanishing breed. Autocracy in the strict sense had virtually disappeared many centuries before, even where it had ever existed, in Western Europe. Feudalism, with its recognition of the contractual rights of vassals, was very far from autocracy in spirit. European absolutist monarchs were always limited to some degree by the fixed rights of independent subjects, whether nobilities, corporate cities, or the Church (which had its own independent canon law). The Ottoman sultans, admired for centuries despite their different faith by Russian tsars envious of their complete dominance over their subjects, were soon to be replaced by a modernizing secular elite. It may be objected that in the twentieth century there have been many personal autocracies in developing countries, ranging from Duvalier in Haiti to Kim Il Sung in North Korea. True enough, but the Russian autocracy differed from the vast majority of these in its deep historical and religious legitimation. As I have discussed in an earlier book, perhaps the closest twentieth-century parallel to the role of the Russian autocrat was the shah of Iran.[2]

In Russia autocracy was not merely practice based on the desire of the ruler for unlimited power, as it has been for many twentieth-century autocrats. Rather, hallowed by multiple strands of frequently inconsistent theological and ideological justifications, by 1900 it had been for almost half a millennium the central myth of Russian political life and also the main cornerstone of social relations. Nicholas II, passive and indecisive by nature, clearly regarded autocracy as a burden placed upon him by God, and before God he was committed to passing it on to his descendants, no matter what his own personal desires. He received almost no inner psychological gratification from the exercise of autocratic power, as his phlegmatic diary amply attests.

It is far from easy to untangle the different strands of autocratic ideology surrounding the office of tsar in Russia by the turn of the century, and even more difficult to give them their due weight in relation to each other. Particularly inconvenient is the rather striking fact that some of its major elements directly contradict each other. Further, specialists continue to debate the relative significance of Christian, Byzantine imperial, Tartar, and Western conceptions of autocratic rule in different historical periods. We are also not fortunate in having, in Nicholas II, a sophisticated and articulate tsar who might have understood and tried to cope with the formidable difficulties involved in the exercise of his role by the early twentieth century.

Whatever the complexities involved, however, for our theme—the fateful impact of the Russian idea on the country's efforts at modernization—the question of the conception and nature of autocratic power is inescapable. For precisely within the very institution of tsarist autocracy the contradiction between the Russian idea of rule and the imperatives of modern politics played themselves out in dramatic fashion.

The idea of the unlimited power of the Russian monarch had both ancient and modern sources. To the former belong notions allegedly borrowed from the Tartars about the tsar as master over his people and territory. All resources ultimately belonged to him, and his people could be nothing more to him than *kholopy*, slaves. In this context, the idea of representation or rights made no sense: the tsar's power could not be constrained in any way by the will of others.

Quite separate from these notions of the tsar as absolute owner of his realm were a whole constellation of religious notions that gave Christian sanction to autocratic power. The tsar was God's viceroy on Earth, whose vast and unlimited powers were given to him by God in the service of the faith. Just as it would be sinful to rebel against the wisdom of God, so the judgment of the tsar, the protector of the holy faith on Earth, was sacrosanct. Chosen by God, the tsar partook of the divine. Curiously, this symbol of the tsar as God's omnipotent terrestrial regent was combined with a Christ-like image of the tsar as humble sufferer for his people. At the end of their lives many Russian tsars, including Ivan the Terrible, took monastic vows in conformity with this model of the tsar as the suffering servant. Only such a pious and humble tsar, re-creating in his person Christ's self-sacrifice, was morally qualified for terrestrial leadership of his community.

Sophisticated and penetrating studies have been published on the intellectual sources and implications of such views.[3] The issues involved are really far more complex than can be conveyed here. How, for example, to interpret the mandate of a tsar who was clearly not Christ-like in service to the community but exercised his autocratic power ruthlessly? Was he still God's hereditary regent on Earth? What traces did these subtle debates leave on popular political culture? Or did the tsar's omnipotence derive more from his political role as owner of his people?

Whatever the answers to these questions, the ancient justifications of autocratic power correspond in some fundamental ways to the expectations of ruler and ruled over the centuries. The Russian tsar was seen as the embodiment of the faith and the protector of the Russian way of life. He saw himself as ruling over a people united in devotion to him. Unlimited power over his subjects derived from this religious interpretation of his mandate. Opposition was perfidious, initiated only by those who were really outsiders to the people—Jews, perhaps, or Western-educated intriguers. For their part, many of his subjects perceived politics in parallel terms. A true tsar embodied the values and traditions of Russian life. He ruled according to Truth and protected the community from dangerous outside forces. Not a mediator among conflicting social groups, he was to side directly with his loyal people in their just grievances. Neither tsar nor people had any conception of a complex society, but acted in terms of conceptions of social harmony based upon unity.

Clearly, these implications of ancient ideas of autocracy provide much of the foundation for the Russian idea of politics. They not only found acceptance among a large sector of the Russian people, but also became elaborated by intellectuals seeking to define a special Russian path to modernity. But by the end of the reign of Peter the Great in the early eighteenth century, they had already partly given way to a more revolutionary conception of the role of the autocrat in Russian life. These more modern conceptions, influenced by models of rule in Western Europe, particularly in Germany and Sweden, testified to the growing influence of the ideas of progress and utilitarianism.[4]

According to this new model, the ruler had the responsibility to ensure his country's prosperity and protect it from its enemies. Both of these goals required that the country be developed, that its resources be utilized and its people trained and disciplined. According to this modernist conception, the legitimacy of autocratic power did not derive solely from religion, although apologists for the new form of autocracy continued to stress the biblical injunctions on the duty of absolute obedience to authority. Nor was the tsar conceptualized mainly as the spiritual leader of his people responsible for the protection of the Orthodox community, or even less as a humble suffering servant in imitation of Christ. Rather, it was the peace and prosperity of the realm and the welfare of its subjects that required autocratic rule. Just as the head of the household was charged with the welfare of all of his subordinates, so the tsar, wise and powerful like the father, was responsible for the nation.

In this new role, the tsar could break with tradition, if the welfare of the nation required it. He could force the young to be educated in foreign lands and according to foreign ideas. He could try to break the hold of the traditional religion on the society if he believed that it inhibited progress. He could attempt to copy Western institutions, introducing new bureaucratic forms into Russian politics and thus partially depersonalizing the old Muscovite model of rule. He could invite foreign citizens to reside in the country, and even to lead the efforts to reconstruct the military, industry, and culture. New elites and social groups connected to modern trade and industry would have to be created to supplement the traditional social structure of Muscovite Russia.

In short, the new model of autocracy sanctioned a kind of revolutionary break with the past inconceivable to the Moscow tsars—and, throughout two centuries, unacceptable to a great many of his subjects. In the words of Alexander Herzen:

> Torn out of our sleepy and vegetative life by a thunderbolt, or more exactly, by a drumbeat; pulled away from the embrace of our mother (a poor and coarse peasant woman, but nonetheless our mother), we came to see that we had been deprived of everything, beginning with our clothes and beards [a reference to Peter the Great's new laws on proper appearance]. They taught us to despise our own mother and to mock our parents' hearth. They forced upon us a foreign tradition, they hurled science at us. Then, upon departure from school, they announced to us that we are slaves chained to the state.[5]

Such, to Herzen, was the essence of the new vision of autocracy as the source of progress. In another place he described the result: "There has never been any interval in the resistance to the Petersburg culture terrorism."[6] Perhaps having witnessed twentieth-century refinements of cultural revolution imposed from above, we might be more skeptical of his use of the term terrorism. But we cannot doubt the truth of his insight: many Russians saw their own government as waging a war against them.

It was this fusion of ancient notions of autocracy with a new vision of autocratic power based on the promise of progress that eventually made political reform both imperative and impossible. Let us return to Nicholas II's dilemma at the time of the political crisis of 1905. Virtually all of urban Russia was demanding reform, the granting of a constitution. But these groups, whom Nicholas wanted to regard as outsiders, alien to the Russian people, were largely the product of the changes brought about by his government and those of his predecessors. It was the Russian state that had been determined to encourage industry, and since the 1880s it had embarked upon an ambitious program of state-stimulated industrialization. It had welcomed foreign investors and entrepreneurs in the hope that their skills could be transferred to a new native elite. For almost two centuries the state had encouraged scientific contacts with Western Europe and inculcated Western education into the elites, producing, in the process, more than the mere embryo of an educated middle class. By the turn of the twentieth century Russian science had begun to come of age.

And yet, as Herzen stated, educated Russians were still shackled to the state, and the new social groups were not allowed to express their shared interests—themselves created through the processes of modernization and industrialization—in an organized way. They could still only petition the father tsar. In response to these changes, the nineteenth-century tsars did attempt to extend autocratic paternalism throughout the society. They created new offices, such as the land captains in the countryside and the factory inspectors in industry, to detect abuses and redress grievances, insofar as the government felt that they were just. But the autocratic regime could not countenance the politics of representation, and it could not conceive of its subjects as an organized society rather than a loyal people.

The problem for Nicholas was both cognitive and moral. Partly entrapped within the ancient model of rulership, Nicholas did not understand the kind of society that was rapidly emerging around him. He even hated his own bureaucracy, whose complexity and scale were beyond his comprehension. He preferred to deal with officials on an individual basis rather than in institutional settings, such as a group meeting, and he relied on personal relations of trust more than on efficiency or expertise. His moral vision was also sadly outmoded: the expression of group interest for him was merely egotism, to which he opposed the fatherly wisdom of the tsar, able to reconcile conflicting claims and petitions. Outright opposition could only be the work of traitors, who through their violation of the norms of autocratic paternalism lost any right to be heard.

In accord with his almost pre-Petrine political vision, Nicholas explained his acceptance of some form of representative political body in the following way:

> My will, the tsar's will, to summon popular electors is unswerving. . . . Let the union between the tsar and all of Russia be established, as it was in olden times, the contact between Me and the *zemskie liudi* [people of the land], that will underlie the order in conformance with original Russian principles. I hope you will assist Me in this work.[7]

"Union," "*zemskie liudi*," "original Russian principles" (which of course never included the *right* of citizens to be heard): such phrases, which are ubiquitous in the tsar's utterances throughout this time of crisis, alert us to the tsar's utter lack of comprehension of the logic of representative government.

And since Russia never ceased being in essence an "autocracy"—although no one knew of exactly what kind, whether inspired by models from the fifteenth or the eighteenth centuries—the tsar's stance was of paramount importance. Under great pressure from the revolution, on October 17, 1905, the tsar signed the famous October Manifesto, which gave vaguely stated promises of full civil liberties; an inclusive franchise for election to the Duma, the new legislature; and the guarantee that "no law can become effective without the approval of the State Duma." It seemed that, almost overnight and at the initiative of the tsar, Russia had become a constitutional monarchy.

Yet less than two weeks later Nicholas could write to the dowager empress that after the issuance of the October Manifesto, "the whole mass of loyal people came alive," "outraged by the impudence and audacity of the revolutionaries and socialists"—"nine-tenths of them kikes."[8] These good people, the real Russian people, not the trouble-making Jews and intellectuals, still favored autocracy, Nicholas believed. "Why were they silent before, the good people?" In the following few months Nicholas came to the astounding conclusion that the manifesto and the changes that it granted implied no diminution of his autocratic powers, but only limited the government that would be formed on its basis! In his own mind, he was still the Orthodox tsar of all the Russias, the defender of Truth and the protector of his united and harmonious people, who rejected the Jews and revolutionaries.

Yet these convictions, which signaled a revival of his own sense of himself as a true Muscovite tsar, did not lead Nicholas to try to reverse his reforms. An electoral law was indeed promulgated, and the Duma established. But the enactment of these reforms, which in theory might have saved the regime through the creation of a constitutional monarchy, thus appeasing the liberal opposition and giving legitimacy to the government, in fact solved nothing. Nicholas, his Councils of Ministers, and the Duma were in constant conflict, unceasingly vying over both particular measures and general principles. Nicholas's own political stance was erratic, alternating between fatalistic passivity and blustering threats. The political system could not accurately be described either as an autocracy or as a constitutional monarchy. Rather, it had lost its coherence and was founded on no clear principles. The constitutional struggles and his own concessions had clearly undermined the tsar's claim to autocratic power, but the outcome was not greater democracy, simply political decay.

As is fitting in the context of Russian history, the responsibility for the paralysis of government in the late tsarist period must rest with the autocrat. If he had been a strong and consistent supporter of constitutional reform, state and society might have ceased to regard each other as divided by an unbridgeable gap. But embodying a more traditional political culture, Nicholas could not come to terms with a politics based, not on tsar and people, but on state and society. His own efforts to conserve the Russian idea of politics played no small part in plunging his people into political chaos.

AUTOCRACY AND THE LABOR QUESTION

In the preservation of autocracy and the social ideals linked with it, the role of Nicholas II was paramount. When we turn to another vital issue confronting the regime, the labor question, we see that many of these same perceptions and assumptions permeated both the government and the labor movement. Many government officials believed that it was the responsibility of officials to define and regulate social relations in industry according to a familial model of society. They were unable to perceive that a new social logic, that of class, was emerging in Russian industry, and they attempted to deal with the new forms of social conflict according to their traditionalist assumptions. At the same time, broad sectors of the labor movement also conceived of themselves according to basic elements of the Russian idea: they were a homogeneous righteous community oppressed by outside forces (the industrialists); they alone had a right to government protection; a just government would act to defend them against the forces of falsehood. These were not the only assumptions underlying the actions of either government officials or workers, but they were extremely significant in hindering some kind of positive response to the labor question.

In the context of mature industrial or "postindustrial" society, it is hard for us to recapture the significance of the labor question for the evolution of industrial societies in earlier periods. Wage labor and large-scale factory production created new social groups and new patterns of relations that did not fit in well with older models of society. Patriarchal relations between masters and dependents were in large part undermined because of the larger scale of enterprises. Workers became subject to the uncertainties of market determination of wages. Further, there were opportunities for new forms of association based on horizontal ties of shared interest. These primarily class-based associations partly replaced the previously dominant vertical ties of dependence. Factory workers, particularly in cities, were also exposed to all kinds of new influences and came to have greater access to education. Virtually everywhere, these fundamental changes gave rise to new kinds of social and political demands expressed through new forms of collective action.

Workers sought civil and political rights in order to defend their class interests, and they engaged in strikes, created organizations, and supported political parties in order to promote their goals.

All of these changes posed new questions for states and elites. It is these issues, taken together, that defined the "labor question." What rights were workers to have—the right to strike, the right to form unions, the right to participate in politics, the right to negotiate with owners? What was to be the role of government—how was it to respond to social protest, what rules would it create, what would be its role in the class struggle? The answers given to these questions were vital in shaping the economic and political trajectories of all industrializing countries.

Responses to the labor question were of two basic kinds: liberal or hierarchical. The liberal response, pioneered in England, involved the gradual extension of civil, social, and political rights to the contending classes, so that each group was in the position to defend its interests. The government made rules, but it left much of the outcome to the play of contending forces and actors: market forces, levels of political influence, organizational capacity. The hierarchical response, typified by Germany and Japan, involved some combination of government and capitalist protection and regulation of labor relations, whether through protective legislation, the development of paternalistic employer policies, or the creation of worker organizations under the control of employers or the government. The goal of such schemes was not to liberate, but to protect workers, and to attempt to replicate the old paternal relations between master and dependent in the new context of large-scale industry.

In the roughly thirty years that the labor question loomed as one of the central social and political issues of late imperial Russia, neither the tsarist regime nor the industrialists were able to undertake effective positive measures to resolve these issues vital to the future of the country. Report after report was made; officials clearly recognized the miserable material conditions of industrial workers and the dangers of social protest. Conference after conference was convened in order to respond to the threat, but effective measures were virtually absent. And when the government did manage to pass a law legalizing trade unions in 1906, after the perils of worker radicalization were clearly visible, in the following years it did more to hamper than to allow the development of an organized trade union movement, in the process violating its own laws.

As in the inability significantly to reform autocracy, much of this failure to come to terms with the labor question stemmed from the pervasive social and political assumptions of the Russian idea. For officials imbued with the image of a homogeneous people united behind a tsar embodying their values, the first challenge was to recognize that the labor question had even come to exist in Russia. Such a recognition does not merely mean that officials noticed the existence of labor conflict: even the most obtuse local policeman could hardly fail to observe it. Rather, to conceptualize the existence of a "labor question" it was necessary to understand something of the logic of the new kind of social relations that were developing. Such insight was completely beyond the capacity of those who thought in the time-honored ways.

What did typical officials understand when they saw a strike? They did not see it as an expression of "interest" and the result of organization. Rather, they saw the workers' actions as a product of the workers' legitimate material grievances; the spontaneous combustion of their accumulated anger; and the insidious influence of outside agitators, who sought to make political use of the workers' discontent for their own purposes. It is worth inquiring into the assumptions behind such an interpretation and their prescriptions for action.

First, it should be emphasized that the government was by no means hostile to the workers' actual complaints. Indeed, government officials charged with dealing with factory affairs often sympathized with the workers and excoriated the factory owners for their heartless exploitation. Sometimes their denunciations sounded much like Marxist propaganda, as in the March 1898 report of Ministry of Internal Affairs official Panteleev. Employers, he said, exploited their helpless workers for their own benefit, paying them almost nothing despite their own enormous profits. Their conduct was especially unjust, said Panteleev, because it was only the "vital forces of the workers" that made the factory's prosperity possible.[9] Not infrequently the worker-employer conflict was interpreted in terms of a binary opposition between the innocent people and the outside, frequently foreign, exploiter. For example, the head of the Moscow secret police, Sergei Zubatov, attacked the arrogance and selfishness of the factory owners and through his organization's efforts hoped to establish a community of loyal subjects in which "all the oppressed and insulted will find . . . paternal attention, advice, support, and help in word and in deed."[10] According to such views, to feel grievances was justified, but to act upon them independently was not, for it was the mission of the paternal government to right wrongs. "Interest" was a category foreign to this way of thinking, for the term has no moralistic overtones and is defined by the actors themselves rather than by a paternalistic overseer.

Interpretation in terms of "grievances" rather than "interests" lay behind the official view of worker protest as irrational, spontaneous, unpredictable. The workers "felt" their exploitation, but to officials they were incapable of rationally judging it. This required the intervention of the impartial agents of the state, who could weigh all claims on the basis of a higher standard of justice. In a famous statement mocked by revolutionaries, Witte appealed to textile strikers in 1896 to recognize that the "law defends the workers and indicates the path by which they can discover the truth if they feel themselves to be injured. . . . The government will occupy itself with the improvement of their situation and the lightening of their work insofar as this is beneficial for the workers themselves."[11] Action, particularly political action, was not necessary, for it was inherently divisive and irrational; the government, representing truth, would determine the justice of the competing claims. Such a view of social groups and social action completely undercuts any idea of rights inherent in the subject; the subject is even deprived of the legitimacy of his or her own interests. Interest, after all, may be at the basis of society, but truth and justice are the roots of community.

Protest was ultimately, then, the result of two sets of agents foreign to the community of subjects: capitalist exploiters and revolutionary agitators. The state's program of action to deal with labor unrest was accordingly twofold in nature. First, it must protect the workers from capitalist exploitation through the development of protective legislation and the administrative apparatus to enforce it. Second, it must deal ruthlessly with the revolutionaries, who were seen to be foreign to the inherently loyal workers. But such a response to the labor question was hopelessly outmoded and ineffective. It implied that the government could know, judge, and act upon the workers' grievances, but it had neither the knowledge nor the power to carry out this utopian program of social engineering. Further, its diagnosis of the appeal of revolutionary ideas was simple-minded in the extreme: in part because many revolutionaries were in fact full members of the worker "community" and in no sense outsiders; and in part because many of the workers' grievances stemmed from the fact that they did not have *rights*, including the right to define and act upon their own interests. Without the recognition of new rights, no progress could be made in coming to terms with the labor question.

Some high government officials did begin to perceive the logic of the new social relations and came to espouse liberal reforms, which would have granted more civil and political rights to the workers. The high tide of such sentiment was reached in the spring of 1906, in the deliberations of the Fedorov Commission, called to propose solutions to labor conflict, which during the 1905 revolution had broken all world records. The commission concluded that primary culpability for the unrest lay with the government, whose assumptions had been completely misguided: "our industrial structure needs, above all, the greatest possible freedom from excessive administrative tutelage."[12] Worker activism was natural in industrial society, it said, as workers sought to defend their own interests. The solution to the labor question, the freeing of the two sides to defend their own interests, and thereby to reach compromises based on their relative power, was also deemed to be natural. The commission was therefore in favor of the legalization of strikes and trade unions as legitimate instruments of the class struggle.

In just the same way, liberal reformers during the same period urged the establishment of a constitutional monarchy to replace the autocracy. And also in the same way, many of the reforms were ambiguously granted on paper, only to be violated by the resurgence of the old assumptions after the revolution had been defeated. Until the 1917 revolution, the government outlawed strikes and repressed organizations that were formally legal. It continued to act upon the view that labor protest was fundamentally illegitimate and could be eliminated through a correct application of autocratic authority. In such a way, it was felt, exploitation could be wiped out and revolutionary agitation suppressed. The tsar and his working people could be united in a just and harmonious community based on ancient Russian ideals, thereby avoiding the conflicts and chaos of class relations in Western Europe.

In fact, the scale and radicalism of working-class protest in Russia dwarfed that of any country in Europe, despite the fact that the proletariat constituted a much lower percentage of the population than in the most advanced capitalist countries. Marx was wrong: working-class militancy did not grow apace with the development of capitalist industry. Rather, Russia taught another lesson: the link between relative "backwardness" and radicalism. Backwardness does not only mean the relative poverty and miserable working conditions of Russian industry at the time, important as these were in generating discontent. In addition, emphasis must be placed on the inability of the tsarist regime to reshape labor relations to meet the challenges of modernization. New rights had to be granted to compensate for the workers' helplessness in capitalist society. The government itself recognized that the rights to strike and to form trade unions were indispensable, but the laws that it passed in this regard were systematically violated. Workers rightly saw the government not just as ineffective in protecting them, but as unjust in breaking its own promises.

The failure to provide workers with modern rights reinforced in them a traditional sense of entitlement. Recall that government officials frequently attacked the capitalists for their unjust exploitation of the workers and urged the workers to turn to the government for the satisfaction of their grievances. Such an approach encouraged the workers to think of themselves as the tsar's privileged subjects, in opposition to the pariah factory owners. In legislating new rights the government had made new commitments to the workers, once again strengthening the idea that the workers' aspirations were just.

If the government had been able to protect the workers and had abided by its own laws, the workers' sense of legitimate grievance would have been turned against the factory owners. But because the government did not fulfill its commitments, its moral stance was turned against itself. The righteous workers opposed themselves to a government of falsehood, which protected not them, but the exploiting class. The working people had a right to demand a Government of Truth, which meant a government that would promote only the workers' interests according to a higher vision of community. The government's failed efforts at reform thus unwittingly reinforced the workers' sense of isolation from the rest of society, their sense of unique entitlement, and their belief that a just government by definition would defend their interests against all opponents. In this view, the only legitimate government was a class government of the proletariat, an idea that in Russia was rooted more in fundamental assumptions of the Russian idea than in Marxist theory, for it did not envision the abolition of the state so much as its transformation into a Government of Truth. Thus, in acting according to basic tenets of the Russian idea, the autocratic regime reproduced them among the workers in a radicalized version.

The Peasant Commune

The Russian serfs were liberated by a decree of Alexander II in 1861. The political debates and the tsar's personal campaign in the preceding years had created an enormous sense of expectation among the Russian peasants, who wanted not only their freedom but full possession of all manorial land. To them it seemed that the tsar-father, now become tsar-liberator, had risen to bring justice to the land, destroying with a mighty blow the power of their enemies. They met the actual terms of the emancipation with literal unbelief: upon the announcement that the landowners would keep their right to roughly half of the land and that the peasants would be responsible to repay the government for what became theirs, rumors began to spread that this was not the tsar's true deed, that deceivers were at work spreading lies. The peasants recognized neither the right of the nobility to possess any land at all nor any duty on their part to pay the government for what was by their moral standards theirs. According to a noble official writing at the time:

> What they have been granted appears not to correspond to the size of the transformation which they had expected; and so they refuse to believe what is written. According to them, because for once fate has turned the natural force of supreme power to their advantage, they now have the right to expect from it every kind of benefit and generosity.[13]

In allocating land to the nobility, the tsarist regime sought to shore up what it regarded as its main social base. It was virtually inconceivable that the government could supervise the destruction of its own servitors in the army, bureaucracy, and provincial life. But in preserving noble estates in the countryside, even if diminished in size and number, the regime perpetuated a social elite that was utterly without legitimacy among the peasantry. The peasants regarded the nobles as an alien force that was responsible for all their ills—for their lack of land, their poverty, and their hunger—even though in fact rural overpopulation and economic inefficiency were far more significant causes of their woes. On several occasions in the twilight period of tsarism, the peasants acted decisively to eliminate their enemy, expropriating land, burning estates, and sometimes murdering the landowners. Contrary to the hope of conservatives, who saw in it the source of social stability in the countryside, the peasant commune led these massive rural revolts.

What was the peasant commune, in Russian the *mir* or *obshchina?* Although it long predated the abolition of serfdom, let us describe it as it existed after the emancipation. By the terms of the 1861 decree, land was vested not in the individual peasant household, but in the commune, which had authority over its use. The commune consisted of former serfs and their descendants, who usually lived in a single village, although sometimes there was more than one village in a mir. The mir allocated land to its household members and periodically redistributed it according to size of family, need, and ability to utilize more land. It is important to emphasize that the mir was not socialistic in nature, for the land was allocated to and worked by individual households, who were fully entitled to the fruits of their labor. Unlike the Communist *kolkhoz,* this was not a system of collective labor. Nonetheless, it was not private property, for the land could not be sold or alienated without permission of the commune.

By the terms of the emancipation, a wide variety of administrative powers were also vested in the commune. It was made responsible for the collection and payment of taxes for the village as a whole, with the right to interfere in household affairs in order to ensure compliance—for example, by forcing a household to hire out one of its members for wages. Also because of this collective liability for taxes, it was given the right to withhold or authorize departures of peasants from the village. Equally fateful for the male peasant, it was responsible for levying recruits for the army. All sorts of local administrative matters were also in its purview. Decisions on these matters were taken by the village assembly, composed of heads of households, and the elected village elder.

Since as late as 1905 roughly three-fourths of peasant households in European Russia lived in communes of this type, we are clearly dealing with one of the most significant institutions in Russian history, in many respects the fundamental building block of the society. Thinkers sought to appraise its overall meaning for Russian life; the government sought to regulate and control it; revolutionaries of various stripes attempted to mobilize it; and modernizers of all categories became committed to transforming or even abolishing it. It was also the ideological focus for three competing versions of the Russian idea, all of them attempting to chart a separate historical path for Russia on its basis.

The first version was authoritarian in nature and had its natural appeal among the nobility and ruling elite. They embraced the idea that in Russia social relations were more familial than in the West, less cold and impersonal. But "the family" was interpreted in a paternalistic way rather than in terms of the competing model of brotherhood. According to this paternalistic view, authority and hierarchy should penetrate the society, permeating all social relations. The peasant should regard the noble in this light, just as both should look to the tsar, and ultimately God, for direction. The bottom rung of this chain of authority was to be the peasant household, ruled by the head of the family. The peasant commune was to be a mediating link in this hierarchy, composed of heads of households, and subordinate to authorities above and below. Thus, in perpetuating the commune after the emancipation, they assumed that it would reinforce hierarchy and ensure social stability. The peasant world, operating by the same principles as the tsarist system as a whole, would be the expression of truth and the foundation of order. The miscalculation in this view could not have been more gross, for authority in Russia did not extend in an unbroken chain. Rather, in peasant eyes God's authority and the authority of the tsar directly opposed and undercut any moral claims of the nobility. For the tsar, as the representative of Truth, must surely be on the side of his loyal people rather than on the side of the usurping landowners.

The second moral vision based on the peasant commune was Slavophilism, especially prominent in intellectual circles before the emancipation of the serfs, but in one form or another widespread in Russian culture up to the present time. According to the Slavophile world view, the mir provided a superior model of society to that of the West, because it was based on harmony rather than conflict. This harmony was based on universal access to property, equality (ensured by the practice of periodic repartition of village land), and quasi-familial social ties based on shared cultural and religious beliefs. Russia, they claimed, was without a proletariat and without class conflict. Instead, it embodied social harmony based on patriarchy, with the nobility safeguarding the welfare of the peasants. Russia could therefore avoid the political upheavals disfiguring Western history. The main danger facing the country, they argued, was the Petrine state, bent on distorting native Russian institutions in the interest of a false and unjust model of modernization. From this standpoint, the *ideal* of tsarist authority was legitimate, since the tsar embodied and protected the principles of the Russian way of life, but the Petrine bureaucracy and actual government policy were seen as corrupt. It should come as no surprise, then, that the government of Nicholas I regarded the Slavophiles' doctrines as subversive and censored many of their writings. This official disapproval only added to the authority of these ideas in many circles and added to the penumbra of sanctity surrounding the peasant commune, even if Slavophilism seriously underestimated the impact of serfdom and romanticized the role of the gentry in rural life. The Slavophile vision of the village was potent mythology, if bad sociology.

Finally, the village commune inspired populist visions of total revolution, providing both a theory of resistance to injustice and a model for the socialist reconstruction of society. Like the proletariat in Marxist theory, for revolutionary populists the peasant already embodied the moral principles of the society that the peasant's revolutionary action would bring into being. Unlike conservative government officials, the populist revolutionaries knew that the authority of landlords and officials was weak among the peasantry; unlike the Slavophiles, they did not look back to a golden pre-Petrine past of unsullied natural community. Rather, they believed that the peasant commune, if properly built upon, could provide a natural basis for socialism. Theirs, then, was a doctrine of "progress." Indeed, the innately communal character of Russian peasant institutions would allow Russia to bypass altogether Western capitalism, with its exploited proletariat and bitter class divisions, and directly transform itself into a country of self-sufficient worker and peasant communes. But the revolutionary populists, too, were misled by their own myths: the peasants opposed the nobility and local officials, but they did not support or understand the idea of political revolution. Nor were the peasants socialistic. They wanted the protection of communal institutions but also favored the maintenance of an individual household economy. In this sense, the Marxist attacks on the "petit bourgeois" peasantry showed a keener appreciation of the peasants' aspirations.

Such were the myths imposed upon the village commune. They exemplified the influence of the binary logic of anti-Westernism within the government and among the intelligentsia more than they displayed empirical sociological acumen. For in fact, the peasant commune was in fundamental ways antithetical to the overall direction of change in Russian society toward a market economy and a more differentiated and interdependent social order. It inhibited individual initiative; strengthened the polar opposition between the quasi-familial known world of the village and the hostile outside world beyond it; undermined abstract legal awareness in favor of a reliance on personalized authority; and rejected the hierarchies of wealth and position inherent in large-scale societies. Its natural inclination was to close in upon itself, indifferent to other groups and to political questions that did not directly touch it, inclined to a natural economy based on local self-sufficiency. Village society was therefore hostile not just to the status quo in imperial Russia, but to any version of modernization based on a complex division of labor and a unified political community.

The tsarist regime was therefore caught in a web of contradictions. Peasants might have been loyal to the tsar, but they were hostile to modern government. They were in many ways conservative, accepting the authority of God, the tsar, and the village elders, as well as the legitimacy of private property, but against the nobility they were Jacobins. Thus, peasants were neither conservative in the way that the government hoped nor revolutionary according to the dreams of the populists. To add to the government's dilemma, even if it had been true that the commune was a source of social and political stability, it certainly seemed to hinder economic progress, both by providing an automatic welfare mechanism for families that were too large and by creating obstacles to individual initiative. But even if, on balance, the government's assessment turned out to be negative, what could justify it in once again upsetting the time-honored traditions of Russian life?

The answer to this question was given by the peasants themselves. To the shock of the tsar, in 1905–1906 his loyal narod, acting through the authority of their communal institutions, rose up against the landlords in a mighty wave of vengeance. In addition, they elected to the Duma not supporters of the status quo, but deputies adamantly demanding the immediate expropriation of noble land. The conservative myth was exploded, just as, in reciprocity, the peasants' faith in their tsar-protector was dramatically undermined by his stiff-willed defense of private property—at least, private property of the nobility. The tsar now saw peasant demands as socialistic, although they were nothing of the sort. Clearly, in the eyes of the political elite, whether disillusioned conservatives or modernizing reformers, peasant communal institutions were now a clear political as well as economic liability.

This dramatic switch of perspective soon culminated in one of the most ambitious efforts of social engineering of the many centuries of tsarist rule: the Stolypin reforms, named after the prime minister who sponsored them, which sought to undermine the peasant commune and encourage the rise of individual peasant household farming. The details of these complicated reforms, initiated in November 1906, need not concern us here. In broad outline, they sought to accomplish the following: to encourage the consolidation of landholdings within the village (Russian peasants traditionally worked separated strips of land); to give legal title to individual peasants who wanted to leave the village commune; and to stimulate agricultural productivity through credit and education. Through these changes, the Stolypin government hoped to stimulate the rise of a prosperous rural elite of independent farmers, who would provide a stable and conservative social bulwark for the regime.

As with the constitutional reform and the legalization of strikes and unions, the government was now enunciating principles directly at odds with those that previously had been heralded as the traditional foundations of social justice. In economic life, peasants were to be self-sufficient farmers or wage laborers, depending on luck and talents. In politics, the constitutional reforms and electoral laws made them citizens, entitled to form and vote for parties that would represent their interests in a competitive political process. They were to be free to leave the village and seek work in the cities, and thus shed their hereditary peasant status if they so chose. Therefore, the peasant world was not to be closed in upon itself, but continuous with the rest of changing Russian society. The tsar, who still preferred to think of himself as the embodiment of Russian tradition, had himself approved these changes.

No more than in the case of the constitutional reforms or the new labor laws can we know what the implications of these changes might have been had the regime survived longer. As a result of the reforms, millions of peasant households did receive individual title to land, but the number of independent farms established was far, far smaller. Further, much resentment and social conflict was unleashed within the village between those who wanted to separate from the commune and those who did not. Whatever the conflicting evidence, which is still being debated by historians, there was simply not enough time before the outbreak of revolution for the full implications of Stolypin's program to be realized. In the meantime, rural Russia was a divided society: old Russia survived even while the new institutions were being born. Unfortunately, there could be no easy birth during this transition period. The old and the new principles did not support, but undermined, each other—for we recall that much of the support for traditional Russian institutions had been precisely because they opposed capitalist modernity. Consequently, rural Russia never became that stable bulwark of the status quo that Stolypin dreamed of.

In 1917 the commune took revenge upon its enemies. Perhaps even more hostility was aroused by the peasants who had chosen to separate from the village community than even by the nobility. The lands of both were of course returned to the community through forcible expropriation, but there was particular enmity toward the brother peasants who had betrayed their own kind, threatening to pauperize their fellows for self-enrichment. And once again, the village attempted to turn in upon itself, although in the context of revolution and civil war its goal of economic and social autarchy was as utopian as any revolutionary dream. But, just as always when faced by crisis, the peasant sought solace in the *rodnoi* village and in the all-protective commune: "motionless in expectation, slow but self-assured in its own development, conservative like a mother bearing a child in her womb, and enduring much, enduring everything, besides the denial of her own foundation."[14]

The tsarist government had never known quite how to deal with this "female principle and cornerstone of the whole edifice, its monad, the warp of the enormous cloth named Russia."[15] Although the commune was compelled by alien forces coming from the government to take on paternal functions of discipline and control, the crisis of political authority brought on by the revolution allowed it to resume its sheltering and nurturant functions. Thus, the peasant commune would survive the revolution, interpreted at first by the Bolsheviks in terms of the class struggle of the poor peasantry against the capitalist elements. But the Communist leadership would soon come to understand that this purest social embodiment of the Russian idea was in clear conflict with its own version of modernity, one much more ruthless than that of the ambivalent tsarist regime. Only then would the real war against the commune, begun by Stolypin, find its consummation in a bloody campaign against virtually the Russian peasantry as a whole.

Intelligentsia, State, and Revolution

The Russian intelligentsia, like intellectual leaders elsewhere, has often been interpreted as an isolated priesthood of ideologists seeking to impose their ideological visions on an uncomprehending people. In this view, the "people," whether peasants or workers, have been seen as concerned only with their own narrow interests, unconcerned with the great questions of politics and certainly uncommitted to parties and ideological programs. Following Alexis de Tocqueville's analysis in *The Old Regime and the French Revolution*, Russian intellectuals have been accused of rootlessness and abstractness, partly the product of the tsarist system's prohibitions on political participation, which otherwise might have tempered these traits. A series of oppositions is then offered: the people were uneducated and of modest class background, the intelligentsia were from the nobility or the middle sectors; the people, still steeped in Russian folk culture and religion, had hardly been touched by Peter's reforms, the intelligentsia were imbued by Western ideas; the people embodied the authentic principles of Russian life, the intelligentsia were rootless and alien; and so on. The political implications drawn from this kind of analysis are clear: the intelligentsia did not speak for the people. Thus, the Bolshevik revolution, the work of a small sector of the revolutionary intelligentsia, was never a people's revolution. Communism was a conspiracy.

Much of this analysis is true. Peasants and workers did look at the revolutionary intelligentsia across a class divide. For them these odd intellectuals were never *rodnoi*, never trusted in the same way as their brother peasants or workers. As one older worker remarked, referring to the intelligentsia activists among them, "I must say that we workers should not trust these mother's girls and boys and well-groomed idlers, who have come from the class of exploiters, since they and we don't have the same interest. We must relate to them with great caution, since they can turn out to be false defenders of the workers' interests."[16] It was notorious that peasants were at least as likely to report revolutionary agitators to the police as to listen to them. Nor can there be any doubt that the workers and peasants had no real understanding of the implications of revolutionary teachings, no matter how appealing radical slogans might have been to them. It should also be remembered that the intelligentsia and the masses had had very little contact with each other: we recall that mass politics had only begun to emerge in the last decade of tsarist rule.

And yet stopping at such observations would seriously distort our understanding of social change in late imperial Russia. Indeed, this whole analysis has been rooted in a quite different perspective: that whatever the cultural and social differences, peasants, workers, intellectuals, government officials, and the tsar himself shared certain cultural elements of the Russian idea. As has been repeatedly pointed out, these elements were not always the same and they did not always mean the same thing, but the shared grounding in what was *not* Western nonetheless gave rise to important similarities. The main group that did not really belong to this universe of overlapping perspectives was the liberal Westernized intelligentsia, whose isolation and rootlessness led it to political oblivion in the 1917 revolution.

The worldview and values of the Russian intelligentsia have been expertly analyzed in countless studies. They were, of course, variegated and by no means fixed in time. For example, after the defeat of the 1905 revolution, liberal ideas gained more appeal, particularly with the continued growth of the liberal professions. Nonetheless, certain generalizations about the culture of the intelligentsia are universally accepted and even became the basis of their own self-critique: the contempt for bourgeois society and its main cultural components (interest, individualism, rationalism, and the like); disregard for law; a vision of community based on shared commitment to the truth; opposition to the modern bureaucratic state; a high degree of moralism, which led to black-and-white judgments on people and institutions; expectation that a just world could be brought about on earth through righteous action; and total commitment to abstract ideologies as blueprints for change.

Certainly not all of these traits would endear the intelligentsia to the people. One implication, for example, was that the intelligentsia was the heroic bearer of truth to a pure, but benighted, people. No one appreciates such condescension. Similarly, their certainty in their own mission did not encourage receptivity to the people's own perspectives and experiences. Indeed, the very concept of "the people," so dear to the intelligentsia, is at heart demeaning, for it reduces the natural diversity of any social group to an ideologically filtered homogeneity.

Despite these caveats, the correspondences between popular mentalities and intelligentsia visions can hardly be denied. In the peasant dream of a homogeneous and egalitarian community cleansed of bureaucrats and nobles, protected by the tsar in accord with the truth of religion, we find much that resembles the teachings of many revolutionary populists. For the workers, too, the good society would embody the values of the worker community, whose interests were directly opposed to those of the factory owner. A just government would not mediate among interests, for the competing interest of the factory owner had no legitimacy. Neither the worker nor the peasant had any respect for procedure, law, or private property: community and justice transcended all of these formalities. And both workers and peasants, like the revolutionaries, believed that these visions could be brought to Earth immediately. It was only the ill will of evil-doers that obstructed change. Destroy the old, and the new will emerge of itself, cleansed of the impurities of the former life.

Even Russian Marxism, despite its European origins, acquired this Russian cultural tint. Its Bolshevik variant, in particular, emphasized the moral qualities of the party elite over the rigid laws of economic change. It celebrated will and consciousness over determinism. It exhibited die-hard hatred for the bourgeoisie, hardly recognizing—unlike Marx himself—that this class had made any contributions to the development of society. Everything was interpreted in terms of a binary conception of class opposition, which ruled out any compromise and, for Lenin, any real cooperation with the bourgeoisie, even in order to overthrow the autocratic system. The Bolshevik movement's mode of struggle was not so much organized mass collective action, as Marx had urged, but the exemplary sacrifice of heroic martyrs who would win popular support to the true cause.

In its Bolshevik variant Marxism was not sociology, but a substitute for religion. It did not spring from experience (most of the intelligentsia had little experience with workers), but served as a guide for the transformation of reality. Anyone who did not accept the priority of ideology and the party against the desires of the workers and purely economic interests was a tail-ender, not a leader. So profound were these cultural modifications of the tenets of Western Marxism that for almost a century they have given rise to passionate debates about whether Bolshevism had not betrayed its own ideological patrimony.

Menshevism was, of course, quite different. It placed more emphasis on the contributions of bourgeois society to the future than did Leninism. It understood that the flourishing of legal consciousness and the enrichment of organized political experience were critical for the development of the workers as an independent class. Cooperation with the industrialists and the liberal intelligentsia was not utterly ruled out, as it was for Lenin. In short, the Mensheviks were closer to European evolutionary socialism than were their Bolshevik rivals, all of which explains why in the contest for mass support in 1917 they never had a chance with the Russian masses. Russian workers, in particular, did not want or choose European Marxism, but Russian Bolshevism, which was an odd jumble of Marxism and the Russian idea.

Ironically, in its struggle with Western political ideals the Russian state had historically proclaimed many of the same values as had the revolutionary intelligentsia. The state and the intelligentsia alike sought to incarnate the truth of a separate path to modernity, one that would overcome the injustices of Europe. But we have seen how the tsarist regime crippled itself in its efforts to bring about modernization without sacrificing key tenets of the Russian idea. The government promised to protect workers and peasants while sponsoring capitalist industrialization. It committed itself to political reform, even though the tsar was not able to renounce autocracy. It created new institutions, but these institutions worked according to conflicting principles. Even the ancient institution of autocracy was no longer comprehensible, especially to the autocrat himself. The government was constantly racked by debates over the most central social and political questions. Consequently, no decision was irrevocable; all measures were subject to reinterpretation and change. The government repeatedly broke its own word and violated its own laws. Losing any semblance of coherence, it suffered from a lack of credibility in all quarters, becoming truly, in the famous phrase, a "government of facades."

Ultimately, then, the tsarist regime became victim of the Russian idea, which was turned against it. It did not represent truth, but falsehood. It did not protect the people, but their exploiters. It did not embody the principles of the Russian way of life, as Nicholas II claimed, but foreign values. During World War I, Nicholas II and his family were assigned a German identity, just as Peter the Great, or Patriarch Nikon, who had sponsored the seventeenth-century church reforms, had been interpreted as foreigners. For some, Nicholas was even anti-Christ.

By 1917, all of the changes that seemed to be transforming Russia in a European direction had done little to weaken the hold of these older assumptions about Russian life. Rather, as peasant and worker protest as well as intelligentsia ideologies and political action all show, this cultural matrix so rooted in the opposition of Russia and the West had served to give focus and unity to social and political opposition to the regime. It was precisely on this basis that a temporary rapprochement of the people and the Bolshevik Party against both the old regime and the possibility of Western-style liberal democracy would triumph. In true Russian fashion, this strange and contradictory alliance of social groups held fast to a shared faith in the promise of an utter transformation of the old world of corruption.

The Russian idea, then, was not simply a set of abstract cultural principles to be found in books. Rather, it provided the conceptual and moral foundation of the actions of the most important political leaders and social groups of late tsarist society. Because of his continuing adherence to a set of images about the nature of autocratic rule and the ruler's relationship to his people, Tsar Nicholas II was unable to comprehend the new world emerging around him. He had even less capacity to initiate policies that might have created a new basis for Russian society. Yet the problems of a modernizing industrial society could not be ignored. Many reforms were undertaken, but they all turned out to be halfhearted and internally contradictory. For this reason, they activated the opposition of virtually all social groups, from elites who saw their positions threatened to workers and peasants who wanted deeper changes.

As we have seen, the Russian idea also lay behind various visions of change. Peasants and workers opposed the government on the basis of this older vision of truth and justice, which identified legitimate rulership with protection of the people. They never developed any sense that modern political life must be based on compromise, and they never accepted the legitimacy of the industrialists and landowners who threatened the unity of the community and the coherence of its way of life. This kind of transformation of consciousness was impossible in a society in which the government inhibited the development of new kinds of social and political organizations.

Finally, whatever the superficial Westernizing claims of Russian populism or Marxism, they too displayed considerable continuity with the underlying principles of the Russian idea. It was for precisely this reason that communication between the revolutionary intelligentsia and the masses was possible, despite all their social and cultural differences.

The continuing vitality of the Russian idea, particularly as it was interwoven with policies and institutional practice, thereby prevented the emergence of a new social logic based on the division of labor, abstract social ties, generalized trust, and compromise among competing interests. For all these reasons, the Westernization of Russian society in the late tsarist period was always superficial, for a set of older principles contrary to the new practices continued to pervade society. The modernization of Russia under the auspices of the tsars never acquired a firm social and cultural foundation, and it fatally undermined the legitimacy of the autocracy and all the social elites identified with it.

CHAPTER THREE

The Logic of Soviet Communism

> Nonetheless we have studied Marxism a bit, we have studied how
> and when opposites can and must be combined. The main thing
> is: in our revolution for three and a half years we have in practice
> repeatedly combined opposites.
>
> —V. I. Lenin[1]

AT LEAST since the time that Peter the Great had set Russia on the course of significant modernization, Russian society had been beset by fundamental contradictions and split apart by schism. In the political realm, the government had repeatedly proposed, and sometimes enacted, reforms to give social groups more autonomy, but the rulers had never been willing to accept any fundamental restrictions on the principles of autocracy. Economically, Russia had entered the age of markets and capitalism, but the government was suspicious of capitalist elites, frequently sought to infringe upon market principles, and until its last decade severely restricted the development of capitalism in the countryside. Culturally, there were dramatic divisions between those who insisted on the distinctiveness and superiority of Russian culture and those who believed that Russia should join the Western world. This deeply rooted cultural schism also found its political expression, as tsarist governments shifted between liberalizing and reactionary tendencies. In fundamental ways, then, tsarist Russia was a contradictory amalgam of principles that defied easy comprehension. What was Russia, and where was it going?

Until 1917 the rulers of Russia avoided any systematic exploration of these questions. The tsarist regime relied upon its traditional authority to introduce policies that undermined tradition. Especially under Nicholas II, it was remarkably passive in its inability to give some kind of coherence and legitimacy to the new social and political patterns that were emerging. Unlike Peter the Great, Nicholas II was unwilling to present himself as the modernizing monarch, bringing progress to his people. And although he may have seen himself as the embodiment of Russian tradition, he was unable to safeguard its fundamental principles.

No one could accuse the Communist leaders of passivity. They proclaimed themselves to be the champions of modernity, the rationalizers of Russia. They declared explicit war against Russian "backwardness" in a way that had not been seen since the time of Peter the Great. But unlike Peter, they justified their changes in terms of a modern ideology of justice and equality that held forth the promise of authentic human community. And yet this vision of community had much in common with premodern values and in some ways harked back to the old Russian ways that Peter had done so much to destroy. Even more paradoxically, this ideology of progress was defined and promoted by a government that seemed to have a great deal in common with the ancient model of Russian rulers as embodiments of supreme truth.

And, like the tsars, the Communist leaders from Lenin to Gorbachev envisioned Soviet *society* as a united and loyal *people*, thus imposing a normative vision on a complex empirical reality. Although the formula of a united people was surely in part conscious ideological ruse, it also diminished the rulers' ability to perceive the society around them. The two chief Soviet reformers, Khrushchev and Gorbachev, were shocked and greatly damaged by the political and social cacophony unleashed by their calls to reform.

Thus, despite its explicit advocacy of a new set of values, the Communist regime seems no less enigmatic than its tsarist predecessors: perhaps even more so, because of the way that its doctrinal pronouncements concealed or distorted actual social relations. Embracing so many opposites, Soviet Communism defies easy conceptualization. It is not surprising that everything imaginable has been said about it. To some, the Soviet regime until the death of Stalin was the logical outcome of Marxist ideas of class struggle and opposition to capitalism; to others, the classical period of Soviet Communism represented an attack upon Marxist principles. Many scholars have traced the roots of Communism to the Russian past, drawing parallels between such rulers as Ivan the Terrible or Peter the Great and Stalin. Others have argued that the Communist regime's attack on religion, peasant society, and the old intelligentsia marked a fundamental break with the Russian tradition on the basis of an alien set of values rooted in Western ideas of progress: "It is beyond my understanding how some Soviet publicists have managed to find something peculiar, Russian, patriarchal, and national in Stalin's conceptions of socialism," wrote the contemporary Russian philosopher Alexander Tsipko.[2] Yet recall Kopelev's judgment, cited in the introduction, that Stalin's collectivization of agriculture followed the traditional logic of Russian serfdom.

Similarly, a highly influential group of thinkers has seen Stalinism as a modernizing regime called forth by the imperative to overcome Russian backwardness for the sake of national survival;[3] a rival current has emphasized the archaic and antimodern elements of Stalinism, its rejection of fundamental aspects of modern rationality, such as market principles of efficiency.[4] The list of contradictory interpretations can easily be multiplied: Eastern despotism versus Western ideological dictatorship; totalitarian dictatorship based on police terror versus class government embodying many elements of popular participation; internationalist regime based on an antinational ideology, which even oppressed the Russian nation, versus a dressed-up Russian great-power imperialism.

My point in introducing this list of contradictory interpretations is not to argue that all analyses of the Communist experiment in Russia were conceptualized in such binary terms. On the contrary, a great many analysts tried to understand how such conflicting principles and practices were related to each other: how modernization, for example, could reinforce archaic practices; or how, as the émigré Russian philosopher S. L. Frank saw the Stalin period, Asiatic despotism could lead to the Europeanization of the country; or how, as the Polish philosopher Leszek Kolakowski argued in his magisterial study of the whole Marxist tradition, the attempt to realize Marxist principles inevitably led to totalitarian dictatorship. I would also add that the current tendency in Western scholarship is to avoid such grand interpretations altogether. Now that the Soviet archives have been largely opened, an empirical approach seeking to describe events, policies, and popular responses more carefully has begun to bear fruit. Many corrections to our understanding of the social workings of Soviet Communism will come to light, and it is possible that new understandings of the nature of the Soviet system will emerge to replace older interpretations.

The more cautious and empirical approach of Western historians lies at the opposite extreme from public discourse in Russia, where there has been a tendency for thoughtful analysis to give way to reckless allegations blaming Stalin and the Communists one-sidedly for everything. Hitler and then the Cold War: for much of contemporary Soviet public opinion these loom as evil emanations from the Communist regime, without history, without complexity. (For example, see the extremely popular book by Viktor Suvorov, *Ledokol* [Icebreaker], which completely blames the Communist regime for World War II.)

Yet I do not believe that any amount of new research or any attempt to oversimplify the past to fit new ideological stereotypes will ultimately lessen our sense of the enigmatic and contradictory character of the Communist regime, particularly in the period of Stalin's dictatorship. The old questions will continue to puzzle our understanding, and the moral issues raised by the attempt to combine terror and progress, to create a good society through lawless means, to introduce Communist ideals into backward Russia, will continue to trouble our consciences. And the words themselves—progress, Communism, socialism, equality, proletarian dictatorship, classless society—will remain imprecise and morally clouded as a result of this experience.

Whatever else it was, Soviet Communism shared with Slavophilism or Russian populism the sense that Russia could pioneer a path to modernity different from and superior to that of capitalist Europe. For many Russians, it was able to prolong the belief that Russia had a historical mission that set it apart from other nations. In a great many respects fully congruent with the central tenets of the Russian idea, it claimed that Soviet society was based on a higher model of community and ruled by a supremely just government. And just as many exponents of the Russian idea in tsarist Russia had committed the profound error of identifying the ideal and the real, so actual practice in Soviet Russia was proclaimed to have realized socialist ideals, thus creating another continuity between tsarist and Communist Russia: the pervasiveness of double-think, of dual consciousness. This insidious kind of hypocrisy, enforced politically, silently but potently eroded both systems' legitimacy.

I conceptualize Soviet Communism as a strange amalgam of Communist ideology, the Russian idea, and the commitment to the logic of modernization. By modernization I have in mind such traits as the following: industry, science, the expansion of centralized state power, mass political participation, and mass education and communications. I do not assume that modernization either is uniform or constitutes a final goal with an end point.[5] Yet whatever the variants and possibilities, it has some universal imperatives. For example, modernization gives rise to increasing social complexity. A regime that ignores or opposes this process will eventually run up against manifold dilemmas. Similarly, economic imperatives based on scarcity and the need to make choices among alternatives are implacable foes of purely ideological decision making. At the end of his life, Stalin officially recognized some objective truths of economics, ominously attacking those who did not accept "objective laws of value." As Lev Kopelev noted, "that affirmation was a contradiction to everything that had been affirmed by our propaganda before."[6] That earlier propaganda had been much more congruent with the Russian idea, emphasizing enthusiasm, belief, and equality.

Ideas and practices based upon all three of these social logics were embraced by a modernizing dictatorial state and made the basis of government policy toward society. Individuals and social groups responded to these policies according to their own interpretations of this same set of values. In the name of Russian traditions and ideals of justice people sometimes accepted, and could also come to oppose, the Communist system. Similarly, commitment to Communist ideals could be a basis for either loyalty or opposition to the regime—which, after all, in its pursuit of modernization seemed to be violating the main tenets of Marxism. In the same way, people committed to modernization and progress could easily come to different conclusions about the merits of the regime, for both the conservation of elements of the Russian idea and the ideological campaigns justified by Marxist values frequently interfered with social and economic rationalization.

Analyses of Soviet Communism that leave out any of these three elements—Communism, the Russian idea, or modernization—will fail to do justice to both the strengths and the weaknesses of the regime. For example, theorists such as Robert Tucker have analyzed Stalin's Russia in terms of the return to traditional Russian patterns of dictatorial rule and lawlessness; for them, Stalinism constituted a kind of revenge of the Russian past on the dreams of Marxism.[7] Yet single-minded emphasis on the continuity of Soviet Communism with prerevolutionary political culture misses all of those aspects of state policy connected with the ideology of class conflict and the commitment to rapid modernization.

Equally, however, an interpretation of the Stalinist dictatorship purely in terms of the logic and imperatives of modernization, with the implication that it was in fundamental respects simply part of a whole class of modernizing dictatorships, ignores the cultural and ideological particularities of the regime. Therefore, it leaves us powerless to understand such momentous and tragic events as collectivization or political terror. Although the Soviet regime clearly had parallels with modernizing dictatorships the world over, its position as the inheritor of Russian political culture and as the fountainhead and fortress of Communist values made its position and policies unique.

It would also be a grave mistake to understand Soviet Communism as simply the product of Marxist ideas. We have already seen that from the beginning Russian Marxism was deeply impregnated with elements of the Russian idea. Further, Western Marxism never had to confront the problem of underdevelopment: from its German inception, European Marxism envisioned socialism and then Communism as the result of modernization, the product of all the accumulated wealth and political experience of developed capitalism. It did not need to develop theories of socialist economics or Communist dictatorship as ways of overcoming backwardness. But in Russia the Communist leaders from the beginning were faced with an entirely different set of problems: not how to socialize the means of production, but how to develop them; not how to bring a skilled and educated proletariat to power, but how to create one. Soviet Marxism was fundamentally shaped by the need to modernize a society not fully prepared for science, technology, and industry.

Whatever their incompatibilities, then, Marxism, the Russian idea, and the imperatives of modernization were yoked to each other. Although this linkage is inconvenient for our ability to construct a simple theory of Soviet Communism, it will help us understand the underlying dilemmas of the Communist regime more fully. For all of the one-factor theories were premised on an idea that we now know to be false: that Soviet Communism provided a relatively permanent solution to the problems of modern Russian society. For those who emphasized continuities with the Russian past, the return to old social and political patterns of statist dictatorship and collectivist culture expressed an irreplaceable core of Russianness. It constituted a Russian version of modernity. For those who emphasized the Communist roots of the regime, Communist values and practices were often seen to provide a viable alternative to the liberal, capitalist West. The party-state and central planning could substitute for competitive democracy and the market. And for those who saw the Soviet regime as a response to the challenges of modernization in an economically and culturally backward country, Communism could be interpreted as an effective mechanism of modernization, one that could substitute for capitalist entrepreneurial elites.

By contrast, if we emphasize the interpenetration of these different principles, we will be alerted to the dilemmas and contradictions of the Communist regime, and therefore be in a better position to understand efforts at reform and why these efforts failed. We will also perceive the profound parallels between the fall of the tsarist regime and the collapse of Communism. From this vantage point, we can begin to understand why these two superficially imposing political colossi collapsed virtually without struggle.

The attentive reader will have perhaps noticed a bit of sleight-of-hand in the discussion so far. I have repeatedly used terms like "the Communist regime," "Soviet Communism," and the "Soviet system," and I have by omission implied that these terms all refer to a uniform and unchanging phenomenon, defined by the interweaving of three sets of principles. But in fact, of course, the history of Soviet society should be divided up into a number of different periods, all with quite distinct traits. Yet in pursuing a definite line of argument we will be concerned less with strict periodization than with the overall logic of change. In this respect, three moments are decisive: the consolidation of this contradictory system under Stalin; the attempts to create a viable model of society under his successors; and the failed effort to reform its fundamentals under Gorbachev.

The present chapter is devoted to the "classical" period of Soviet Communism, the Stalin regime—with an emphasis on the 1930s, the crucial decade in Soviet history. The following chapter will take up the dilemmas and ultimately dissolution of this form of society in the entire post-Stalin period. Although some comparisons with the pre-Stalin Communist experience will be offered when relevant, it would take us too far afield to pursue these themes in the earlier period, when social and political institutions had not yet acquired more fixed shape. As well as being the formative period that gave shape to the culture and practice of Soviet Communism ever afterward, it is only during the Stalin years that the combination of rapid modernization, the revival of key elements of the Russian idea, and class-based Marxist doctrines were powerfully linked together. During the period of War Communism (1918–21), the Communist regime was too preoccupied with its own survival to be able to sponsor rapid social and economic modernization. The New Economic Policy period (1921–29) witnessed a doctrinal retreat in the assertion of Communist values, allowing for the introduction of widespread private trade and market production in many spheres of the economy. It was therefore only during the classical Stalin period that the creative and destructive potentials of this threefold combination were most visible, and the strengths and weaknesses of the Soviet Communist model of modern society most clearly expressed. However much later Soviet rulers tried to introduce changes, they could never escape from the logic of this system nor solve the contradictions that it created.

THESIS, ANTITHESIS, SYNTHESIS: THE RUSSIAN IDEA,
MODERNIZATION, AND COMMUNISM

Russian and foreign observers in the two decades following the revolution marveled at what they saw as a transformation of the Russian character after the revolution. To the émigré philosopher and historian Fedotov, the change seemed to mark a catastrophic break with Russian cultural traditions. Instead of the old values of selflessness, modesty, and compassion, Soviet Communism had ushered in a stage of crass Americanization of values. Young people especially seemed to be absorbed with technology, athletics, and practical results; they had no time for the moral dilemmas explored by classical Russian culture. "No generation in Russian history has been more divorced from what some foreign observers have regarded as the essentially Russian trait of mysticism," wrote the perceptive American journalist and historian William Henry Chamberlin in 1930.[8] Many young people felt that life had begun anew, on the basis of new values oriented to a boundless future. The literary scholar Raisa Orlova later recalled her education and her feelings about the past in the mid-1930s: "In 1917 a line had been drawn. This past was of interest to a few, to historians, for example. But it was of no interest at all to me. Everything that was important was in the present; the measure of everything would begin with us. I wasn't the only one to feel that way."[9]

Such witnesses and participants would be most shocked at the following analysis, which traces the imprint of the Russian idea on Soviet Communist political, economic, and social life. Orlova was unaware that her own sense of a complete break with the past, and the possibility of creating a purified society in the future, is itself a constant theme of Russian cultural history, traceable in the ideas and practices of such towering figures as Avvakum or Peter the Great. Indeed, it was partly this very sense of the ease of re-creating the world after the sources of evil had been destroyed that allowed many of the prior cultural assumptions to make their way into the new society in subterranean ways. As Freud taught us, unconscious ideas are often more powerful than conscious ideas, for the former cannot be confronted openly. As with the individual personality, they return to haunt social life in hidden and distorted ways.

Perhaps the most visible aspect of this subterranean imprint of the past was the cult of the leader, which emerged under Lenin but acquired its mature form in the 1930s under Stalin. The leader of the Communist Party, like the tsar, was granted an almost religious sanction to rule. Reports have come to us from the 1930s of homes in which the "red corner" decorated with icons and candles was replaced by the Communist corner, prominently displaying pictures of Lenin and Stalin as well as the holy writs of Marxism. "I once stood in a factory church which had been turned into a workers' club," writes William Henry Chamberlin, "and here again the substitution of new objects of reverence for old was very striking. Instead of pictures of the saints, pictures of Marx and Lenin. Instead of the rich decorations of the typical Orthodox church, red streamers proclaiming that with Communism would come the final liberation of humanity."[10]

With Stalin the return to a sacramental idea of rulership becomes more calculated. In his biography of Stalin, Robert Tucker has shown that Stalin assiduously read Russian history and was particularly fascinated by the aura surrounding tsarist power and the use of it made by such giant figures as Ivan the Terrible or Peter the Great.[11] He sought to emulate the hallowed model of tsarist rule: the tsar alone in communion with his loyal people, both of them opposed to the corrupt world of officialdom and local authorities; the tsar as bearer of justice and protector of the people. In line with this logic, Stalin loved to receive delegations of "simple" peasants or workers, and to fulfill their petitions out of his own magnanimity. On a more ominous note, he also attempted to use this logic in the terror unleashed in the 1930s against party and government officials: workers and peasants were encouraged to denounce local authorities so that the great leader could rectify wrongs. Indeed, the vicious campaigns of denunciation in the 1930s, with their frequently bloody outcomes, were only an exaggerated form of the traditional logic of Russian politics—they were a time-honored way for rulers to keep control over their officials and also to establish paths of personal communication between ruler and ruled.[12] They were based upon and reinforced the idea of the ruler as the embodiment of a higher justice.

Stalin's way of speech, in part surely a product of his seminary education, seemed to reinforce for many Russians this quasi-religious aura surrounding the ruler. He spoke in simple dichotomies, laconically repeating fundamental truths over and over again. His speeches were laced with rhetorical questions and characterized by plodding and predictable argumentation. Yet the constant repetition of simple "truths," the logical certainty, the citations from the "sacred" texts, seem to have had their effect. He was described as a shaman; his words were incantations. His whole style communicated inscrutability and mystery, as if his authority were rooted in higher powers not subject to rational comprehension. "Among theosophists, persecuted and far from supporting the regime, there was a rumor that Stalin knew something that no one else guessed, that he was the incarnation of the Great Manu of India."[13] Writers and memoirists have recorded the extraordinary awe and devotion that Stalin could inspire among many people, and even those who hated him could have difficulty believing that he was a mere mortal, with bodily functions like all the rest of mankind. For the great composer Shostakovich's jailed nephew, "Comrade Stalin is light without shadow, the pure light of wisdom and goodness."[14] Clearly, there was nothing modern or Communist in the image of the supreme ruler; rather, it was an exaggerated and sometimes outlandish version of ancient Russian ideas of kingship.

Much else in Soviet political life under Stalin can also be interpreted through the prism of the Russian idea. Fundamental to the Russian idea of politics was a rejection of the Aristotelian formulation of the essence of political life: the problem of the one and the many. How is it possible, asked Aristotle, to make decisions binding on the community when the community is heterogeneous in nature? In Aristotle there was no attempt to answer this question through an appeal to a unified truth or knowledge as the basis of political life. The Russian idea was more Platonic in nature: it sought to base political life on truth and a uniform life based on truth.

Under the tsars this "truth" was essentially religious and traditional in nature, and it did not by itself threaten the way of life of the people. The danger to popular traditions came from elsewhere, from the urge to modernize regardless of Russian customs. Peter the Great did not try to transform Russia on the basis of a claim to a higher ideological vision, but for essentially pragmatic reasons. In this sense the Communists were true innovators: in preaching a "Red Gospel" and "Red Truth," they sought to transform Russian society, but they did so on the basis of the very traditional idea that the ruler was the repository of truth. While Nicholas II undeniably brought together autocracy, modernization, and the Russian idea, the Communists yoked them together in much closer unity. Initially more effective, at least in a gross way, their bold departures had costs and dilemmas of staggering dimensions.

Accordingly, much of the logic of Communism in Stalin's Russia has a very traditional ring to it, despite the ideological and technocratic jargon. Marxism was not a set of scientific tenets rationally chosen, but articles of faith to be accepted and believed. Opposition to its principles as interpreted at any given time was regarded as sinful or criminal and could be punished if expressed openly. On its basis many people believed not just that they were on the verge of a better life, but that their generation could construct a paradise on Earth.

Of course, few people read Marx, or for that matter Lenin, carefully. It is not even certain that Stalin himself ever read *Capital*, the central work in the Marxist tradition. So it is not surprising that Marxism came to be popularly interpreted as very close to many native Russian utopian traditions. Society would be like a *rod*; all people would be brothers and sisters to each other. Truth was not multiple and complex, but simple and accessible to the common people. Even further, the common people, the working class, embodied this truth to a higher degree than did the wavering and spineless intellectuals, who thought too much and were cut off from the people. In particular, the proletarian class instinct was celebrated above knowledge or diverse experience as a source of truth. In his memoirs Lev Kopelev gives a multitude of examples of the anti-intellectualism and preference for simple answers that stemmed from these attitudes. Class instinct meant agreement with the Central Committee in whatever it decided; books and thinking meant the possibility of sympathizing with the opposition.[15] The sophisticated writer Ilya Ehrenburg recalled that he often heard the following kind of remarks: "Why be so complicated? It's all rotten intellectual rubbish. Have you seen the papers? Well, then, everything's perfectly clear. All these whys and wherefores are just bourgeois talk."[16]

If the revolution's goal was to make men brothers, what should be done about those who did not share the same values or did not act in the prescribed way? One answer was cultural revolution: they should be reeducated to conform to the authentic Soviet way of life. Art and literature in the Stalin period were mobilized for just this purpose: to create the "new Soviet man" through adherence to the doctrines of Socialist Realism—art that is infused with party values and is true to the purity of popular, especially proletarian, consciousness. Such literature illustrates once again a more general trait of Soviet life: the real and the ideal were collapsed together, despite obvious empirical contradictions. Literature, like culture more generally, did not benefit from the imposed inability to distinguish between reality and what reality was ideologically defined to be.

But not everyone could be reeducated and become brothers, and for those who did not embrace Soviet values and the Soviet way of life, separation from the community was the only answer. Thus, a dualistic conception of society was built into the logic of Stalinist politics: friend versus enemy; we versus they; loyal worker versus saboteur; and the like. All problems were caused by ill-intentioned people, by enemies of the people. Poor performance was not rooted in weak organization or lack of resources, but in sabotage by enemies. The classic question of Stalinist Communism was not "What is going wrong?" but "Who is guilty?"[17]

The guilty, knowingly departing from true values and the correct way of life, should have no rights. In the words of a song cited by Kopelev, "And if you won't be my brother/ I'll crack your skull open."[18] Formal rights, procedures, and laws also have no place in a world where what is good and right is already known, and where it is assumed that any deviance is a willful departure from the values of the community. Democracy, in the sense of procedures for the expression of a diversity of social voices, is also only necessary in a society in which complexity, and not homogeneity, is of primary value. For the same reason, it is not necessary for separate groups to express their interests; insofar as their aspirations are legitimate, they are known to and will be taken account of by the leadership.

It is necessary to spell out two further implications of this ideological version of traditional Russian political ideas. First, there is no room here for a legitimate independent social elite. Authority and privilege stem from the regime, not from the personal qualities or energies of individual actors. Even more ominously, if the people are loyal and the political leaders wise, bad results must have their source in corrupt officials. In attacking specialists and party elites, the Stalin regime repeatedly used this logic to attempt to reinforce its ties to the population. Within the contours of this political logic, no real elite could emerge until the post-Stalin period—and even then, its very existence was seen to violate widespread standards of justice based on Russian tradition.

Second, this same binary separation between what belongs to the community and what is foreign was transferred to international relations. The outside world, particularly the West, was seen to be hostile and threatening. Soviet Communism took over from the Russian idea the sense that its way of life and institutions were unalterably opposed to European civilization, that they could be defined in large part according to this binary opposition. Until Gorbachev it was always a convincing argument for Communist orthodoxy that, if it was done in the West, it must be bad.

There was also much in the culture and practices of Soviet economic life that harked back to fundamental assumptions of the Russian idea.

Large sectors of the prerevolutionary Russian peasantry, workers, and intelligentsia did not accept the logic of an economy based on private property, the free pursuit of individual material interests, and market relations and institutions. Such a model, they felt, would put the individual at odds with the community, create a class of privileged exploiters, augment uncertainty and insecurity, and debase the higher human motivations. The ability of individuals freely to pursue their interest meant chaos and injustice, not freedom and prosperity. (Not all Russians, of course, held these perspectives; again, I am referring to deeply rooted cultural tendencies, but they were always opposed by other ideals.)

For many groups in prerevolutionary Russia, the "natural economy" was the implicit model: universal access to the land; household production largely for use; exchange through barter, with limited monetarization; and a large degree of local autonomy. This image of the natural economy, which itself amounts to something like a utopian vision, clearly left its mark on Soviet Communism. During the period of War Communism, economic life in many ways corresponded to this model: rationing and barter largely replaced money; there was equality based on universal poverty; property was in the hands of the people; and production and exchange were localized. And this reversion to premarket economic patterns was identified with socialism![19] Whereas in European Marxism socialism was called upon to make use of the achievements of capitalism, in the practice of Soviet Communism the aim was to negate them.

Such a conception of the economy was clearly inconsistent with the requirements of modern industry, and during the great modernization campaigns of the 1930s other economic mechanisms came into play: centralized planning, unequal pay, one-person management, and the like. But even in the economic life of the industrialization period it is not difficult to identify precipitates of the Russian idea. Now, however, there was a new ingredient: the powerful state that was breaking down local communities and self-sufficiency in the pursuit of different goals. Nonetheless, this state had eliminated private property in the means of production; it proclaimed the goals of equality; it justified its actions not by utilitarian interests of individuals, but by the collective values of the community; and there was still little room for the divisive play of market forces. People were asked to work and produce on the basis of community needs, belief, and enthusiasm. Economic life was to be based on "truth," not interest, and so it would avoid the capitalist war of all against all and the capitalist anarchy of production.

Therefore, economic life did not have an autonomous logic—it was defined by the political leadership in accordance with higher values. To work hard was a political duty and a moral obligation. Economic performance out of line with the plan was a sign of political disloyalty. "Wreckerism" and "sabotage" became crimes. But loyal workers believed that their activity truly was imbued with higher values. Although to observers like Fedotov the devotion of young workers to five-year plans and machines may have seemed like a break with the Russian past, in fact this new faith was in part a revival of the Russian idea, whereby economic life should not have its own separate sphere and logic. The building of socialism, with its plans and directives, with its elimination of private interests, became a kind of faith whose meaning far transcended the growth of the gross national product. For Kopelev, the vision of socialist progress "was essential to me as a source of spiritual strength, of my conception of myself as part of a great whole."[20]

This moralized meaning of economic life also served to set the Soviet people off from the rest of the world as the bearers of progress, and so reinforce the sense that their nation had a superior mission in the modern world. We are very far indeed from a purely utilitarian conception of economic life centered on the expanding production and consumption of individuals. Indeed, the definition and motivation of economic action in terms of final goals excluded the category of the pursuit of individual interest, as this idea was explained in the introduction. Similarly, the emphasis upon the final state, the end point, catastrophically minimized the significance of efficiency and utility in favor of gross production.

The survival of older Russian conceptions of the economy into Soviet Communism would be a source of great strength to the regime in its efforts to transform the society in the relative absence of material rewards, but it also left it deeply vulnerable to moral criticisms of injustice and hypocrisy. Capitalism, went the old Soviet joke, is the exploitation of man by man, but socialism, guided by the party, is the opposite. It is impossible to build a modern economy without a recognition of the partial independence and separate logic of economic life, which cannot without great costs continue to be submerged in politics and morality.

In its ambivalent loyalty to Russian tradition, the government of Nicholas II had been unable to embark on a consistent path of economic and political modernization: everything was done by half-measures. By contrast, the Communist regime's commitment to fight Russian backwardness could not have been more clear-cut. Nor did it ever have to present itself as the defender of Russian values against the threat of modern civilization. The imprint of the Russian idea was subterranean and largely unconscious, and so antimodern elements, such as the tsar as protector of his loyal and passive people, were not directly used to combat modern institutions. Rather, the regime consciously set itself against those elements of old Russia that it felt inhibited the modernization of the country, even while unconsciously many of these same elements were imported into its practices and institutions in unrecognized ways.

Publicly and consciously, however, the break with the past was total. Symbolic of the new values was a major campaign to melt down church bells in order to use the metal for industrialization. The worthless past was to be utterly destroyed in order to create a new and just society. A new activist conception of the world came to triumph: we must become conquerors of our selves and then of our country in order to defeat the enemy of backwardness. "We must discover and conquer the country in which we live. It is a tremendous country. . . . And the Five-Year Plan is one of the first great battles in the war. We must burrow into the earth, break rocks, dig mines, construct houses."[21]

The first order of the day was rapid industrialization, so that the Soviet Union could protect itself from the hostile capitalist powers and also "in order that there may be no poverty, no filth, no sickness, no unemployment, no exhausting labor—in order that life may be rational and just."[22] For this goal a cultural revolution was also necessary, the creation of a new human type. As Nikolai Bukharin said in 1928, "in our system of scientific planning, one of the first priorities is the question of the systematic preparation of new men, the builders of socialism."[23] These new men would no longer be imbued with religious passivity, which taught them to accept misery and injustice, but would actively struggle to create the new world on the horizon. Literate, educated, and confident in their own powers, they would display discipline and initiative. The slack work habits of the past and the old passivity would be overcome: human beings would now become adults, masters of their own fate.

Such conquerors of the world must also become active citizens, involved in the life of the nation-state. They should participate in large-scale organizations, such as trade unions or political parties, so that their loyalty and enthusiasm could be coordinated with that of others. Willing support based upon belief, and not simply submission to authorities, should guide people's actions. Localism and social divisions of all kinds would be replaced by the overarching shared identities stemming from participation in the new society: no longer would city and countryside, lower and upper classes be antagonistically opposed to each other, but all would have their place in socialist interdependence. Science, progress, activism, universalism, abundance: these were the dreams of modernity in the new Soviet Russia.

There are obvious contradictions between this modernist project and the residues of the Russian idea that were also an important part of Soviet Communism. In the economic realm, for example, modern industry required a highly developed division of labor, which included different levels of rewards and authority. But how was this social differentiation compatible with the older vision of community, which was hostile to inequality and suspicious of elites? Culturally, how was belief and enthusiasm to be sustained in the context of the need for subordination, discipline, and the performance of uninspiring tasks? How could people conceive of themselves as something other than passive cogs in a larger process over which they had no control? Politically, how could the vision of a homogeneous community united behind certain shared values be reconciled with the differentiation of interest and perspective inherent in societal complexity? And did not party dictatorship based upon ideological truth undermine the potential political initiative of the masses? Further, was not the bureaucratic routinization necessary for orderly economic and political administration inconsistent with the older ideas of the unlimited power of the ruler, who stood above all rules and formalities in his dispensation of justice?

The dilemma might be put in the following way: if modernization and the attack on backwardness was the consciously stated "thesis" of the Communist regime, the unconscious "antithesis" was provided by numerous elements of the Russian idea. Although I am purposefully overstating the tension—for in fact the Russian idea and modernization were not in all respects antithetical to each other—nonetheless the potential dangers were clear. How could a set of cultural orientations that were in part prior to modernization and in part an explicit reaction against them fit together with the logic of modern technological society? What would happen to the older idea of community? Upon what would political authority be founded in a profoundly changing society, with rapidly increasing levels of education and social heterogeneity?

Marxist ideas were peculiarly suited to mediate between the Russian idea and the commitment to build an advanced industrial society. They partly owed this capacity to their own ambiguous relationship to modern institutions. Marx praised the achievements of Western bourgeois society and believed that socialism could only be built on its political and economic foundation. On the other hand, in his vision of the coming socialist society he clearly made use of ideas of community rooted in premodern "primitive Communism": the end of class conflict and the division of labor; social relations based upon a harmony of values and interests; the elimination of market exchange in favor of a natural economy; and the replacement of the modern state and bourgeois law by nonantagonistic administration in the interests of all. No wonder that toward the end of his life Marx came to accept the view that the Russian peasant commune might indeed be the seedbed of socialism!

How did Marxism come to play this role as synthesis of two conflicting logics of social organization? I certainly do not want to argue that the political leadership was explicitly aware of this dual nature of Marxism, which could both look back to premodern society and look forward to scientific socialism, and therefore consciously used it for its own political purposes. Rather, I believe that the answer to the question is simpler: Marxism in Russia was not just a doctrine imported from the West, but was itself deeply rooted in the Russian idea. It was worked out by Russian thinkers who had little of Marx's appreciation for bourgeois society, and it appealed to a great many Russians because of its resonance with their traditional political and economic values. The modernity promised by Marxism in Russia was always in part a Russian version of modernity—economic life largely without economics, political life largely without politics. It follows, therefore, that the version of modern society that eventually emerged in the Soviet Union preserved a great many cultural orientations and institutions of the Russian past, many of them in great tension with the more general logic of modern society.

Let us first examine how, for the first time in Russian history, Communism created a moral basis for modernization. This was one of the key ways that modernization became connected to the Russian idea, according to which utilitarian goals are not enough to give meaning to action. The essential point is the following: Communism embraced modernization, not as an end in itself, but dialectically, as the demiurge that would eventually give birth to the good society. It therefore had the capacity to bring together two dimensions of life that had historically been split in Russia: the world of secular, this-worldly activity and the world of higher values and belief. By contrast, under the tsarist regime the state's efforts to modernize society had been based on fundamentally utilitarian motivations: the desire to keep up with the West, the need to maintain Russia's status as a great power. Modernity had been seen as separate from and often antagonistic to the truth and integrity of the Russian way of life. Modernizing rulers such as Peter had been regarded by many of their subjects as the embodiment of evil, as the anti-Christ returned to Earth. State efforts at rapid modernization had led to profound schisms in the society: between Russian traditions and Western ways; between the city and the country; between the intelligentsia and the people.

The link forged in Communism between modernization and a higher vision of truth was a new departure in Russian history and marked one of the fundamental ways that Communism mediated between the Russian idea and modernization. According to its logic, the Stalin regime's modernization program could be interpreted as a painful transition period on the way to an ethically higher form of society. In this context, the personal sacrifices necessary for industrialization—the dislocations of rapid urbanization, low wages for the sake of investment, poor living conditions—had moral meaning. They were part of the struggle for a higher form of society and so could be connected to belief, not just interest. Never before in Russian history was hard work or the squeezing of living standards given this kind of higher meaning.

In this regard, it has been frequently and correctly pointed out that Communist ideology provided a socialist substitute for the Protestant ethic of the West, which also gave higher ethical sanction to worldly activity. Whereas previously Russian religion had not invested this-worldly activity with any particular ethical value, now Communist ideology could connect secular effort with transcendent historical meaning. Hard work, self-discipline, and the accumulation of wealth (now in collective form) were no longer simply condemned as narrow traits of bourgeois materialism, but were directly connected with the coming triumph of human brotherhood. For the same reason, science and technology, previously interpreted as symptoms of Western rationalism and materialism, were now given a quasi-religious significance.

A similar alchemy was at work in the political realm. Communism was able to associate an essentially prepolitical vision of politics as brotherhood with the requirements of the modern state. It did this through the elaboration of the concept of the dictatorship of the proletariat, which acquired a new and broader significance in the 1930s. In the 1920s many Communists lived in expectation of the coming triumph of the socialist millennium, when law and the state would be abolished in favor of the harmonious relations of social community. As had theorists of the Russian idea, so had Marxist ideologists believed that the modern state was an expression of a deep alienation between people and government. Slavophiles wanted a people's tsar in communion with the people; Marxists hoped for a harmonious and self-regulating community.

But there were others in the Soviet Union of the 1930s who understood that the coercive apparatus of the state still had many tasks to perform. Here is what Stalin said in a speech to the Sixteenth Party Congress in 1930:

> We stand for the withering away of the state. And at the same time we stand for the strengthening of the proletarian dictatorship, the most mighty and powerful of all hitherto existing state regimes. The highest development of state power for the purpose of preparing conditions for the withering away of state power—that's the Marxist formula. Contradictory? Yes, "contradictory." But a contradiction of real life, entirely reflecting Marx's dialectic.[24]

What was the meaning of this "dictatorship of the proletariat"? First, since it was based on Marxist dialectic, it partook of the truth. Therefore, it was not to be contested, not even by the proletariat itself, but to be believed in. Policies that seemed "contradictory," that seemed to violate the workers' own interests, had to be dialectically understood in terms of its overarching historical logic.

Second, it was "of the proletariat"—in two "contradictory" senses: it embodied the authentic values and will of the proletariat in its commitment to a classless society; and it involved the widespread participation of the proletariat in government and society. If these two dimensions are taken together, and not separately, there is only one logical conclusion: workers should actively and unanimously support the policies of their government. This was how one very important circle was to be squared: democracy and participation were encouraged insofar as they were in line with the participants' own ultimate class goals. Participation on the basis of values foreign to the proclaimed true interests of the proletariat was thus forbidden.

Finally, that this was a dictatorship of the *proletariat* meant that it was exclusionary: it sought to separate out an ideal community based on class from all other groups in society. These other groups would be tolerated or favored only insofar as their activities coincided with the proletariat's historical mission. Because of this exclusionary policy, because politics could not simply be the expression of a harmonious class in a homogeneous society, the state had to be preserved and it had the right to use force.

Stalin was right that this concept was fundamentally contradictory: it represented the transfer of essentially premodern political ideas based on social harmony to an increasingly complex and heterogeneous modernizing society. The concept of dictatorship recognized actual social heterogeneity but also affirmed the desirability of homogeneity. It could therefore be used to justify either class truce or class warfare. And at different times the proletariat was asked either to accept the authority of bourgeois specialists or to participate in bloody purges against them. This dual policy exemplifies the ways that this concept could be used as a very flexible instrument of state power in its commitment to modernization.

In his comments on the dictatorship of the proletariat, Stalin naturally left out another fundamental contradiction: his own role as autocratic leader of the people, a political ideal completely foreign to Marxism. But we can easily see how it fit in. If Marxism was ideological truth and the embodiment of the authentic values of the community, then Stalin's personal rule was merely service to the doctrine and the people. His role, too, was thus hybrid and multiple: tsar, modernizer, Communist leader. The logic of the regime tried to work against the separation of any of these dimensions of his role. In the state's major modernization campaigns, all of these images and legitimating ideas were brought into use. But the victims of these policies were under no obligation to accept Stalin's dialectical logic. Many, particularly in the countryside, came to define him as their enemy in both the traditional and modern senses.

The same "dialectical" logic was at work in economic life in the Stalin period: the regime promoted a policy of economic modernization on fundamentally premodern economic principles. Again, a potpourri of divergent economic practices and ideas, often seeming to come from entirely different archaeological periods of human economic development, were thrown together and announced as economic truth based on party principles. At one time or another equality and inequality; the need or the obsolescence of economic incentives; one-person or collective management; and economic laws or purely political will were all propounded as the most effective means of reaching the promised land. How can we attempt to understand this conceptual chaos?

The essential point, for economic life as for politics, is that Communist ideology, facing both backward to the vision of a harmonious premodern society and forward to the communal society of abundance, provided a bridge between elements of the Russian idea and the requirements of rapid economic modernization. Although its key exponents were not aware of this irony, it therefore facilitated the transfer of much of old Russian economic culture into modern economic practices and institutions. Until its very demise, the Communist regime was never able to solve the resulting dilemmas.

In the economic realm, too, paradoxes and contradictions abound. Appearances rarely corresponded to reality. What to the external gaze looked one way, when more deeply understood was seen to have an entirely different meaning. Western visitors, most famously Bernard Shaw and the Webbs, were frequently completely misled by the world of appearances that seemed so clear-cut to them. Nowhere can the deceptive quality of standardized concepts be better observed than in the idea of a "planned economy." The concept itself is in the best traditions of Western rationalism. As opposed to the Russian idea, which was suspicious of such utilitarian practices as strict accounting, optimal use of resources, and the like, the idea of a plan was in fact perfectly consistent with much of the logic of Western capitalism. For centuries Western firms had been, on the micro level, learning how to count up, organize, and deploy their resources for maximum advantage, often over a long time frame. Ever since the early modern period, European governments had sought to encourage and complement these practices of economic rationality through their own fiscal policies for the sake of national growth and power. It is symptomatic that socialist thinkers first came to work out theories and practices of overall economic planning after observing the German economy during World War I: it was in a capitalist society that the demands of war led to the extension of government planning over much of the economy. Why could socialism be not even more rational than capitalism, asked many socialists, and completely eliminate the anarchy of the market in favor of the rationality of elite policy-making?

The idea of plan rationality seemed to its adherents to transcend cultural boundaries; it was a logical deduction from the universal values of the enlightenment, which favored the expansion of material welfare as a central dimension of progress. It was not, then, an exclusively socialist ideal. Indeed, two of its main intellectual innovators were the German businessman Walter Rathenau and the Russian economist Grinevetsky, the latter an opponent of the Bolsheviks whose book was published in Kiev during the time that the city was under White army control.[25] But despite this dubious provenance, Lenin ordered the work of Rathenau to be translated and Grinevetsky's treatise to be brought to Moscow and studied. He felt that as neutral technique, economic planning could be a tool in the construction of a just, rational, and efficient society on the ruins of the capitalist system.

The First Five-Year Plan was adopted in 1929, five years after Lenin's death. By that time it had lost many of its German traits and been imbued with Russian belief and Communist dogma. Even in its initial formulation it was not a careful plan based on an accurate assessment of resources and a reasonable forecast of potentialities. One group of economists had in fact opted for this kind of rational plan—they were called "geneticists," as opposed to the "teleologists," who believed that belief, enthusiasm, and political will could overcome allegedly objective difficulties. The teleologists, who tended to be party leaders rather than economic specialists, may not have had the stronger economic case, but economics was not seen by the political leadership to comprise a separate sphere of social life with its own logic.

A sea-change was worked upon the technocratic vision of the rational use of resources in the name of economic progress. It became transformed out of all recognition in two related directions: it became archaized and ideologized. The archaic practices I have in mind had the following logic: economic life was not determined by interest and commodity exchange, but by political command; these commands were invested with the sanctity of truth, derived from the political leadership's ideological prescriptions; poor performance was regarded as criminal, as was disagreement with economic decisions. This logic, which might have found its closest equivalents in ancient Egypt, were officially interpreted as embodying the virtues of the dictatorship of the proletariat. Class exploitation was eliminated. Authority was based solely on the ultimate interest of the proletariat and had no warrant by virtue of private property or specialized education in themselves. And because of its greater justice, the belief and enthusiasm that it would inspire would lead to economic miracles beyond the comprehension of bourgeois rationality. Anyone who opposed the plan's directives was therefore a class enemy, guilty of opposing the will of the proletariat and therefore hindering the arrival of Communism.

The practical consequences of this fusion of different meanings for the nature of the plan were enormous. Although it was still presented as some kind of product of rational thought, in fact it had no moorings other than in political vision. And the commands of these visionaries, particularly Stalin, were the essence of simplicity: industrialize at break-neck speed, regardless of the costs. Economists or specialists who tried to adopt the rival logic of reasonable outcomes were political enemies. Stalin explained his view without any qualifications: "people who talk about the necessity of reducing the rate of development of our industry are enemies of socialism, agents of our class enemies."[26] Sensible people knew what to do: outbid each other in a flurry of wild claims. We can reach the goals of the five-year plan in four years, it was promised—even though five years was far from sufficient for the actual targets. And those modest goals—said others—why not double or triple them? Anyone with true socialist enthusiasm can easily overfulfill them. An unreal psychological atmosphere of expectations unchecked by objective circumstances quickly enveloped much of the country. There are no fortresses Bolsheviks cannot overcome: this was the famous declaration of the leader that gave blessing to this orgy of unkeepable promises and orders.

Let us think of the differences from the phlegmatic regime of Nicholas II. The Russian and Soviet people were set upon a resolute new path of modernization, one whose logic elevated them above all the other peoples of the world. No longer were they at the mercy of foreign models and foreign capital—these would be welcomed, together with foreign specialists from the bourgeois world, but under the terms of the Soviet government. This separate path was imbued with ethical values: it was for the benefit of the people and sought to transform their age-old passivity and rightlessness into active support. It held forth the hope of a united people, one not torn asunder by rival values or conflicting class interests. Selfish private interests would not be allowed to hold sway over the welfare of the people, and government planning would protect people from the risks and uncertainties of the market. Of the greatest significance of all, this unity, belief, and mass participation were at the service of a historical process that would soon usher in a collective good life, one that would compensate for temporary sufferings. It was for broad sectors of the population an entrancing vision, one filled with prospects of personal advancement as well as idealistic hopes for the future of the country. But even for those who did not advance or did not care about advancement, there was still the prospect of being, in the memorable phrase of Osorgin cited earlier, a "naked hero."

However, this ardent association of practices and values that in truth did not fit together, this only partly conscious synthesis of contradictory models and orientations, gave rise to its own enormous problems. It created a new basis for decisive action in the name of noble goals, but it also inevitably gave rise to cruel and ultimately self-defeating policies. A brief discussion of two of the major social campaigns of the 1930s, the collectivization of agriculture and the attempt to industrialize the country at breakneck speed, will reveal the sources of both the power and the tragedy of the Stalinist model. Each topic illustrates the intricate interweaving of elements of the Russian idea, the commitment to modernization, and Marxism. Despite the inconsistencies among them, their association together during drastic campaigns of social transformation inspired not just cruelty, but also idealism. And the insoluble contradictions surely made these campaigns less amenable to cool-headed analysis, since they were fundamentally so incomprehensible. Boris Shragin was not alone in confessing that "I can still hardly explain to myself how all these things coexisted in my mind in a more or less harmonious state."[27]

Stalinism at Work: Collectivization and Industrialization

Collectivization

One can easily imagine the dismay of a rank-and-file committed Communist in contemplating the countryside in the late 1920s. Considered from the standpoint of "progress," the proletarian revolution had actually led to a certain socioeconomic regression. According to the main contemporary Soviet authority: "If peasant family economy predominated quantitatively before the Revolution, afterwards its predominance was absolute."[28] The peasant family economy was still organized around the communal mir, which had taken on a new lease of life after the revolution.

If one took a classic Marxist perspective, this change was in the wrong direction. At least the development of capitalism would increase agricultural efficiency, stimulate commercial links between the countryside and the city, and ultimately prepare the way for a communal life of abundance after capitalist exploitation was eliminated. By contrast, the revival of the peasant household economy and the traditional communal mir posed ideological and practical dangers to the development of socialism. For a Communist, the peasant had interpreted the nationalization of the land in the entirely wrong way: it did not belong to the whole people, but to the peasants who worked it. For many peasants, taxes were illegitimate; and decisions about how much food to produce, and whether to sell it and at what price, should be left entirely to the small producer. This mentality, traditional for the Russian peasant (and not just the Russian), threatened to create an autarchic peasant world, cut off from the city and with no modern ties of interdependence, much along the lines of the Russian idea of the united homogeneous community. In addition, our Marxist would be convinced—rightly or wrongly—that such an organization of agriculture inhibited technological modernization and perpetuated small-scale inefficient agriculture. One possible way out of the bottleneck of inefficiency was to permit the emergence of a peasant rural bourgeoisie, who would produce and market a surplus in the interests of accumulation. In this case, the weak and inefficient peasant, as elsewhere, would simply be squeezed out.

There were some Communist leaders, such as Nikolai Bukharin, and a school of agronomists, led by A. V. Chayanov, who believed that small-scale peasant agriculture could be coordinated with the regime's commitment to industrialization, the accompanying growth of cities, and the interests of its target social base, the working class. They believed that with government support peasant agriculture could become more efficient, and that the peasantry could be persuaded through examples and incentives to develop communal practices and institutions compatible with a modern economy. Such moderates tried to assuage skeptics with the hope that socialist practices could develop organically in the countryside and fuse with the logic of the dictatorship of the proletariat.

There are many scholars who believe that these moderates were correct, though closure on these debates is nowhere in sight.[29] Whatever the scientific merits of their case, the policies ultimately adopted by the Soviet government in favor of dekulakization, collectivization, and forced grain requisition bespoke an entirely different spirit: not compromise, but war; not organic development, but heroism in the service of a cause; not purely utilitarian logic, but the higher truth of political consciousness and will. Once again, behind the trappings of modern socialist doctrines can be discerned the familiar sediment of the Russian idea.

The dilemmas of Soviet agriculture were ruthlessly interpreted in terms of the logic of class war. In the late 1920s there certainly were profound dangers stemming from the unwillingness of peasants to sell their grain at the unreasonably low state-mandated prices. Further, there was little in the way of industrial products that peasants could buy with their money, and so little incentive to sell at all—far better to consume their product or barter it on the local level. In a certain sense, these were rational peasant responses to the breakdown of interdependency between city and countryside, but such an interpretation did not correspond to the binary logic of Communist enthusiasts, whether at the mass base of the party or among the leadership. They had a much simpler diagnosis of the problem, and radical solutions that followed from their diagnosis with an iron consistency.

How to interpret the shortcomings of agriculture? Willful sabotage of the class enemy. And who was the class enemy? The rich peasant, taking advantage of the freedoms of the New Economic Policy to exploit neighbors, to buy up their land, and then to starve the working class. Ultimately, by such actions they could overthrow Soviet power and restore capitalism to Russia. It was necessary to defeat these enemies of the new society, and to establish rural collective farms that would restore equality among peasants, perform the socialist duty of providing grain supplies to the city for the building up of industry, and provide the organizational nucleus for the application of science and technology to the countryside.

These class enemies, the rich peasants, were thus thrice cursed: they exploited their neighbors and so destroyed the harmony of the rural community; they opposed modernity and so condemned their fellow citizens to backwardness and poverty; and they violated Communist ideology, which fused together the values of brotherhood and science in a more general truth. In this fusion of values, the reverse logic also came to operate: anyone who opposed the government's policy was by definition a kulak, a rich peasant. The term came to have a moral and political, much more than an economic, definition.

Tragic consequences followed from this icy logic. Hundreds of thousands of better-off peasants, denounced by their neighbors or identified by the authorities, were shot or deported. In a campaign of dizzying speed, the peasantry as a whole was compelled to join collective farms, where they lost their individual allotments and much of their livestock (what they would be allowed to keep—chickens, a cow, a horse?—was heatedly debated within the party leadership in these years). Finally, to combat the greedy instincts of the class enemy, party activists were sent to extort absurdly high quotas of grain from the peasantry, thus initiating a massive famine in 1932–33.

Many people believed the mythology upon which these cruel measures were based. They believed, in accord with the commitment to modernization, that progress depended on the pumping out of more resources from the countryside. As Marxists, they believed that class conflict was rampant in the countryside, and that the rich peasant was the enemy of socialism. And they believed that the Communist state aimed to create a collectivist rural society that would embody both ancient Russian values of community and the modern Communist vision. Stalin's political goals—in his words, to "transfer from small, backward and fragmented peasant farms to consolidated, big, public farms, provided with machines, equipped with the data of science and capable of producing the greatest quantity of grain for market"[30]—seemed progressive and just.

The allure of the party vision was all the greater because the solution seemed so simple: remove the class enemy. Imbue the countryside with socialist values by attacking the church, the cultural bulwark of the old exploitative order. Such goals, which promised creation on the ruins of destruction, had the power to animate, in different ways, the best and the worst of people, those who acted out of idealism and those who acted out of hatred. Lev Kopelev, who himself participated in these events as an enthusiastic young Communist, has given us unforgettable descriptions of both extremes. Of himself he wrote:

> It was excruciating to see and hear all this. And even worse to take part in it. . . . And I persuaded myself, explained to myself. I mustn't give in to debilitating pity. We were realizing historical necessity. We were performing our revolutionary duty. We were obtaining grain for the socialist fatherland. For the five-year plan.

Around him "were people who in my eyes embodied, personified our truth and our justice, people who confirmed with their lives that it was necessary to clench your teeth, clench your heart and carry out everything the party and the Soviet power ordered."[31]

Less elevated was the perspective of the "one-eyed commissar" Cherednichenko, who was called by the party to participate in collectivization but balked at first. "I don't like hayseed bumpkins. Don't trust 'em. Every one of 'em is only out for himself, his own sweet home—yeah, and his own little hole in the ground and his own small change. But I'm a proletarian from my father's father's father and don't give two hoots about their dung shoveling."[32]

Building on such attitudes, the Communist regime was able to accomplish another first in Russian history: it penetrated deeply into the countryside and yoked the peasant to the purposes of the state. But only in a mechanical sense. It is indeed true that the countryside lost the capacity to rebel against state power, and that eventually the rural economy recovered slightly from the devastating catastrophes inflicted upon it in the early 1930s, although never enough to satisfy the needs of the country. Even if very poorly, the workers were fed, and the cities were assured basic food supplies through the workings of the political apparatus. But although the regime tried to portray the new system of collective farms as an embodiment of Communist ideals and explained to the peasant and to the rest of the world that they were now masters of their own communal life, its game of mirrors could only work outside the countryside itself. The peasants knew that they had no real say over their own affairs and were well aware that, as they had been under the tsars, they were second-class citizens, with inferior rights. They were not legally allowed to leave the village and were not granted the economic and social rights of the rest of the population. They regarded the system of collective farms as a second serfdom and hated the man who had imposed it upon them. They also knew that his promised mechanization and modernization of agriculture had not taken place, that emergency priority was given to industry and the cities.

As a result, just as the regime had found its enemy, the evil force responsible for all the ills of rural Russia, so the peasants identified their own anti-Christ. According to the most recent study, based on newly available Soviet archives, "The prevailing opinion, as expressed in rumors, was that Stalin, as the organizer of collectivization, was the peasants' inveterate enemy: they wished him dead, his regime overthrown, and collectivization undone, even at the cost of war and foreign occupation."[33] The myths propounded by the ruler did not work. Stalin was not the good tsar protecting his loyal people, nor was he the great modernizer or the instrument of class justice. For the peasant he was guilty of the crime for which he had sent so many to their deaths: he was the enemy of the people.

Industrialization

Logically, the industrialization campaign of the 1930s should not have been as tragic as the attack upon rural Russia. The workers were, after all, the regime's targeted social base, and it was to industry that it endeavored to devote all available resources. Yet a similar logic of class war was applied to industry, and together with some real triumphs there were incalculable injustices, stupidities, and barbarities. In industry, too, a similarly potent fusion of cultural and political models connecting the Russian idea, modernization, and Marxism issued in an appallingly destructive movement, but this same fusion gave wing to flights of idealism and self-sacrifice. With staggering human costs and deeply flawed in its basic mechanisms, the Soviet state's industrialization drive transformed the country into one of the world's great industrial powers.

The Stalinist regime's industrialization campaign (for this is a much more appropriate term for its policies than "strategy," which implies more coherence and consistency) was beset by contradictions from the beginning. Its fundamental postulate was that, in the famous statement of Stalin, there are no fortresses that Bolsheviks cannot storm, for theirs is the truth. Class consciousness and will can overcome any objective impediments. In Russia, as Alexander Panchenko explained, nothing whatsoever depends on the economy, everything on consciousness. At the same time, modern industry has more exacting requirements than those of a largely backward agricultural sector, and so the reign of belief, as well as extremes of compulsion and violence, could wreck havoc on industry. Expertise and material incentives, two concepts certain to arouse the suspicion of Bolsheviks of the War Communist cultural persuasion, just as they would set on edge any good Slavophile, were indispensable ingredients of industrialization.

Nonetheless, in the first two years of the First Five-Year Plan, the Communist spirit triumphed over the requirements of efficiency and rationalization. Those who spoke up for economic balance, realistic output directives, and unequal wage incentives were tarred as class enemies. An atmosphere of "specialist baiting," which culminated in some dramatic show trials, showed that the logic of class war was temporarily transcendent. Workers who refused to accept egalitarian wages combined with unrealistic new production targets were also in danger of being branded as saboteurs or wreckers. Factories were purged of alleged class enemies, whether managerial or worker in actual class background. This turmoil, which removed many of the best-prepared people from the industrialization effort, created an atmosphere of fear and mistrust, which undercut cooperation and initiative.

But this same logic of class war also unleashed enormous reserves of enthusiasm and self-sacrifice, particularly among the young. Many ardently believed in the socialist dream and were convinced that the enthusiastic efforts of their generation would speedily bring it into existence. Popov, a welder encountered by John Scott in the Urals, recognized that there was a great deal of injustice in the new society: "A lot of things happen that we don't hear much about. But then, after all, look at what we're doing. In a few years now we'll be ahead of everybody industrially. We'll all have automobiles and there won't be any differentiation between kulaks and anybody else."[34] Naked heroes could once again perform miracles through suffering! To buttress their sense of the superiority of the new regime, it was not difficult to draw unflattering comparisons with the tsarist past or appeal to the miseries of Western capitalism, especially if one was not familiar with actual conditions.

The chaos and even threat of economic collapse produced by the class war approach to industrialization in the early stage of the First Five-Year Plan have been described many times. Unrealistic targets created confusion and uncertainty among managers. Egalitarian wage scales, no matter how much in accord with time-honored Russian values and Marxist doctrine, led to an exodus of skilled workers away from many branches of industry. There were repeated shortages of vital materials, and no sensible way to make choices among competing uses for supplies that far from met essential demand. The financial system was in complete disorder, with factory deficits automatically covered by a centralized credit system that embodied no controls over factory performance. Rapid expansion of the money supply and currency devaluation took on dangerous dimensions. Instead of centralized control, the "planned" economy gave birth to all kinds of centrifugal tendencies that directly contradicted its rationalist aims: hoarding, mutual protection, local improvisation, and the like.

In responding to this crisis, the Stalin regime was incapable of charting a fixed course. It was caught between its own contradictory principles and the choice of either a rationalizing strategy based on the logic of modernization or a class war approach involving great risks for its own survival. The first would threaten utterly to eliminate the ideological basis for its rule as well as risk the alienation of its main social base in the party and the working class. The second was incompatible with the expertise and authority necessary for effective economic performance and might also plunge the country into even more political chaos. The regime, with Stalin's blessing, therefore lurched from one extreme to the other, cavalierly violating the prescriptions that it had embraced a short time before.

One strategy, attempted in the first years of the five-year plan and then again toward the end of the decade, built upon the enthusiasm of class struggle and socialist construction. Its destructive side was the purging of specialists and managers who did not adhere to the official line. It appealed to the class egoism of the workers as the pure bearers of egalitarian models and urged them to participate in the purges against the class enemy. This anti-elitist vision of the cohesive proletarian family united with the leader, familiar to us in logic from Zubatov's program of police socialism under Nicholas II, served to mobilize some sectors of workers in the service of the regime's goals. As well as this emphasis on purges and popular control of the elites, there was also a creative side to the class war strategy: the emphasis on shock work, storming methods, socialist enthusiasm, and proletarian values—in short, a complex of beliefs and practices that stimulated heroic service to the cause.

Yet such heroic methods were also divisive, separating the proletariat from other classes, and even creating new conflicts within the proletariat. In addition, they were based on a serious undervaluation of the long-term complexities involved in industrial development, which involved coordination and standardized practice more than enthusiasm. As a result, these campaigns, like the Zubatov experiment which undermined capitalism, were short-lived, although the values associated with them always survived to contest the rival logic of social relations meant to replace them. They were in substantial degree replaced by a second orientation, whose fundamentals were explained by Stalin in a well-known speech of the summer of 1931, "New Conditions—New Tasks in Economic Construction." Reacting to the excesses of the recent past, Stalin advocated the rehabilitation of bourgeois specialists, the elimination of wage leveling, and the introduction of cost-accounting measures in socialist factories. In the following years, various methods of industrial administration and types of material rewards consistent with this alternative logic were instituted: wage differentials, piecework, one-person management, the de-skilling of the labor process through mechanization (which was presented as an example of "collective," "egalitarian" models of industrial organization), and the introduction of severe penalties for absenteeism, tardiness, and other forms of misbehavior. Workers were no longer to be mobilized in campaigns against factory authorities, who were now seen to be essential in a rational industrialization program—at least, not until the next orgy of political repression of bourgeois managers and specialists in 1937.

Throughout the 1930s Soviet industry often grew at an impressive rate, but it would be hard to qualify this change as "development." For industrial development implies that a solid foundation is being created for future progress on the basis of sound fundamental principles and workable institutions. Certainly there were some elements of development in the 1930s: the level of skill and expertise increased dramatically, and the political leadership seemed to be more willing to listen to the specialists that it had trained.

Nonetheless, the industrial structure that emerged was rife with fundamental contradictions. In theory, it was an administrative command system, where decisions were taken at the top on the basis of overall goals and executed through various bureaucracies and administrative structures. But as scholars such as R. W. Davies have shown, managers and other administrators at all levels were forced to improvise and violate both the letter and the spirit of their orders. Effective administration, even if based on command, requires that there be reliable links through all levels of the system. While this goal is in some senses utopian in any organizational system, the departures from the ideal were especially marked in the Soviet case.

In theory, too, industrial relations had been recast to fit a more modern model. People had the right to participate, they acted in terms of standardized norms of behavior, and different groups and classes were held to be indispensable and interdependent. But in fact such a set of principles, which form part of the general process of rationalization in modern societies, with its good and bad effects, did not displace a set of more traditional Russian orientations: a quasi-familial model of social relations; a suspicion of inequality, combined with a restoration of authoritarian social relations throughout the society; hostility to elites, who were seen as interlopers between the ruler and his people; group exclusivism and egoism, which worked against a wider sense of interdependence; an emphasis on belief, enthusiasm, and heroism, more than interest, as the roots of behavior; and an unwillingness to measure results on purely utilitarian principles. All of these traits made Russian industrial life jerky, inefficient, and unpredictable, despite the formal existence of a rational plan.

Finally, the Communist regime was based upon a claim to truth and an appeal to justice. Yet its constant backtracking and violations of its own principles were clearly visible to anyone who wanted to pay attention. It was perhaps for this very reason—the evident contradictions not just between words and deeds, but even between deeds and deeds, and words and words—that the regime committed itself to control the thoughts of its people—not for the sake of truth, but in the interest of its own survival. Perhaps, too, it was necessary for Stalin to cultivate an air of personal mystery, which could then envelop the contradictory society over which he ruled and prevent too much rationality from entering the darkness. Millions and millions of people continued to believe in the justice of Stalin and his socialist system, but they believed blindly, without clear comprehension. Ideology had no clear meaning, and for many it was replaced by simple loyalty. "Almost no one thought anymore of a program, of ideals, of the principles of Marxism."[35]

Concluding Remarks

Reflecting in 1980 about the victims of Stalin's terror, Vyacheslav Molotov, the political leader closest to Stalin for many years (himself, by his own recognition, probably slated for extinction if Stalin had not died), stated: "Poor things! Pity them? Don't forget, they worked to ruin the cause!"[36] And what was this cause? It was virtually everything: it was the truth of Marxist-Leninism; it was support for the five-year plan; it was hard work at the factory; it was loyalty to the party line, whatever its shifts; it was defeat of the fascists in war; it was rejection of whatever was culturally alien, the product of foreign or bourgeois influences. In such a vision of the world, there can be no differentiation of spheres in society and no neutral behavior. Science must be party science; economic behavior must be in accord with the dictatorship of the proletariat; surrender in war when surrounded by the enemy means betrayal of "the cause."

This vision of the world arose from social and political schism, and it also reinforced it. All belief and all action were interpreted in terms of binary logic: party versus nonparty, city versus country, kulak versus poor peasant, proletarian versus wrecker—the categories were endless. But whatever the concrete form of the opposition, the logic was always the same and at heart extremely primitive. It simply boiled down to a radical distinction between what is "ours" and what is "alien" and so bore the imprint of tribal ideas of community transferred to the modern world.

The lack of differentiation of separate spheres of society had negative effects for the modernization of the country. Scientific progress was impeded and economic decisions could not be based on strictly economic reasoning, although, as we have seen, economic truths had a way of influencing practice no matter how strong the emphasis on Communist goals. Throughout the society, the hypertrophy of political will prevented open debate and inhibited means-end rationality. For these reasons, science and technology could never possibly keep up with world standards; at most there could be spheres of great achievement in particular areas. The politicized economy could accomplish certain tasks very well, but it was extremely inefficient, wasted enormous quantities of resources, and inhibited initiative and innovation. The party-directed campaigns to eliminate religion and control culture were powerless to spread modern rationality throughout the society, for they reinforced magical and dualistic ideas—which were in fact much more in line with the overall atmosphere of the regime than rational evaluation.

Here is a letter published in a major newspaper in 1937 that eloquently demonstrates the irony:

> We repudiate the writings about God and we assert that there was not and there is not any such person. This fact has been established on the basis of scientific data concerning the origin of man as well as the origin of the universe. But what interests me is another thing: Do sorcerers and conjurers really exist and what is the power they possess by which they corrupt people and transform them into swine, dogs, etc.? You may, perhaps, deny this, but these are facts.[37]

The new modernist ideological dualism had the effect of reinforcing traditional peasant dualism, for both of them were absolutely distinct from a genuinely pragmatic and rationalist worldview.

The Stalinist model, with its modernizing and archaizing elements, could therefore not have endured for long. It required a leader with considerable powers of mystification—one who had some of the qualities of the Great Manu.

> In memory the pain and horror of 1933 and 1937 had not grown cold. I remembered, knew and to a certain extent understood how he had schemed, how he had deceived us, how he had lied to us about the past and the present, when together with Hitler we had routed and divided up Poland, when we had waged a shameful war on Finland. And nevertheless I believed him all over again, as did my comrades. I believed him more than at any time in the past. . . . This belief and even heartfelt devotion could not easily be broken. It was not broken even by many years of prisons and camps."[38]

The Stalinist system probably required some such combination of mysterious personal qualities in the top leader but also ensured that only mediocrities without such qualities were likely to survive.

The Stalin regime also rested on mass terror, which was essential to the working of the regime for many reasons: as a component of the policies of class war in the countryside and industry; to prevent the resistance that inevitably emerged within the party and among various social groups to the contradictory model of Communist modernization; to enforce silence and reinforce the monolithic culture imposed upon a diverse population; and as a logical outcome of the ruthless division of the world into friends and enemies.

Equally essential: the Stalinist model could only work for the short period when resources were unlimited and economic growth could be "extensive" rather than "intensive"—that is, based on the use of vast quantities of land, labor, and capital to reach an intermediate industrial stage. For the efficient use of resources and the transition to more technologically sophisticated stages of economic development it was greatly handicapped. Its very emphasis on quantitative growth inhibited real "development." Similarly, the time horizon for success was short because the promises upon which the model was based—the need to sacrifice for the immanent creation of the socialist society of abundance—could not be postponed indefinitely.

Finally, the survival of such a system depended upon a Manichaen conception of the capitalist world as utterly evil and the regime's willingness to keep the country completely isolated from foreign influences. Stalin was ruthless in this respect: he even sent Soviet soldiers who had been prisoners of war in Germany to labor camps so that they would not infect the rest of the population.

At Stalin's death in 1953, all the Communist leadership, even the notorious secret police chief Lavrenty Beria, knew that fundamental changes in the regime and its relationship to society had to be introduced at once. They did not understand one of the great tragedies of this incoherent system: its very fragility, born of its contradictions, ruled out effective reforms. Its ancient roots in Russian culture, as well as its ideological dogmatism, in fact contradicted the vision of modernization that the Communist leaders promised this nation of expectant, though still naked, heroes.

CHAPTER FOUR

A Viable Form of Modern Society?

Of Stalin's death in March 1953, Solzhenitsyn later recalled:

> This was the moment my friends and I had looked forward to even in our student days. The moment for which every zek [prisoner] in Gulag (except the orthodox Communists) had prayed! He's dead, the Asiatic dictator is dead! The villain has curled up and died! What unconcealed rejoicing there would be back home in the Special Camp! But where I was, Russian girls, school-teachers, stood sobbing their hearts out. "What is to become of us now?" They had lost a beloved parent. . . . I could have howled with joy there by the loud-speaker; I could even have danced a wild jig! But alas, the rivers of history flow slowly. My face, trained to meet all occasions, assumed a frown of mournful attention. For the present I must pretend, go on pretending as before."[1]

No doubt these extremes of grief and jubilation epitomize the mood of the country as a whole, for the Stalin dictatorship, whatever its achievements, had deepened the schisms and splits of Soviet society. No more than in 1700 or 1900 had the gaps between town and country been healed, and we can speculate that the country celebrated Stalin's death (quietly, of course) much more than the city. Nor was the governing bureaucracy seen as any closer to the "people" than it had been under the tsars: the old split between "we" (the innocent people) and "they" (the distant and inscrutable rulers, perhaps excluding the totemic father Stalin) continued to characterize Russian and Soviet political culture. Indeed, one of the common fears after Stalin's death was that the new ruler of the country would not be able to rein in the bureaucrats, as Stalin was seen to have done. Nor did the state's forcible efforts to inculcate a new set of beliefs remove the classic split between the true believers in the official truth and the heretics, driven underground but not eliminated. Finally, the split between Russia and the rest of the world had only deepened during Stalin's rule, posing the most difficult questions about the future place of the country in the larger world context.

The reinforcement of schism during the period of the Stalinist dictatorship of the proletariat had prevented the elaboration of ties of interdependence throughout the society. Although there had been many winners—for example, ambitious young people from among the workers who had risen to dizzying heights in the new society—there had also been millions of victims. And so the worry—what will become of us now?—came naturally to the minds of everyone, even those who had suffered from the regime's lawlessness. The somber expression on Solzhenitsyn's face may not have been entirely feigned after all. No one knew whether the social and political patterns that had emerged under Stalin's watch could provide the foundations for a "normal" life.

It is clear that precisely this—a normal life—is what people desired above all. The poet Boris Slutsky expressed the overall mood: "The time for circuses is over, it is now the time for bread; a break for smoking has been granted to all those who were storming heaven."[2] But what were the implications of this desire for a stable, predictable life? Were the institutions and ideas of the Stalin period, developing during a time of the "storming of fortresses," capable of sustaining a society based on routine? Was it true, as many later commentators believed, that there had already emerged the foundations of a separate Soviet model of modern society, one that provided a viable alternative to Western capitalism, even though it was based on an entirely different logic? What changes would be necessary for the transition to a stable socialist society?

As we have seen, this separate Soviet model of modern society was not, as some have argued,[3] a rational alternative response to the challenges of modernity. Rather, it was a complex association of Russian antimodernism and the commitment to modernization mediated through Communist ideology. But the classical model of Soviet Communism could not synthesize these different elements. Instead, this untidy misalliance of elements distorted both the Russian idea and Communist values. The Soviet institution of the dictatorial party state, culminating in an absolute ruler, parodied and perverted the old Russian idea of the Government of Truth, as well as the Marxist idea of the administrative state superintending a harmonious society. The planned economy, with its complex roots and symbolism, embodied neither rational planning nor the older Russian idea of a society based on higher values. Thus, far from being "a natural form of society,"[4] every practice and institution was invested with uncertain meaning. The discrepancies between ideal and reality were expressed in a pervasive dual consciousness, which gave life a theatrical sense.

There was widespread recognition, even in the most unexpected circles, that dramatic changes were essential. The ruthless head of Stalin's secret police, Lavrenty Beria, acted quickly to introduce some elements of normality and even envisioned a series of other changes that would have gone far beyond what his political rivals after Stalin's death would countenance. Although, based upon his atrocious record under Stalin, Beria has conventionally been seen as a hard-liner who had to be eliminated for the reformers to come to power, recent archival research has suggested that his orientations were more complex. Beria would have pioneered, and much sooner, some of the reforms that would later be announced by Khrushchev. For example, less than three weeks after Stalin's death Beria sent a memorandum to the Presidium of the party's Central Committee arguing that, of the 2,526,402 prisoners in labor camps, only 221,435 were "especially dangerous state criminals." He therefore urged a broad-scale amnesty.[5] In addition, in a series of initiatives that followed each other with remarkable speed, Beria sought to reduce the arbitrariness of criminal procedures, to cut back on the Stalinist cult of personality, to strengthen the position of government ministries vis-à-vis party officials, to cancel a number of Stalinist mega-projects that made little economic sense, and to grant important concessions to non-Russian nationalities in the Soviet Union. The sweep of these reforms, which for Beria's rivals would have had unsettling effects throughout the Soviet empire, particularly in Eastern Europe, helped cement the eventual alliance against him.

But if Beria was in some respects in the lead, many of his aims and proposals were universally shared. Reduction in the level of terror and greater economic rationality were obviously necessary for the creation of a stable Soviet society after Stalin's death. But beyond such obvious considerations, what changes had to be introduced for the sake of social stability and political legitimacy?

On a very broad level, the sacrifice of the present for the sake of the future could not continue indefinitely, for no society can forever live in the future. The poet Alexander Tvardovskii, later editor of the journal that published Solzhenitsyn and who came to represent the hope for reform under Khrushchev, wrote of Stalin: "He said, follow me/ Leave your father and mother/ Leave everything transient and earthly/ Leave it, and you will get to heaven."[6] But there seemed to be little evidence in the early 1950s that the generations who had built industry and won the war against Hitler were about to cross this celestial threshold. It was now time to think about food, not just tractor production, and about housing, not just industrial construction. The tremendously high rates of investment in industry had to be decreased for the sake of present-day consumption. Present and future welfare could not continue to be opposed to each other, but somehow had to be linked together more organically. Unrealistic tempos and unbearable pressure for the fulfillment of hastily thought out programs must give way to a realistic assessment of present possibilities for future development. The commitment to higher ideals and heroism over vulgar materialist calculation, crucial in the vision of a separate Russian-Soviet path to modern society, must be diluted.

Crucial to this link would be a new orientation toward work. No longer a heroic struggle against nature and historical backwardness, it would now become the source of real material rewards. There had been constant debates and numerous policy shifts throughout the 1930s about the relative significance of enthusiasm and interest in the motivation of labor, but material interest and rewards had never been completely legitimate, no matter what the current doctrinal positions had been. And there was always the fear that any encouragement of self-enrichment would be followed by a campaign against the new kulaks or entrepreneurs, whose relative prosperity would once again be interpreted as the result of bourgeois tendencies. Assistant minister of economics Frumkin exposed the illogic that was obviously not lost upon the population as a whole: we tell peasants to produce more, and if they do they are kulaks; we loosen up the possibilities of trade and production in the interest of economic growth, and then we attack those who respond to the incentives.[7] Work and material incentives had to be more consistently linked once the heroic stage of socialist construction had been largely superseded.

The state also had to modify its class-war approach and recognize that it ruled over an increasingly heterogeneous society. Industrialization was not producing a community of workers, but a complex division of labor based on fine-tuned interdependence. Engineers should no longer yearn for an inseparable "fusion with the proletarian collective," as Kopelev described the aspirations of the building designer Kolya Melnikov.[8] Nor should peasants feel that they were regarded as a potential petit bourgeoisie opposition, or in any way inferior to some kind of hegemonic proletarian class. The outflux of the most active and productive peasants from the countryside had had a devastating effect on Soviet agriculture, and no stable modern society could evolve on the basis of such extreme dualism. No matter how hypocritical and unconvincing to the workers themselves, the regime's efforts to glorify the role of the proletariat inevitably led to resentment and fear on the part of other classes. When might the proletarian state once again mount an attack against them?

All of these changes implied a new role for the state in Soviet society: no longer would it base itself on social schism, and on this basis further divide the community, but it would come to regard itself as the government of the people as a whole. If this were the case, it would not just impose a "proletarian" policy, but listen to the aspirations of the population as they were in reality. Pragmatism and a willingness to compromise would flow as a matter of course from this altered relationship to society. Mass terror against whole social groups, abstractly defined in terms of ideology (kulaks, bourgeois specialists) would have no place in such a political system. According to a new logic of representation, the Government of Truth must soften its efforts to define and control society.

Considerations such as these were behind Beria's reform program, and they would also underlie many of the changes in Soviet Communism in the Khrushchev and Brezhnev periods. Reforms in these directions were inevitable if the society was to acquire a degree of stability and the political system a modicum of legitimacy in the absence of the totemic leader. But these were not the only challenges confronting the new leaders, whoever they might turn out to be. For in an odd way, the Stalinist system had revealed itself to be not only revolutionary, but also extremely conservative. Both its revolutionary and conservative elements were in tension with (although not diametrically opposed to) the goal of the creation of a dynamic socialist system.

These conservative elements of the Stalinist system were recognized long ago. Shortly after the Second World War Nicholas Timasheff published an important book called *The Great Retreat*,[9] which catalogued and analyzed the multiple ways that the Communist regime was moving away from its revolutionary goals and transforming itself into a rigid status quo. Growing appeals to nationalism; the end to cultural experimentation; rigidity in the educational system; the return to rank and decorations in the army; backtracking on the issue of equality: these were some of the signs, thought Timasheff, that a stable and conservative social order was emerging in Stalin's Russia.

The empirical indicators of such a transformation were indeed everywhere, although Timasheff has been retrospectively criticized for underestimating the revolutionary drive of the party, made painfully apparent shortly after his book was written. But if his interpretation turned out to be flawed, the phenomenon itself was present. Further, the regime's radicalism, both in the last years of Stalin and under Khrushchev, can hardly be understood outside of the context of its battle with threatening elements of a conservative social order, which were undermining the hallowed social and political ideals of the alternative Russian tradition.

Particularly dangerous to partisans of the idea of a separate Russian path to modernity was the emergence of privileged groups of party functionaries and economic managers. Sometimes dubbed the "new class"—although the term is misleading in its broader implications—this new Soviet elite was of an entirely different stripe from the old revolutionary party leadership, which had been largely destroyed and completely demoralized in the purges of the 1930s. Educated in Communist-created schools and institutes, and thus trained to think according to the party line, they owed their careers to the system that had so rapidly advanced them. Narrow in outlook, and with a clear stake in the status quo, this new elite posed little threat of political independence. On the other hand, like any elite they had power and influence, and therefore the capacity to act in their own interests, which did not always correspond to the goals of the party leadership.

Equally important, the emergence of this new elite posed an ideological threat to the regime, which, strangely enough, could be turned to the regime's own advantage. There was nothing in Marxist doctrine to justify the privileges of such a stratum, and the Russian idea had always been inimical to intermediaries between the ruler and his loyal subjects. The danger was that this privileged new elite would undermine the legitimacy of Communism and those who ruled in its name. The potential advantages for the regime were obvious to a ruler as shrewd as Stalin, and expeditiously taken advantage of: the hostility of the masses to the dictatorship of the proletariat could be channeled against the "corrupt" and "unprincipled" managers and bureaucrats, who were distorting the will of the just ruler. As noted in the previous chapter, the trick did not always work, especially in the countryside, but Stalin, and then Khrushchev, would continually resort it, no doubt because of a certain degree of efficacy. Naturally, the mobilization of the indignant workers against their betters also had the very important extra benefit of controlling and motivating the conduct of this potentially self-serving and inefficient social elite. The dangers inherent in their ascendancy for the dynamism of the Soviet system became all too apparent under Brezhnev, when the top party leadership and the Soviet elite, for the first time, fully accommodated to each other.

The Stalin regime's very repressiveness and drive for superhuman levels of change unintentionally gave birth to another source of conservatism: the preservation and even strengthening of the closed, quasi-familial group structure of Soviet society. The natural reaction of people being asked to do more than they reasonably could under the threat of terrible penalty was to form illicit networks of personal connections for self-protection. A high degree of threat to security, we know, was the source of both European feudalism and the Italian mafia. The response of Soviet people, whatever their social positions, had an identical logic: the formation of hierarchical systems of mutual protection that could provide alternative ways of operating and shield the participants from outside scrutiny.

Throughout the whole history of the Soviet Union, such unofficial and indeed often illegal relationships proved to be both essential for the working of the system and fundamentally subversive of the overall goals of the regime. The ills were attacked under various names: departmentalism, localism, familism. Creative methods were employed to counteract their effects, but to little avail.

For even though the Russian idea cum Communist ideology was grounded on anti-elitist ideals of equality and community, in fact the very notion of a Government of Truth encourages the creation of such closed networks based on personal ties. These networks subvert the larger ideals of both equality and community. At the same time, and somewhat paradoxically, a number of social traits celebrated by the Russian idea were preserved, even if in distorted form: the importance of personal ties over purely formal relationships; the rejection of abstract organization and rules; the perpetuation of paternalistic bonds, which seemed to replicate Stalin's political role throughout the social system; and the collective (if not strictly communal) character of social life.

Eloquent testimony to the utopianism of the idea of a truth-bearing government protecting a united people, to many observers the particularism and collectivism of this unofficial pattern of social organization have brought to mind the logic of the peasant village, with its hierarchical structure and its immense capacity to cut itself off from outsiders. Whatever its advantages, this unexpected perpetuation of older social patterns was subject to stricture from the standpoint both of the regime and of the individuals involved. From the ruler's point of view, the density of informal networks obstructed the transmission of orders from the top to the bottom of the social hierarchy. They were always distorted by the "noise" of these informal social patterns. In the Soviet Union, as in Russia throughout its history, the regime was always less powerful than it appeared on the surface.

For the individual the system also had its drawbacks: although it might provide protection from the rigid application of unreasonable norms, it also subordinated the individual to the collective and its local leader, thus undercutting individual initiative. As has been recognized countless times, this theoretically centralized system gave rise to a plethora of little Napoleons able to exercise arbitrary power in their own domains. The individual's sense of impotence helped transmit and reinforce those same traits of Russian individual behavior so ardently attacked by Lenin: irresponsibility, laziness, passivity. Clearly, no real revolutionary could rest content with the reassertion of this very potent form of conservatism within the embryo of Communist society.

In other respects, too, Soviet society had come to mimic some of the conservative traits of tsarist society, in particular in the rigid state definition of the position and rights of different social groups. For example, as in the nineteenth century the peasant was most definitely a second class citizen, subject to the arbitrary will of local authorities and the object of numerous restrictive laws on mobility and property ownership applicable only to this group. More generally, Soviet law was highly particularistic in its designation of the rights and responsibilities of different groups. This particularism bears striking similarities to the logic of the tsarist estate system, which also sought to freeze the position of every social group in a state-ordered hierarchy. Under both the tsars and the Communist leadership these rules were inconsistent with the fluidity of a rapidly industrializing society and so were violated with great frequency.

Was it conceivable that these numerous indications of the emergence of stable and conservative social patterns could provide the foundation for a stable Soviet social order? Could Russia recapitulate the experience of nineteenth-century Japan, when a samurai elite under the Tokugawa regime was able to displace the shogun and transform itself into a dynamic ruling group? Could the dense networks of quasi-familial social relations be somehow reshaped to serve the interests of economic development rather than self-defense? In this respect, Meiji Japan had decisive advantages over mid-twentieth-century Russia, for the authority of institutions and elites was well-grounded in Japanese culture. But in Russia all institutions were called into question by the Russian idea of truth; and elites, interfering between the state and the people, always had tenuous legitimacy. And was the Japanese samurai ideal, parallel in some ways to the Russian emphasis on heroism, so opposed to routine everyday work?

The use of social conservatism as a way of combining socioeconomic transformation with a return to normalcy had little chance of success in the post-Stalinist Soviet Union. Because so many of the conservative elements of Soviet society had emerged as efforts at self-protection against an aggressive state, they in fact tended to work against modernization. For example, it was by means of networks of personal trust that factory managers could understate productive capacity, hoard resources, and disguise poor quality. Similarly, the self-enclosed local worlds protected their own internal interests and inhibited the emergence of broader patterns of interdependence. Thus, the weakness of markets and of horizontal ties more generally worked against the expansiveness and openness of Japanese enterprise, where the hierarchical micro world was forced to integrate itself into the broader economy. For these reasons, the conservative elements of Russian society presented especially formidable obstacles to social and economic rationalization.

Still more serious doubts arise in the political sphere, for social conservatism in the above senses, although in part engendered by the Communist Party, clearly contradicted the party's mission. Stable elites and localized centers of autonomous power would undercut drives for permanent revolution and, perhaps even more significantly, deprive the party of its ideological legitimacy as the fountain of knowledge and the demiurge of progress. For these reasons, no matter how many concessions Stalin may have granted to the "new class," he prevented its consolidation as a stable and independent social group with the capacity to perpetuate itself through time. The Brezhnev regime permitted the emergence of this kind of elite, with disastrous consequences for the effectiveness and legitimacy of the Communist system. Khrushchev, in his attacks on the positions of party and bureaucratic elites, had a much keener sense of the underlying logic of the system, for which real conservatism was self-annihilation.

I have not yet addressed the most weighty obstacle to a conservative consolidation as a response to the problem of normalcy in Soviet society. The poet Slutsky had urged that the time of circuses was over, and that the people longed for a break from the repeated attempts to perform miracles. Yet neither Russian traditions nor the experience of Communist modernization could easily be combined with a world of sober calculation, careful plans, and tempered progress toward reasonable goals. The writer Ehrenburg expresses the heroic alternative, one rooted both in the Russian idea's rejection of bourgeois rationalism and in Communist dreams for a brilliant future: "The men who had slogged all the way from the Volga to the Spree could not in their hearts reconcile themselves to obtuse bureaucracy, to the huge imaginary figures of published statistics, to the familiar words 'better not do it.'" The Soviet people had "performed such feats that it may rightfully be considered the hero of the twentieth century."[10]

There is abundant evidence that, whatever its crimes, the Stalinist regime had been able to inspire belief in huge masses of people, and through this belief many people's lives had taken on heroic meaning, even lives led isolated in the village or shut up inside factory walls. For such humble people had also participated in the struggle for socialist construction and the war against fascism. In their own view, they had given their labor or their lives not for material advantage, but for a larger goal that had conferred transcendent value on their efforts. They had performed miracles and thereby proved to the doubting Westerners that the Soviet path to modernity was superior. Realizing the dreams of Slavophiles and Eurasianists, they had thrown off the European yoke and become masters of their own fate. Could such people, thirsting for equality and longing for participation in a collective goal, reconcile themselves to the existence of a conservative new elite and a rationalized social order based upon the pursuit of material welfare?

However puzzling or perhaps ethereal such questions may be to many Western readers, I am convinced that they were at the heart of the cultural, social, and political debates of the entire post-Stalin period. Unfortunately, the attempts to resolve them operated according to a binary logic that is by now painfully familiar.

Nikita Khrushchev attacked Stalin's cult of personality, with its terror and voluntarism, and attempted to replace it with a kind of makeshift populist Communism that threw together elements of the Russian idea and a crude version of Marxism. His egalitarianism, attacks upon the stability of the state and party elites, and hastily thought-through economic improvisations were branded by his successors as hare-brained experimentation.

The Brezhnev regime, once again originating in an act of negation, sought to construct a stable socialist society on the basis of "stability of cadres" and a broad compromise with the population. But this regime, in theory based upon a synthesis of Communism and modernization, in fact violated the premises of both alike, as well as those of the Russian idea. For this reason, there was a strange triumvirate of dissident voices raised against it, composed of advocates of authentic socialism (such as Roy Medvedev), rational progress (such as Andrei Sakharov), and a return to the Russian idea (such as Alexander Solzhenitsyn).

Gorbachev also began with an act of negation: the Brezhnev regime, having claimed to usher in the period of "developed socialism," was now labeled as the "period of stagnation." But once again the act of negation, which under Gorbachev came to embrace not just his own immediate successors but a good part of the whole Communist tradition, was much easier than creation. No more than his predecessors was Gorbachev able to cobble together a compromise between all the different conflicting elements of Soviet modernization. Although he claimed to believe that consensus and a cohesive society had already been largely achieved, Gorbachev was defeated by the logic of *raskol* (schism). His failure suggests that there was no way out of the contradictory system bringing together the Russian idea and modernization on the basis of Communist values. Gorbachev was surely right that the patient, Soviet society, was terminally ill. But the illness was long-term, and the efforts to operate on it merely hastened its death.

KHRUSHCHEV AND THE PEOPLE: UNRESOLVED CONTRADICTIONS

Stalin had labored tirelessly to ensure that none of his lieutenants could threaten his rule. Among his changing entourage, most were of mediocre ability. Of the few exceptions to this rule, some, like Foreign Minister Maxim Litvinov and chairman of Gosplan Andrei Voznesensky, were removed from office or eliminated. The very shrewd Beria would almost certainly have fallen victim to Stalin's paranoia. Satraps like Malenkov or Khrushchev hid their talents behind fawning subservience and streams of flattery.

It was not necessarily to be expected, then, that a new absolute leader, a *vozhd*, could emerge after Stalin's death. Nikita Khrushchev surprised everyone, from Beria, who seriously and fatally underestimated his talents for political intrigue, to foreign diplomats, who often mistook his uncouthness for stupidity. The contrast with the former "father of the people" could not have been more absolute. Stalin was aloof and mysterious, even to his closest associates, and even more so to the Soviet people, many of whom ascribed semimagical powers to him. His was the decisive word in social and political affairs, but his authoritative utterances were often hard to interpret, especially in conjunction with his own conflicting statements and policies. Khrushchev was an interminable chatterbox, a self-appointed expert on everything, with boundless energy and curiosity. He loved nothing better than to travel throughout his country, meeting with milkmaids and engineers at cement plants, explaining to them the details of their jobs. He was an authentic man of the masses, of humble worker origin himself and illiterate until his twenties. He liked to contrast himself with other heads of state, raised in the best families and educated in elite schools. He was proud that his country could raise such a man as he to the top, and he was convinced that his life experience gave him the edge over his foreign counterparts.

Unlike Lenin or Stalin, he had never participated in the revolutionary underground and could not have understood the ideological debates that raged in the country in the 1920s. Notwithstanding a brief flirtation with Trotskyism, he was for the "general line" of the leadership, a loyal supporter of official policies. Even after he became general secretary of the party, his only books were collections of speeches, and then, published abroad, his memoirs. No theoretical tracts, no matter how crude, came from his pen. He saw himself not as an ideological innovator, but as a man who had been raised according to the true values of a superior system, whose duty it was now to put them into action. Khrushchev was a believer, and it was in large part his attempt to remodel society according to these beliefs that led to his downfall: in part, because he intruded on the vested interests of others; and also because these beliefs, rooted as much in the Russian idea as in Marxism, were naive, inconsistent, and unrealizable in the context of a complex modern society. His ten-year career as leader of the party illustrates, in a different way from that of Stalin, the unresolvable tensions among the Russian idea, Communism, and modernization.

Khrushchev's verbosity and bluntness do not make his rule easier to interpret, for there were numerous contradictions and reversals. But these were not the Sphinx-like policies of the Stalin years, with their mysterious unpredictability. Rather, inconsistency and indeed hypocrisy flowed from Khrushchev's simplistic social and political outlook, which served as a poor guide for the creation of a "normal" modern society. As opposed to Stalin, whose vapid and often contradictory utterances seemed to mean something profound, "Khrushchev was garrulous, and so gave the show away."[11] Thus, it is by no means clear how Khrushchev will be judged by history. During perestroika, there was a flood of articles and letters in the Soviet press expressing different evaluations of Khrushchev's rule, some praising his efforts to end Stalinism, others stressing his dictatorial style and ruthlessness.[12] Perhaps the best emblem is the famous sculpture at his grave in Moscow, designed by Ernst Neizvestnyi, whom Khrushchev had viciously attacked: Khrushchev's bust is set off by two slabs of marble, one black and one white, symbolizing the warring tendencies within him.

Although he never achieved it, in some measure due to his own flaws as a leader, it is clear that Khrushchev did pursue a certain vision of normalcy. He wanted to end government based on fear and terror, and he also believed that the party had an immediate responsibility to improve the life of the people. He therefore embarked on a dual policy of removing the threat of terror and attempting to whip the party into shape as a tool of social transformation.

Khrushchev's efforts to curb political violence and lawlessness had both sociological and political sources, which were not fully consistent with each other. He proclaimed that, while the dictatorship of the proletariat had been historically necessary to build socialism, now a new stage of social development had been reached. Previously exploiting classes had indeed existed, and it was right that they were eliminated. In his speech to the Twenty-second Party Congress, he praised the "voluntary cooperation of the peasantry" as "the outstanding event in the social economic history of mankind."[13] Because of this transformation, capitalism had been eliminated in the countryside. Since force was applied only against exploiting classes, the dictatorship of the proletariat had been "deeply democratic."[14] Further, because of socialist industrialization and the increasing use of science and technology, the gaps among workers and between them and white-collar employees were narrowing. Socialism, therefore, had achieved a fundamental social consensus based on class harmony, and so dictatorship could be replaced by the "government of all the people." Once again there was the temptation to identify an ideological ideal with empirical social reality.

Violence against the masses, at one time justified, was now no longer necessary. But for Khrushchev there had never been any basis for the violence against the party in the 1930s: this had been the result of Stalin's "cult of personality," which Khrushchev denounced at the Twentieth Party Congress in 1956. At his extraordinary speech at this meeting, one of the turning points in the history of modern Communism, and even more graphically at the Twenty-second Party Congress, the high point of the official denunciation of Stalinism, Khrushchev and his allies gave chilling descriptions of ruthless terror against the party. While the peasants and bourgeois specialists were still regarded as real enemies of the people, countless victims of the party purges had been loyal Communists fallen victim to Stalin's malevolent will.

Could such a stance provide the basis for normalcy? Could it really heal the wounds of the recent past? The hypocrisy was especially galling when it touched Khrushchev's and his allies' own roles. They, of course, had not really known. They had been kept in ignorance. Only their present political enemies, the "antiparty group," had been fully complicitous in Stalin's crimes. Nor, given the political implications of such a choice, could all of Stalin's victims be rehabilitated: luminaries such as Trotsky and Bukharin were not among those now pronounced innocent.

With such enormous shortcomings and contradictions, Khrushchev's de-Stalinization policy inevitably strengthened social and political splits within the country instead of healing them. The Stalin question continued to polarize Soviet society until the end of Communism, with no compromise possible between those who saw Stalin as the father of their country and those who regarded him as an enemy of humanity. Khrushchev's half-hearted policies satisfied no one.

The same ambivalent conclusions can be drawn about Khrushchev's attempts to reform the legal system. Normalcy certainly required that specific laws be enacted and enforced, to replace the use of vague concepts like "enemy of the people." According to the new criminal code, promulgated in 1958, people had to be accused of specific crimes and tried by duly constituted legal bodies. Certainly many advances in legal procedure and consciousness were evident, but there were still setbacks. Particularly worrisome to Soviet legal reformers were the new law on parasitism, which could be used to punish anyone troublesome to the authorities, and the extension of the death penalty to new categories of crime, particularly serious economic offenses. Khrushchev wanted this new law applied retroactively to a couple of famous swindlers, and despite opposition to him he prevailed. The Soviet people still did not live under a predictable legal system based on accepted legal principle, in part because Khrushchev, like Nicholas II, identified the Government of Truth with the people.

Although one of Khrushchev's favorite words was *vpered*—forward— he also committed the party to the improvement of people's living standards in the here and now.

> If we do not guarantee our people a higher living standard than in the developed capitalist countries, what kind of Communists are we? For Communism isn't something unearthly. We are not priests who teach that earthly life is temporary and eternal life must be earned by earthly suffering. We destroyed the bourgeoisie not just in order to take power, but to remake the economy in order to guarantee the highest level of living for our people.[15]

Among his earliest policy innovations was to raise the prices paid for agricultural goods to the collective farms. More attention was given to the production of consumer goods, redressing some of the imbalances of the Stalinist economic model. He constantly hectored party members that they were to be economic activists responsible for raising production. When criticized by rival leaders for neglecting ideology and party work, he replied that theory and ideology could well wait while the party fulfilled its promises to the people.

There was much talk during Khrushchev's rule of the law of value, economic accountability, rational planning and administration, and the like, but the leader himself fell far short in these respects. There was much justice in the later charges that he was impulsive and voluntaristic, for he energetically embarked on unrealistic and poorly thought out campaigns, which bore all the marks of the old Bolshevik storming mentality and the traditional elevation of belief over rationality.

Famous examples were the feverish efforts to get Soviet farmers to plant corn even where it made no sense and the sowing of the virgin lands in Central Asia. Khrushchev's own lack of realism translated itself into enormous pressure on those below, who also often took flight from economic rationality. The "Riazan affair" was a notorious example. In his desire to win the approval of the general secretary, the local party chief A. N. Larionov made promises to produce that were as fanciful as any of the targets announced under the utopian First Five-Year Plan. To fulfill the commitments for meat, breeding stock and milk cows were slaughtered, and cattle were bought from neighboring areas. Larionov was decorated for his overfulfillment of the plan, but the deception soon became clear, and he committed suicide. The whole absurd and tragic episode showed that hastiness, overenthusiasm, and deception, promoted from on high, could still overcome sober economic calculations. Further, Khrushchev himself displayed an inability to distinguish between his own ideological hopes and real economic possibilities. Hero-socialists could still, in his view, perform any task.

The culmination of this Khrushchevian commitment to a utopian breakthrough in the standard of living of the population was the 1961 program of the Communist Party, the first party program drafted since 1919. The first sentence of the program read: "The building of a Communist society has become an immediate practical task for the Soviet people." Immediate—it was held—because the development of Soviet socialist society had already prepared the necessary prerequisites of a Communist society of unheard of abundance and equality. By 1970 the living standards of the Soviet people would surpass that of Americans. By 1980 "a Communist society will, on the whole, be built in the U.S.S.R." A political anecdote of the time chronicles one kind of reaction: "An official lecturer explained to the audience that under Communism people will have everything, homes, cars, even helicopters. An old woman asked: Son, why do I want a helicopter? Granny, he answered, suddenly you'll find out that there's macaroni in Kiev and you can fly there immediately to get some." According to the later recollections of Politburo members Alexander Shelepin and Vladimir Semichastnyi, high party officials at the time understood that such claims were nonsense.[16] How could such hyperbole be the basis for a sound economy and a stable modern society?

Perhaps our sympathy for Khrushchev's policy will increase if we consider another side of the problem: his fear of conservatism. Khrushchev favored normalcy and so sought to replace key elements of the dictatorship of the proletariat, but, having risen through the party ranks, he also understood that stability could easily turn into stagnation. The main danger, he knew, came from the party elite, which could insulate itself from criticism and wallow in its own privileges. But the mission of the party, as the vanguard of progress, was always to be close to the masses, so that it could lead and inspire them in the struggle for Communism.

Stalin had also worried about the powerful elite that his rule was bringing into being, although he was probably not overly concerned about its lack of inspirational ties with the masses. His strategy was not to attack the privileges of the party and governmental elite as such, but to control individuals through intrigue and fear. Khrushchev acted differently: party purges were relegated to the past, but he enacted one measure after another to undercut the structural position of the party and governmental elites as a group. Regional economic councils were formed to decentralize economic decision making, thus reducing the power of the almost omnipotent ministries. New rules for term limitations in office at all levels of the party hierarchy were introduced. The party was divided into agricultural and industrial sectors, and both were told to go to work to get the economy moving. Local party organizations were enjoined to take a more active role in social affairs, not just awaiting instructions from on high. Further, party activists should take over many of the functions of full-time party officials, so that the number of professional party administrators could be reduced in preparation for the Communist "self-administration" of society.

Western commentators at the time often evaluated these measures as Khrushchev's attempts to develop a more consistent totalitarianism, with a more active party controlling the government and penetrating society more effectively. (One eminent American writer on Soviet affairs even called the 1961 party program Khrushchev's *Mein Kampf.*) But such judgments missed the crucial point that Khrushchev combined his assault on conservatism with a commitment to normalization. Why, mistakenly, did he think that these two goals were consistent with each other?

The answer lies in his vision of Soviet society, which was a kind of crude populist fusion of Marxism and the Russian idea. Bureaucratism, self-serving, narrowness: all of these were foreign to the collective. As phenomena of the "old," they could be magically removed by an attack on the cult of personality. They were thus artificial brakes on a society for which all the prerequisites of an active community based on shared belief already existed. There is ample evidence that Khrushchev could simply not imagine the possibility that large sectors of the Soviet people did not share these values. He was convinced, just like the Slavophiles, that morality in the West was a mere abstraction, since the root of action was individual self-interest, whereas in the Soviet Union values were actually embodied in social life. He also believed that participation in the collective opened up all possibilities, whereas purely individual activity was ultimately impotent. Shelepin recounts an illuminating episode that occurred when he was with Khrushchev in his native village of Kalinovka. Khrushchev called a general meeting, at which he spoke for two hours, trying to convince the *kolkhoz* farmers to give up their private plots and livestock, for the collective could produce more efficiently and sell to them at government prices. A shout was heard from the crowd: "Nikita, what happened to you, have you gotten stupid?" The villagers departed, leaving behind a furious Khrushchev.[17]

"For everything to be shared—this was the truth and salvation," so a veteran Russian commentator summed up Khrushchev's worldview.[18] The corollary of this proposition was also unquestioned by Khrushchev: truth and salvation were also to be shared. Accordingly, Khrushchev could be extraordinarily harsh with his opponents, whether religious believers or independent intellectuals. For them socialist legality did not apply, for they violated socialism. "There will be no peaceful coexistence in questions of ideology. None, comrades," Khrushchev warned a group of writers and artists that he had assembled for a meeting in Moscow in 1962.[19] On other occasions he explained why: who are you to present your own point of view? he asked the poet Voznesensky. You are nothing, of no significance, ignorant and incompetent like a new army recruit in need of training. What is of significance? The people—that is who should decide in our country. And who is the people? The party. And the party? That is us. That means that we will decide, that I will decide. Understood?[20]

We have encountered this antipolitical vision before, if in much more sophisticated terms. Truth, the ruler, and the homogeneous community are one. Social elites who break the unity of the people are alien. Freethinkers who question shared beliefs are outsiders. The control or removal of such evildoers will ensure the victory of the good, for the people and the ruler are pure. Participation is only legitimate if it accords with the people's truth. It is extraordinary to find such sentiments in the heart of the ruler of a highly complex country in the latter half of the twentieth century. It is both remarkable and tragic that he was in a position to act upon this worldview at a time when a wiser and more accurate appreciation of his own society might possibly have led to fruitful paths to normalcy and progress.

No one came to Khrushchev's defense when he was removed from power in October 1964. He had done much to reestablish the power of the party, and he certainly had made party life much safer, but his chimerical attempts to mold this huge body into a revolutionary organization had gained him much more enmity than support. He had done much for the peasantry, but he had been unable to understand their diverse aspirations, for he had no concept of societal complexity and insisted upon interpreting them in terms of his own preconceptions. Intellectual life was much freer than it had been under Stalin, and we know from memoirs that many people experienced exalted hope for the future. But because of Khrushchev's arrogance and his high-handed attacks on the intelligentsia, as well as his inconsistencies and backsliding, by 1964 few artists and intellectuals pinned their hopes on him. Technical and professional groups were similarly ambivalent: although specialists such as economists, criminologists, or lawyers had been able to participate in the most open debates since the 1920s, had been able to influence government legislation and policy, and had even gained the independence to criticize the party and the leader, they too were appalled by Khrushchev's arbitrariness, irrationality, and crude judgment.

More generally, he had taken steps to establish a normal society, but his own primitive utopianism had undermined social stability and created much uncertainty. Tragically, it had been his very idealism that led him astray, for despite his energy and intelligence he was unable to perceive the world apart from his own values. And these values had something fundamentally antimodern about them, elements reminiscent of Avvakum or Aksakov, no matter how dressed up in Marxist concepts. "In his energetic faith uncouth Khrushchev possessed something ancient, open-hearted and majestic. But Lord, how he irritated us, how he wore us out!"[21] Whatever the majesty, this faith could ensure neither stability nor progress, and the failures to which it gave rise contributed in no small part to the mood of disillusionment that was to follow.

BREZHNEV: NORMALCY OR STAGNATION

Whatever the underlying dilemmas of Khrushchev's reform program, in many ways these were years of genuine achievement and hope. Living standards were on the rise; industry continued to grow, if not "develop"; intellectual and cultural life had been partly freed from its political shackles; the space program was attracting the admiration of the world; and the Soviet Union's international influence was greater than ever before. If few could believe the exaggerated claims of the leader, nonetheless there was a general mood of optimism about the future. Perhaps some workable combination of normalcy and progress could at last be established in this country that had experienced so many tragedies.

There were different interpretations of the fall of Khrushchev, and different expectations for the course that the new regime would take. According to the most optimistic view, Khrushchev had been removed from office because of his voluntarism and unpredictability. The new leadership, it might have been hoped, would be more committed to systematic reform and consistent rationalization, thus jettisoning the legacy of utopianism. Campaigns and extreme methods would at long last be eliminated, and the Stalinist legacy would be superseded. The presence in the new leadership of Alexei Kosygin, known as a man of ability and experience who favored economic reform along market principles, buttressed such an interpretation.

Although experts and rationalizers would have an important part in the new regime, it was not yet their hour. Instead, the tone was set by Leonid Ilyich Brezhnev, who managed to remain the dominant figure in Soviet politics for almost two decades, thus outlasting all Soviet leaders except Stalin. With Brezhnev's tightening grip on the party, it became clear that the fall of Khrushchev did not simply mean the end of adventurism, but also the waning of belief and enthusiasm, to be replaced by a stultifying conservatism masked by a pro forma allegiance to Communist values. Under Brezhnev, the return to normalcy came to mean the triumph of a fundamentally conservative elite and the consolidation of an increasingly hierarchical society. The real goal of this political elite was not so much progress as order. Characteristically justifying his regime's efforts to stamp out competing ideas, Brezhnev remarked that "if everyone starts doing what they feel like, there won't be any order in our country."[22] For the first sustained period in Soviet history, the drive for perpetual transformation seemed to have lost its momentum, in favor of this ideal of a sterile order.

Although the ascendancy of a settled conservatism may have been new in Soviet history, the whole period has an eerie resemblance to the regime of Nicholas II. Is it purely by chance that even their characters were similarly mediocre? Both had utterly lackluster mentalities. I have already described Nicholas II's intellectual limitations. Brezhnev easily surpassed him in philistinism and mental crudity. According to Shelepin, who as a Politburo member had occasion to observe him well, his reading was limited to the popular satirical journal *Krokodil*. Like Nicholas II, he felt insecure before people of real ability and chose people on the basis of their personal ties to him. Often these were family members or old associates from the days that he had worked at Dnepropetrovsk. The overall stance of the two leaders is also strangely similar: although there were great pressures for reform throughout their periods of rule, and many concrete proposals were prepared, both played an essentially passive role. They effectively stunted the initiatives of others but made no real efforts to solve the pressing problems of their societies. They did not squash the reformers and occasionally even embraced the substance of the proposals, but they did so hesitantly and against their own natures. For both preferred to try to maintain a predictable situation, concealing problems under the mantle of an official version of truth, rather than to try to grapple with fundamental problems. Brezhnev, for example, was disgusted by the corruption and moral decay of the highest political circles, but, according to his niece, "his normal response to abuse and corruption was, sadly enough, passive acceptance."[23]

Just as significant as such personal traits and styles was the overall set of challenges facing both leaders. In both societies an official value system justified authoritarian rule over what was alleged to be a united people. Like Nicholas II, Brezhnev was apparently convinced that "the official line was correct, that he was infallible, that the people adored him."[24] This "official line," however, did not correspond to a deep belief in Communist values, about which Brezhnev was utterly cynical. "All that stuff about communism," he is reported to have said, "is a tall tale for popular consumption. After all, we can't leave the people with no faith. The church was taken away, the czar was shot, and something had to be substituted. So let the people build communism."[25]

But despite such cynicism, both Nicholas II's Russia and Brezhnev's Soviet Union were officially held to be superior to their Western alternatives in their emphasis on shared values, justice, and community. At the same time, social change in both late tsarist Russia and the post-Stalin Soviet Union forced both leaders to come to terms with the limitations of this set of ideas and practices. For, as we have seen, the imperatives of modernity undermined the naive claims of these official versions of reality and therefore sapped the legitimacy of the rulers.

Yet there was also a decisive difference. Nicholas II's vision of a separate Russian path to modernity was at heart conservative, and the tsar wished to return to old Muscovite models of rule. Modernization ultimately hollowed out this vision, rendering it increasingly irrelevant to the challenges of the early twentieth century. For Brezhnev, the logic was the reverse, even if the effect was very similar. Because the Communist model of a separate path to modern society was by its nature revolutionary, it was the turn to conservatism that eroded the official ideology and sapped the regime's dynamism. If Nicholas II's fruitless attempts to protect a mythologized tradition conflicted with the modernization policy that his regime sponsored, General Secretary Brezhnev's formulaic adherence to a revolutionary ideology was similarly at odds with conservative practices. As a result, ideology and reality did not support but undermined each other, creating pervasive hypocrisy and dual consciousness.

With hindsight the corrosive effects of conservatism on the Soviet system seem self-evident, but at the time the great majority of Soviet people and scholarly observers felt otherwise. They largely accepted the claim that an alternative logic of modern society had been successfully pioneered in the Soviet Union, transforming the country into one of the world's two great superpowers. People generally felt that they could plan their futures on the basis of a comprehensible social logic, even if the official system was filled with illogicality and arbitrariness. Despite its shortcomings, which the ordinary person inevitably perceived and experienced, for the majority of people it was "ours," and decidedly better than "theirs" in the capitalist West, where exploitation reigned supreme.

The recurrent utopianism that repeatedly astonished those observers who kept expecting a normalization of the Soviet Union was finally laid to rest under Brezhnev. There would be no more documents like the embarrassing party program adopted at the Twenty-second Party Congress. Despite the cult of Lenin, the symbolic elevation of the proletariat as the bearer of revolution, and the support for militant Communist movements and states in the third world, ideology was largely transformed into a set of formulaic beliefs and stereotyped norms of behavior that came to constitute the largely taken-for-granted way of life under "developed socialism."

Obedience to local authorities; acceptance of the leading role of the party in social life; rejection of alien opinions and values; dependence on the state for the definition and the satisfaction of individual needs; the official cult of work; belief that the Soviet Union was the most powerful and progressive country in the world: these were some of the everyday ideological stereotypes of a routinized Soviet way of life, with its holidays and rituals. Typical in this respect were these sentiments from a new army recruit in a letter to his parents in the mid-1980s. He was proud to be participating in a parade for the anniversary of the October Revolution. The army could show its strength and invincibility, and together with the spectators they could all celebrate "the dearest of all holidays for the Soviet people. For whatever you say, this was an event of no little significance in our life."[26]

Thus, conservatism was not just a project of the elites, but it also defined and permeated daily life. It provided a kind of folk interpretation for everyday behavior, one that had more parallels with reality than did the official revolutionary ideology. It gave many people a sense of security and also a degree of pride. In addition, it provided a sense of historical continuity and also faith in the future.

With respect to the past, didn't the Brezhnev regime resemble that of the nineteenth-century Russian tsars? The world of facades described by the Marquis de Custine in the 1830s seemed to find all too close parallels in the contemporary situation. To foreign observers writing in the 1970s, such as Hedrick Smith of the *New York Times*, Soviet factories uncannily seemed to resemble Potemkin villages. Despite impressive facades, they might be producing little if anything of value. The same obtuse and unresponsive state, with its mean and petty censorship; the same passive population, nonetheless adept at bending rules and getting by somehow; the same eternally quarreling intellectuals, separated equally from the state and the people: the parallels were indeed striking. And although such parallels could give rise to depressing reflections, they also meant that Russian history and culture were still relevant. People read the classics with great reverence and took seriously the contemporary spokespeople for ancient Russian values.

This continuing vitality of the Russian cultural tradition also stemmed from a phenomenon that has been stressed repeatedly throughout these chapters. Soviet Communism was not nearly so "progressive" as its proponents proclaimed. It surreptitiously imported many traditional Russian cultural values, thus ensuring their survival. For the Soviet people, raised on the values of overarching belief, the collective, equality, and the state as the embodiment of justice, the ideas of the Slavophiles or Dostoyevsky would continue to resonate, as would the attacks on these ideas by nineteenth-century liberals or radical materialists. Is it possible to imagine in the United States that a volume of essays on the moral shortcomings of the intelligentsia, originally published seventy years earlier, would be seen as absolutely contemporary in its relevance? Such was the case with the book *Landmarks* in the Soviet Union under Brezhnev, a book that set off impassioned debates about the nature of Communism and the future of Soviet society.

This rediscovery of many traditional Russian cultural values did not go unchallenged. Ideologically, proponents of Communism attacked the obscurantism of the village writers and neo-Slavophiles in terms not so different from Belinsky's tirade against Gogol. A less dramatic, but undoubtedly much more insidious, affront to traditional Russian cultural values was the growth of Western consumerism, especially among the new elite and their children. No longer with any real connection to the Russian idea, they ran amok amidst the empty trappings of Western culture: "paper napkins decorated with naked women, Touch-Tone phones, Marlboro cigarettes, undershorts with KISS ME or PLAY WITH ME printed on them."[27]

Although the triumph of conservatism seemed to promise predictability and stability in Soviet society, there was nonetheless a serious dilemma in this Soviet model of modernity, a conundrum for which no solution was ever found under Brezhnev: in the Soviet context conservatism inevitably led to the decay of the foundations of the system and the waning of belief. In the catchphrase made current under Gorbachev, the Brezhnev years ushered in a period of "stagnation" that left the country far behind the rest of the world. Although ex-Politburo member Yegor Ligachev is surely right that this broad indictment neglects many signs of improvement in the society, such as an increased living standard and the initiation of major projects of technological innovation,[28] nonetheless the signs of long-term crisis were indisputable. Perhaps most ominous were the party's inability to advance the most competent people to the top (a phenomenon much lamented by Ligachev himself); the clear failure of the Soviet Union to keep up with international technological and scientific innovations; and the widespread cynicism, opportunism, and corruption in this society in principle based upon a higher moral order.

Without Western incentives and cultural traditions of individual initiative, dynamism in Soviet society had always depended upon the efforts of the political leadership, which, in different forms, had always acted according to a Russian cultural model of politics. In the Communist period until Brezhnev, change had been justified by an all-embracing ideology, which synthesized older Russian patterns with a commitment to modernization. Now, with the relaxation of state pressure and the waning of mass enthusiasm based on ideology, what would be the mechanisms of change under "developed socialism"? No answer was ever found to this question, and while conservatism meant predictability and a gradually increasing standard of living, it did not provide the foundation for the future in a competitive world. A great many Soviet people simply surrendered to the logic of the system, asking little of either themselves or the society. Soviet life became privatized to a degree impossible to imagine in the Stalin period, when even families and friendship networks were split apart by the political whirlwind. In the Brezhnev period almost any form of conduct was tolerated, shielded from view, or protected through personal connections—everything except public criticism of the Soviet system, which, as the embodiment of an ideal, was still held to be sacrosanct.

Repeated reference to Brezhnev may have mistakenly given the impression that he occupied the same role as Stalin, or at least as Khrushchev. However, an additional element of the new conservatism was that Brezhnev was no supreme dictator, but the head of a party that now recognized many norms of collective leadership. His conservative orientation was not just a personal choice, but embodied widely shared aspirations within the country's social and political elite, and no doubt among the masses as well—they, too, were well aware of the possible implications of another revolution from above. On the elite level, the catchphrase became "stability of cadres." There would be no further purges of government and party à la Stalin, nor any new measures to activate, inspire, or rotate the established elites, as Khrushchev had advocated.

But stable cadres also had to be reliable cadres: to ensure that there would be no challenges from below, the regime relied upon the famous *nomenklatura* system. Briefly, lists were kept of critical positions throughout the society and of potential candidates to fill the posts. Appointment of an individual to one of these nomenklatura positions required a thorough vetting and approval from above. The positions themselves gave the right to a hierarchically defined set of privileges: suppose that the second secretary had the right to two weeks vacation on the Baltic; then the first secretary might have the right to three weeks on the Black Sea. Medical care, access to food, car privileges, lodging: when we recall that the great majority of resources were ultimately controlled by the party-state, we begin to understand the scope and significance of such a system of allocation. It must also always be kept in mind that, at least in principle, this system was secret. From my own experience I know, however, that there was a pretty good sense among the population of where the special stores were and the extent of the privileges. I will never forget the comment of a Russian friend of mine when we were standing together near a bus stop sometime in the winter of 1981. He pointed to a huge curtained window with no signs and told me that inside was a store reserved for the party elite. "We are blacks in our own country," he remarked.

The nomenklatura system exemplified a more general social pattern under "developed socialism": the classification and grading of the society according to positions, rights, and privileges. An ideally conservative regime would have been able to define all social groups and allocate all resources according to its own criteria. Developed socialism never went that far, of course, but it did succeed in creating large numbers of quasi-estate definitions of social groups, each with its own rights. Not the least significant of these classifications was provided by the internal passport system, which defined who had the right to live in what kind of place. Work status was an equally important way of allocating scarce goods— which meant virtually all goods. But the standardization of this system should not be exaggerated. In practice, it was arbitrary through and through, as connections and mutual favors came to count more than abstract rules.

The cultural hostility to abstract rules and impersonal institutions, which were assumed to represent the dominance of "society" over "community," facilitated the emergence of this highly unjust system of closed social networks. It is as if the famous revolutionary Nikolai Chernyshevsky, who wrote in the mid-nineteenth century, had been describing life in the Soviet Union little more than a decade ago: "Our fundamental concept and our most stubborn tradition is to introduce the idea of arbitrariness into everything. Juridical forms and individual efforts seem to us ineffectual and even absurd; we desire and expect everything to be done on a basis of arbitrary decision."[29] In theory the Russian idea rejected "society" in favor of a higher "community"; in practice, the critique of law permitted petty tyranny and deprived people of a sense of fixed rights. In this regard, it is worth noting that Soviet ideologists always attacked the doctrine of the natural rights of man, preferring a concept of citizenship for which all rights were accorded by the state.[30]

This whole system of hierarchical grading and allocation of resources was in principle controlled by the party elite, and so corresponded to a statist model (perhaps something like the famous Table of Ranks under Peter the Great). Yet de facto every position under developed socialism gave rights of private use of public resources: in other words, it allowed for corruption, and in a certain sense depended on individual initiative. But perhaps corruption is not the right word, for the practice was so universal and accepted that it has to be regarded as part of the conservative self-perpetuation of the system. The saleslady would take the best cuts of meat to give to the doctor who was about to perform an operation on her child. The factory foreman had hoarded spare parts to be exchanged for better food for the factory cafeteria. In the economy of shortages, positions allowed people monopolistic control of resources that could be bartered for other scarce goods. Despite the formally state-run system of distribution, individual entrepreneurship on a universal scale gave the lie to any claims of top-down regulation based on the plan. Negotiation, bargaining, and informal exchange were ubiquitous. Once again, the official logic of social relations gave rise to its opposite in practice.

Although economically irrational, this whole system had enormous implications for social stability: it gave everyone a stake in the system and also made everyone complicitous in formally illegal activity. It therefore served the regime's conservative strategies well, just as it worked against rationalization and dynamism. According to one anonymous intellectual surveyed in January 1979, only about a quarter of the population were not tied in to the system and committed to its preservation. He cited Eduard Shevardnadze's words about the Georgians to describe the Soviet Union as a whole (this was in 1979!): "We were a nation of warriors, and we became a nation of speculators."[31] Belief seemed to have given way to the pursuit of material interest and consumerism—people still thought in terms of this oversimplified opposition.

What happened to the enthusiasts who, despite everything, have continued to emerge in Russian society throughout the whole modern period? Siberian literature of the Brezhnev period is full of material relevant to this theme. Writers such as Vasily Shukshin portray inveterate dreamers, with the *razmakh* of the Russian romantic, who constantly run amok in the prosaic and hypocritical world. In this literature, we are very far from the world of socialist realism, where society and the hero were in harmony with each other. As under the tsars, the main arena for heroism now lay outside the system, in the various movements of dissent.

If this system of private use of legally public resources, based on a formally hierarchical system of positions, had some positive functions for stability, its effects on the moral foundations of the system were highly insidious. According to an anonymous interview taken in April 1981, the system had failed with regard to its great slogan of "to each, according to his work." Instead, the formally illegal but almost universally permitted appropriation of public goods had led to black markets, corruption, and bribery. Those who engaged in these forms of "private entrepreneurship" saw their activity as natural (because everyone thinks about himself or herself first of all) and just (to each according to his or her ability). Honest labor had therefore turned out to be a poor provider, much exceeded by officially sanctioned corruption.[32] Ironically, the social analyst Platonov praised the advanced countries of the West for their development of "social property," which bound the interests of people together in a common enterprise. Our state property, he said, is not socially oriented, but privately appropriated—this in a country where industry was nationalized![33]

Nonetheless, for large sectors of the population this system was one part of a more general mode of accommodation between the regime and the people—an implicit part of the conservative strategy that won a great deal of passive support even while it inhibited rationalization. In exchange for security of employment, a reasonable (and gradually improving) living standard, free (even if low-quality) medical care, guaranteed (even if very cramped) housing, and, very importantly, minimal pressure to work efficiently, the population would accept the system, even with all of its hypocrisy.

And there is no doubt that large sectors of the Soviet population gained a great deal from the new arrangements, which continued in the spirit of Khrushchev's idea of the "state of all the people." Perhaps most significantly, the Brezhnev regime made considerable progress in improving people's lives in the countryside, in large part through huge government subsidies to agriculture. Special treatment was also accorded much of the working class, in terms of both relatively good salaries for many categories of workers and all kinds of extra privileges, such as low-cost vacations. I remember, too, the frequent articles about workers in the press and radio interviews in which they discussed their lives—not always completely openly, of course. Nonetheless, such attention must have given workers some sense that they still counted in the regime. Such special treatment, I recall from numerous conversations at the time, aroused the resentment of more educated groups, whose pay and benefits were much lower. Although by the early 1970s a good part of the intelligentsia had become gloomy about the country's future prospects, there is no evidence that the same mood was prevalent among other sectors of the society, even though everyone was aware of arbitrariness and corruption, and few believed in the ubiquitous slogans of Communism.

The point bears reemphasis. It was not just that the Soviet people had been cowed into a kind of fearful passivity, or that a new personality type based on true inner conformity had been created by the regime. Although there is some truth to such charges, repeatedly leveled by intelligentsia critics of the system, just as important was that, in the spirit of Saltykov-Shchedrin's antiheroes, a great many people were able to maneuver and protect themselves in this strange world that violated many of the official norms of Communism. "You've got to get moving," I was told by a sly Central Asian unofficial entrepreneur in 1981 when I told him my Soviet salary, which was very high by the standards of the time. In fact, vast numbers of people in Brezhnev's Soviet Union had wide scope for movement. And if this did not result in collective forward motion of the Communist type, it did provide space for energetic people who might formerly have acted on the basis of values and enthusiasm.

Much of the intelligentsia's pessimism had its source in the regime's renewed use of censorship and repression against unorthodox voices. It was perhaps because of the obvious contradictions between theory and practice that the Brezhnev regime became so much more protective of ideological purity. Out of a concern for order, they insisted on adherence to outer forms, if to nothing else. If Khrushchev had threatened and fulminated against writers and artists, he still did not have a consistent and thorough policy of repression of dissident voices. Such a renewed wave of repression was inseparable from the Brezhnev regime's commitment to conservative consolidation. Because of the outpouring of criticism of the system under Khrushchev, and also as a result of the role of intellectuals in the Czech defiance of orthodoxy, the government's innate mistrust and fear of the creative intelligentsia was magnified. In a series of visible trials, starting with the writers Yuri Daniel and

Andrei Sinyavsky, it signaled its intention to muzzle skeptics, dissenters, and freethinkers if they attempted to propagate their ideas publicly.

Did this new wave of repression signify a return to Stalinism? Many people thought so, particularly with the mini revival of a cult of Brezhnev toward the end of his rule, when military awards covered his chest and literary prizes attested to his genius as a writer. But these were testaments more to Brezhnev's senile vanity, and perhaps the perceived need to shore up the legitimacy of the system somehow, no matter how ridiculously, than to any serious movement in the direction of neo-Stalinism. For the regime did not have energy of any kind, either ideological or organizational, for a new assault on society; and party leaders without exception wanted to avoid a return to the atmosphere of party purges. Further, the regime had become deeply committed to incorporating expert knowledge into policy-making, whether in the economy or in constitutional reform, and so could hardly attempt a revival of the dictatorship of the proletariat. Although I believe that many Western political scientists drew fanciful conclusions in the 1970s and 1980s about the implications of this expanded scope of political participation—there was even a comparison made with the British cabinet system!—these changes do underline a significant departure from both the Stalinist and Khrushchevian models of politics.

Rumors about the revival of Stalinism were fed by the Brezhnev regime's retreat from de-Stalinization. Now almost nothing was publicly heard about the crimes of the dictator, his legacy, or how to extirpate the remaining elements of Stalinist thinking and policy from the country. Yet retreat from de-Stalinization was not the same as the restoration of Stalin. Indeed, it is my impression that those party and government leaders who defended Stalin, and so were branded as neo-Stalinists, did not aim at a return to Stalinist methods. Rather, they wanted the immense changes that Stalin had introduced to become part of a new conservative consensus on the nature of Soviet society: collectivized agriculture, the planned economy, socialist realism, and the like. While they praised Stalin for his achievements, they did not advocate a return to Stalinism in any real sense. This is the interpretation that should be given to the following 1966 declaration of Devi Sturua, then secretary for ideology of the Georgian Communist Party:

> We are sometimes called Stalinists, but we don't see anything to be ashamed of in that. I am a Stalinist because the name of Stalin is linked with the victories of our people in the years of collectivization and industrialization. I am a Stalinist because the name of Stalin is linked with the victories of our people in the Great Patriotic War. I am a Stalinist because the name of Stalin is linked with the victories of our people in the postwar reconstruction of our economy.[34]

Yet this conservative consensus never really became consolidated in the Brezhnev period. There was still too much sense of fragility, uncertainty. One key obstacle was the continuing propagation of an official ideology that was almost entirely at odds with the real functioning of the society. On a more mundane level, practices did not even correspond with official versions of them. Everyone who worked in the planned economy, for example, knew about corruption, deception, shirking, and other "spontaneous" activities. The party proclaimed its ability to continue to lead the people on toward full Communism (now somewhat delayed), but everyone knew that the party attracted multitudes of careerists. The writer Vladimir Voinovich expresses a not untypical attitude:

> Most of the Communists I've run into bear little resemblance to their counterparts in literature. Either they're dull, slack-jowled bureaucrats who scowl at those beneath them and fawn shamelessly to their superiors, or else they're slinking out of the special stores for the privileged, their briefcases bulging. In general, they are cowed little people who never have anything to say on any subject, great or small.[35]

I vividly recall the general skepticism and distaste with which party activists on the make were greeted in the early 1980s: they must not have any other competence, it was felt, and they must be willing to sell themselves out. I also remember overhearing the "discussions" at the closed party meeting in the room next to the archive where I worked. I and other Western researchers were amused by the passionate harangues of the leaders, and the utter silence of the audience. (I was told that they were all reading or doing their knitting.) Descriptions of party meetings in the Khrushchev period are not like this: participants have described the passionate debates and real concern among the members. I can imagine—I have witnessed numerous such gatherings during perestroika and afterward. Russians love passionate discussion and debate; public obedience and passivity were forced upon them by their insecure political masters.

Although great numbers of people accepted the system as natural, and in any case "theirs," there were also many signs of a moral crisis and spiritual vacuum among those who might in other circumstances have been political and intellectual leaders. A stubborn and insistent dissident movement, divided roughly between supporters of Western-style democratic reform and neo-Slavophiles, who favored a return to their agrarian version of the Russian idea, with some admixture of socialist reformers, attracted the attention of the world. The tragic fates of many of its members reinforced the belief among many that a return to Stalinism was feasible. But beyond such overt defiance, there was also the remarkable spectacle of the flourishing of all kinds of formally suspect or prohibited cultural tendencies, from rock music to Eastern mysticism to Christian sectarianism. Even among established writers, there was an influential group of "rural writers," centered around the journal *Nash Sovremennik*, who questioned the value of modern progress, celebrated many of the traditional values of the Russian peasantry, and posed the question of whether life without religious belief could have any real meaning. A split psychology was predominant in the country: the official belief is empty and meaningless, appropriate only for public discourse; real truth and meaning is not only separate from current orthodoxy, but diametrically opposed to it. No honest person could really accept the values of the regime.

Most significantly for the subsequent fate of the country, there was a large group of technocrats and party rationalizers who were disgusted by the Brezhnev's regime's continual thwarting of their efforts to make planning and administration more efficient and rational. Primary among their goals was the introduction of more market elements into the planned economy, partly through granting enterprises more autonomy. But although proposals along these lines had been approved, almost nothing was accomplished—again reminiscent of the political dead ends of the late tsarist period. The dictate of the party still held sway over science and reason. Many such technocratic reformers had managed to gain entrance into the nomenklatura, and so had a chance to witness the mediocrity and corruption of top officialdom firsthand. Profoundly distressed by what they saw, they came to identify Brezhnevian conservatism with decay and sought new paths of reform. Could they once again mobilize belief and enthusiasm in the construction of a new society cleansed of the impurity of the old? Again, it only seemed necessary to get rid of the corrupt and incompetent old officials, to replace bad people by good, and everything could begin all over again. Such a naive view of social change, pervasive in modern Russian political culture, provided the foundation for a tremendous surge of optimism in the early Gorbachev period.

The desiccation of the revolutionary version of the Russian Marxist idea under Brezhnev did not culminate in revolution, as had the decay of Nicholas II's political vision in the early twentieth century. Perhaps large-scale collapse or revolution would have occurred had there been a crisis of the scope of World War I. Instead, Soviet rulers of the 1980s were faced with a different kind of threat: increased technological and economic backwardness in comparison with the advanced West, made all the more threatening by the erosion of the society's values. If the challenges facing Soviet Communism had not been apparent enough before, President Reagan's new military programs heightened the sense of threat. Just as the nature of the crisis was different from the time of

Nicholas II, so was the initial response: it strengthened the position of those who wanted to instill a renewed dynamism into the Soviet system through a new model of modernization.

GORBACHEV AND THE FAILURE OF REFORM

> Before the reform movement, Soviet people felt theirs was the best society in the world; today they feel it is the worst.
> —Fyodor Burlatsky, December 5, 1989[36]

The roots of Mikhail Gorbachev's program of perestroika are so deep and varied that it is difficult to assign relative weights to them. Retrospectively, from the standpoint of the collapse of the Communist system and the unrelenting barrage of criticism leveled against the Brezhnev regime since the time of perestroika, we can identify a deep systemic crisis that utterly demanded reform. But this is the wisdom of hindsight. And although Western scholars were far from oblivious to the fundamental dilemmas of the system, the general weight of opinion was that Soviet Communism could continue to muddle through for the foreseeable future. Even Boris Yeltsin, by the time of his memoirs an arch enemy of the Communist system, believed that the system had considerable staying power.[37] This is also my own view: Communism had not yet reached its death throes by the mid-1980s, neither because of its own internal weaknesses nor due to external pressures from the Reagan administration. Rather, an energetic leader emerged from the gray party masses who understood that the system could not continue indefinitely and was full of faith that it could be reformed, the sooner the better. By 1991 it was not the Communist system that had failed utterly, but the attempt to reform it.

Reform in Russia: over the centuries it has always failed, sometimes to be replaced by a reactionary regime (Alexander III's reversal of Alexander II's "great reforms" of the 1860s and 1870s), and sometimes culminating in the collapse of the system (1917 and 1991). This historical generalization, tragic in its implications, compels us to analyze the Gorbachev period not simply as the crisis of Communism, but as another episode of the recurrent crises of Russian modernization.

Fundamental to the repeated failure of reform in the modern era have been the dilemmas born of combining the Russian idea and modernization. The political formula of a harmonious people united behind a ruler representing truth and justice has been asserted, in all its sterility, time and again from the tsars to Gorbachev. In reality, however, the very claim to a Government of Truth leading a united people was itself the source of schism between the state and the "enemies of the people," whether Old Believers, capitalists, Jews, or political dissidents. Further, artificially enforced unity—which really meant passivity and silence—exacerbated social divisions, for there was little free and open contact among groups based upon interdependence. Rather, social groups were oriented upward, hoping for government satisfaction of their grievances, without regard to a broader understanding of social compromise.

An additional universal dilemma has been the weakness of elites. Smothered in their self-assertion by the state, they also had no reliable connection to other social groups and thus were in no position to lead them in times of social change. For its part, the intelligentsia was always oriented more toward critique and opposition than to responsible construction, for which task they had no experience in any case. And they, too, were often captive to the mirage of "the people" united behind their ideals, whether Communist or democratic. Victims of their own illusions, they tended to exaggerate their influence in society at large, leading to grave miscalculations.

For these reasons, reform, always initiated by the leader, quickly disappointed everyone. The political elite is astonished to confront the true countenance of the people, not at all consistent with its own image. Society dissolves into a cacaphony of competing voices, all insistently demanding the complete realization of their own goals. Social polarization increases rapidly, thereby splitting the political elite into competing camps of radical reformers, moderates, and conservatives. The state is threatened by these processes of social and political dissolution and either retrenches or falls apart.

Such, in essence, was the fate of efforts at reform in the 1860s, early 1960s, and late 1980s.

To highlight these underlying dilemmas of reform, rather than to identify an acute crisis of the system, is not at all to gainsay the fundamental weaknesses of Soviet Communism under Brezhnev. By the time Gorbachev came to power in 1985, it was not clear that anything vital remained in Soviet Communism, any institutions or forces that could help renew the country. The Communist dream had been twice betrayed, in opposing ways that together sapped much of the life of the system. First, there had been the state-imposed revolution from above, according to the ideological model of the dictatorship of the proletariat. In its wake, this social and political pattern deepened schism and inhibited the emergence of a consensual, rationalizing modern society. But equally, Communist ideals had been betrayed by conservatism, the emergence within the inner reaches of the system of powerful elites, authoritarian micro worlds, and personalistic patterns that effectively protected narrow interests and hindered central planning and direction. The party state had many fewer levers of control than the common appellation "administrative-command system" would suggest. Nor were the different parts of the system connected with each other through abstract rules and actual interdependence. In many respects, the whole was at war with the parts, and the parts with each other. The classic social and political problem—the problem of order—was even further from solution than in other advanced industrial societies. The system was an eerie combination of hypertrophied claims to "order" and a high degree of quasi-anarchic "spontaneity."

Soviet society on the eve of perestroika was not, of course, without its integrating mechanisms, although these all bore the marks of the double betrayal. There was first of all the Communist Party, both feared for its dictatorial role and reviled for its incompetence and corruption. And yet it did in part express the interests of the whole above the parts, providing a degree of centralized political and economic coordination and leadership. The planned economy, whatever its defects, also served to integrate the parts and the whole, to an extent creating horizontal and vertical ties among different sectors of the economy, even if the actual relationships that developed seldom corresponded to the formal plan. The government administration, with its powerful centralized ministries and vast bureaucratic apparatus, in part subordinate to the party but in part acting according to its own interests, also worked to create a certain kind of overall order. Marxism-Leninism itself, no matter how battle-scarred through its incorporation into the party-state modernization program, still provided an official sanction for centralized political leadership in the society. And finally, there was patriotism, reinforced by the awareness that, whatever its flaws, the Soviet Union was one of the two great superpowers. Not accepted by all, of course, especially in the Baltic republics; nonetheless, there was still a reservoir of pride in the achievements of the country.

Could Mikhail Gorbachev, having come to power, reform the Communist system? The question implies a number of corollary issues. What, after all, was the system, what were its principles of operation? We have seen that Soviet Communism was a historically changing pastiche of elements, many of them contradicting each other. The society that had emerged was by no means transparent, with a clear-cut logic that could be easily understood and then somehow transmuted. Further, what was the desired endpoint—still a utopian future, or a more workable model of a stable developed society? And even if the beginning and the end could be so defined, was there a path between them? I doubt that the leaders of any industrialized country have ever faced such a daunting array of questions. The slightest appreciation for the complexities involved increases our sympathy for those who feared to make any changes.

Very few who thought about the nature of the Soviet system appreciated sufficiently that it was in fact a kind of sociological centaur: a vast agglomeration of semi-autonomous micro worlds acting according to their own interests and logics grafted onto a centralized party-state operating a planned economy. Proponents of change tended to focus on the second aspect of the system, arguing that the fundamental problem was, in one form or another, the smothering of society by the state. Two crucial dimensions of the system escaped their grasp. First, that an attack on the role of the party-state would tilt the balance toward local powers and authorities, who were not excessively democratic, efficient, honest, or public-spirited themselves. Second, the weakening of the central party-state institutions would give, not the freedom of autonomous parts, but disorder and polarization. In this regard, Eduard Shevardnadze, one of Gorbachev's main advisers and architects of the reforms, later admitted that the biggest mistake of perestroika had been the weakening of executive power, which paralyzed the political system and made the reformers themselves largely impotent.[38]

In the same interview, Shevardnadze admitted that in the beginning of perestroika he and the other reformers had little idea of exactly what to do and equally little sense of what would happen as a result of their policies. Nonetheless, a number of less highly placed analysts, both Soviet and Western, have ascribed a considerable degree of consistency and sense of purpose to the Gorbachev program. "The basic principles of economic reform have been carefully and realistically formulated. The country contains all the necessary material and intellectual resources for implementing this new economic system and for carrying out a restructuring of industry in conformity with the current needs of scientific and technical progress."[39] Similarly, after a sober and perceptive analysis of the course of perestroika until 1989, Padma Desai, a Columbia University economist, concluded that "the sequencing of the economic reforms is sensible: Gorbachev has a fine strategic sense."[40]

What was this strategy, and why did it fail? We can begin with Gorbachev's highly optimistic first postulate. The socialist system in essence is a superior variant of modern society, one that embodies both social justice and the potential for progress. The theoretical basis for such a society had been laid by the classics of Marxist thought, including Lenin; and, in Soviet society of the 1920s the concrete outlines of such a society had already begun to take shape, if imperfectly. But throughout Soviet history many tragic and unnecessary distortions of socialist doctrine had developed, beginning with Stalin and ending with the corruption and incompetence of the "period of stagnation," the Brezhnev regime. The party, far from being the vanguard of progress, had itself been transformed into a "braking mechanism" that prevented the full development of the potentialities of the socialist system. Thus, socialism must return to its authentic roots, represented by the teachings of Lenin, the experience of the NEP, key ideas of Nikolai Bukharin, and even many aspects of the previously discredited Khrushchev period. Another reversal of history was under way!

In economics, this return of the socialist repressed (to adapt a phrase from Freud) involved the integration of plan and market through greater decentralization of economic decision-making, the introduction of more market mechanisms into the behavior of enterprises, and the legalization of some forms of private economic activity. The deadening hand of the all-powerful party-state was to be kept further away from the economy, although the state sector would still be predominant and centralized planning would continue, albeit in altered forms.

In politics, the Gorbachev reformers renounced the idea that the party leadership already possessed the truth and proclaimed that intra-party discussion and debate was essential if the dynamism of the socialist system were to be restored. Similarly, authentic mass participation was held to be a vital part of vibrant socialism. It was held to have several crucial functions: to impart information to leaders; to motivate the masses economically; to restore popular belief in the system; and also to hold economic and political elites accountable. In the cultural sphere, Gorbachev and his collaborators criticized the party's previous imposition of a lacquered view of society and urged that there be openness and pluralism in cultural life. The intelligentsia, who Gorbachev admitted had been mistreated by Communist regimes in the past, should constructively participate in the debates over the socialist future.

It was Gorbachev's apparent conviction that the debates would indeed revolve around the *socialist* future, for he was convinced that the country had already made its fundamental historical choice, around which there was overwhelming consensus. Together with his criticisms of past abuses, he defended Stalin's industrialization drive, collectivization, and the one-party system. Consistent with these historical views, he did not favor, at least at first, the privatization of land, the denationalization of industry, or the creation of a multiparty system. Yet even without large-scale private property or competition among parties, reform socialism would nonetheless be democratic because (1) there would be a broad network of social organizations expressing the diverse interests of a plural society; (2) party life would itself be highly participatory and full of debate; and (3) the actions of the party and the state would be bound by law.

Not only were all of these changes argued to be compatible with each other, but the transformation of each area of social life was felt to be indispensable for the reform of the others. For example, political democratization was essential for sound planning based upon reliable information, and it would also encourage a more enthusiastic orientation toward work. The restoration of the authority of the party and democratization required greater freedom of cultural expression, just as progress in science and technology underlay economic renewal. Finally, economic progress would provide a foundation for the other changes, particularly by fulfilling the long-delayed material promises of the socialist system. The consequences of this postulate of complementarity and interdependence were of incalculable significance: unlike the Chinese reforms, perestroika would be waged on all fronts at once. And if it was true that success in one area conditioned success in the others, the reverse was also the case: failure in any sphere could have deleterious consequences for all other aspects of the reforms.

The reformers had two arguments for why their version of reform Communism could work, one metaphysical, one historical. The idea of consensus around a "socialist choice" was the metaphysical a priori, not subject, in the reformers' minds, to refutation. The historical argument was more empirical but questionable in its own right. Gorbachev and his allies argued that their version of socialism had always been recessively present in Soviet society, even if always defeated by its enemies. They could point to ideas, experiments, and practices under Lenin, Stalin, Khrushchev, and even Brezhnev to buttress their argument from history: for example, the New Economic Policy, frequent populist campaigns against the elites, and the more market-oriented 1965 economic reforms. These programs, and many more, did indeed foreshadow important aspects of Gorbachev's program, and for obvious reasons. All Soviet leaders from Lenin onward had confronted the problem of how to deal with the emergence of conservative bureaucratic elites within the very logic of the system. They had also wrestled with the question of how to motivate people in the relative absence of market mechanisms.

And yet, as Gorbachev himself claimed, these ideas in many ways marked a revolutionary break with the past, both Russian and Soviet. Never before had a Russian (and certainly not Soviet!) ruler come so close to renouncing claims to rule on the basis of truth. The denial of special sanction was not complete. Marxism-Leninism was still proclaimed to be the correct doctrine of society, and the party, once transformed, was still heralded as the guiding force of Soviet society. But the ruler's and his party's claim to superior knowledge was constantly qualified by pragmatic arguments. Truth is not fully known, so no ideology can be complete. "Creative Marxism-Leninism is always a discovery, and not a screen," wrote Alexander Yakovlev. Gorbachev himself appealed to the inductive nature of Marxist thought: "Karl Marx, as is known, said in response to his daughter's question that his favorite motto was 'question everything.' We consider ourselves Marxists."[41] Science must therefore be independent of party tutelage, so that the party can learn from it and absorb its findings. The social sciences were seen to have a vital part in society's discovery of itself—a tremendous contrast with Lenin's and Stalin's hostility to the bourgeois sciences of sociology and economics. Official peace was made with religion, and many rights of churches were restored, for religion had its part to play in a highly diverse socialist society. Just as scandalous for Communist orthodoxy, it was now recognized that socialism had much to learn from the West—markets, for example, were a major achievement of world civilization.

Mention of the new official orientation toward the West brings us to the second revolutionary aspect of Gorbachev's new creed: it was an unprecedented amalgam of Communism, the Russian idea, and Western economic and political concepts. "Now it is necessary to include in our arsenal of ideas the whole wealth of our own and world socialist and democratic thought," proclaimed Gorbachev in July 1991, in an effort to explain the party's attempts to come up with a self-definition in the new sociopolitical context.[42] Certainly not since Peter the Great had a Russian ruling elite expressed such admiration for Western civilization, whose laws had typically been seen as cold-hearted and formalistic; whose economic relations were traditionally regarded as conflictual and exploitative; and whose claims to pluralist democracy were interpreted as superficial attempts to disguise deeper antagonisms. In the Gorbachev version, the socialist choice, which still largely excluded private property, was seen to be consistent with a larger scope for markets, legal definitions of social and political relations, and political democratization (of the variety discussed previously). Yet people would still have shared goals and so be motivated by belief, and not interest. The absence of private property would still undergird a community based on relations deeper than law. And political life would still be founded on a consensus of values about the nature of the good society, even as it was opened up to alternative voices.

But given the hybrid character of the leadership's pronouncements, was anything really left of the socialist choice? Commenting on the proposed new party program, Gorbachev remarked: "No doubt the comrades have noticed that communism is only mentioned in the Program. It must be admitted that our experience, and others' as well, gives us no reason to believe that this goal is realistically attainable in the foreseeable future. But the communist idea—that the free development of each person is a condition for the free development of all—has been and continues to be an attractive guideline for mankind."[43] By late July 1991, that was all that Gorbachev could say about the bright and shining future!

To Gorbachev and his team, this bringing together of different elements, this ability to learn from other societies and historical periods, indicated the strength and self-confidence of the socialist choice in a mature socialist society. But herein also lay its weakness, for once again the regime combined contradictory elements. Under Stalin, the ruler explicitly recognized the dialectics of contradiction and mercilessly imposed them upon the population, making use of his claim to truth and his quasi-magical style of rulership. But Gorbachev's government had neither the desire nor the capacity to impose its contradictory vision as a truth to be accepted. As with Nicholas II, the regime itself fell victim to the contradictory program of change that it sponsored.

Appearing on television in late 1990, Gorbachev remarked that "over these past six years I feel I've lived several decades, several lives."[44] The same could be said for his country, where once again the pace of historical change compressed events that in normal times, in stable countries, would have sufficed for a century. But is it really appropriate to use the word "change," which implies not just flux and instability, but some new state? On the surface, of course, an enormous amount had been accomplished in a few years: there was a new law on state enterprises that granted them considerable autonomy from the planners; many forms of private cooperatives had been legalized; an elected congress had taken over many of the powers formerly monopolized by the party; a new post of president had been created; the republics had won considerable autonomy within the context of the union. The list could be multiplied. Yet by 1990 complaints that Gorbachev and perestroika had accomplished nothing positive were legion.

The "right"—a strange term indeed for more orthodox Communists—attacked Gorbachev for the destruction of the old system in favor of foreign ideas that imported exploitation and threatened the breakup of the Soviet Union. The "left"—the self-styled democratic forces—assailed Gorbachev's continuous flirtations with conservative elements of the party and his unwillingness to break with traditional Communist hostility to private property and a multiparty system. But beyond these different substantive evaluations, both oppositions agreed on one central point: Gorbachev had not been able to solve the cardinal problem of his reform program, the problem of power. In the last year of his leadership Gorbachev himself stated the problem with utter clarity: "The problem is that our power has been torn to shreds. The chain of command is broken. The electrical current is switched off and the economy is grinding to a halt. . . . We're already in a state of chaos."[45]

The indicators of this vacuum of power were everywhere by 1990. Not only did Boris Yeltsin give Gorbachev headaches with his frontal attacks on the party and his calls for further democratization and deeper economic reform, but Gorbachev's own head of government in the spring of 1991, V. Pavlov, asked for extraordinary powers from the Supreme Soviet, powers that would have infringed on Gorbachev's own legal prerogatives, without even consulting him. "The situation that has developed in our country is simply unprecedented," wrote the Pravda correspondent about the incident.[46] Of equal significance was the lack of clear demarcation between old centers of power, such as the party or the Cabinet of Minsters, and new institutions, like the Supreme Soviet and the president elected by it (Gorbachev, who was both head of party and head of state). The party was deeply divided, split into irreconcilable factions that threatened to form separate parties but could not quite bring themselves to do so. The writ of the Communist Party apparatus throughout the vast country was now so weak that local political administration was in chaos. All sorts of new political clubs and movements had arisen to challenge authority throughout the system, but they had not managed to create political parties or even coherent mass movements that might have provided a real alternative, or even solid support for the regime. The exception was in the republics, especially in the Baltic region, but also in Central Asia and the Caucasus, where nationalist party-movements declared their sovereignty or independence throughout 1990. (It was symptomatic that even in the Russian republic the parliament declared that its laws took precedence over Soviet law.)

Because of this political decay, which meant that the regime had the power to destroy but not create, not the dreams of perestroika but its nightmares were being realized. All of the promises made by the reformers to the public were turning into their opposite: instead of consensus around a new vision of socialism, unresolvable conflict; instead of a revitalization of the economy, declining growth, growing deficits, and increased corruption; instead of moral renewal, a sense of apathy, powerlessness, and hopelessness among the masses.[47]

Although many journalists and scholars have blamed Gorbachev's tactical and strategic errors for the political paralysis and decay that doomed his efforts to reform the Communist system, the root causes of the collapse are much deeper and bear striking resemblances to the sources of breakdown of the tsarist regime. Just as Nicholas II could not combine autocracy and a quasi-Western style of modernization, so Gorbachev's espousal of both the "socialist choice" and modernization based on markets, some degree of privatization, and political pluralism was fundamentally incoherent. This incoherence explains two important facts: Gorbachev's superficially puzzling choice of teams of advisers with completely opposed viewpoints (this was also true of Nicholas II) and his constant hesitancy to make decisions, from which he frequently backtracked after the decision had apparently been made. As a result, it was never clear how far Gorbachev was willing to go to support economic reforms. For a time he seemed to support the ill-fated Shatalin plan, which proposed a dramatic sell-off of state industry and other decisive measures, but he backed off at the last minute, exasperating his advisers. Nor was his perspective on the admissibility of a multiparty system ever clear, although by the summer of 1991 he seemed to have accepted its inevitability. On a broader scale, at times he seemed to side with those who wanted to move further in the direction of Westernization, but as late as the early part of 1991 he seemed to have cast his lot with the party conservatives.

These uncertainties were not simply peculiarities of Gorbachev but pervaded the political system in the absence of some kind of firm direction. Consequently, political institutions and political life at all levels became a constant battleground of competing goals and perspectives, with no means of arbitration or compromise. "Our society is unable to move forward because the existing social and political forces drag it in different directions. Not an addition but a subtraction of forces is taking place. All uncompromisingly fight with everyone else, no one can agree with anyone else about anything. The thoroughly worn out and historically compromised old structures of authority have lost their customary ways of operating, but no new structures have yet emerged. The result is not dual power, but the absence of power."[48] Nothing needs to be added to this description of the decomposition of political authority written in early 1990. As a result of this incoherence, the regime, just like its tsarist predecessor, was completely unable to deal with the vital issues confronting it, whether economic renewal, the challenge of separatism, or the democratization of political life.

The regime's political incoherence was in part cause, in part consequence, of the more general polarization within society, which deepened with the government's inability to act decisively in any fixed direction. Although as late as the end of 1990 Gorbachev continued to affirm that "socialism is ingrained in the people, ingrained in all of us,"[49] either this was an idle wish or the socialist choice lay so deep in people's unconscious that it was of no political use. For it was obvious that the majority of people in the Baltic republics regarded socialism not as an innate part of their values, but an alien system imposed by political occupation.

Within Russia itself, powerful social movements and even large sectors of the party wanted to join world civilization on the basis of capitalism and multiparty democracy. They frequently made no distinction between Marx, Lenin, Stalin, and even Gorbachev: all of them were tainted by the evil teachings of socialism. For in fact, as in previous periods,

Soviet society was still based on the schisms produced by forceful state modernization centered on a claim to truth, and opponents still viewed each other in black and white terms. For the democrats, loyal Communists were complicitous in the historical crimes of the regime and thus morally repellant. For those who adhered to a more conservative version of Communist values than did Gorbachev, both the democratic opposition and Gorbachev himself were traitors to the country who acted in league with world imperialism. In such an atmosphere, fears of civil war were ubiquitous, clearly showing that the regime had accomplished little to create some kind of overall consensus since the time of the Civil War.

The regime's indecisiveness had also reinforced another classic split of Russian history: that between the people and the state. The regime was seen to be acting in its own interests, with little regard for the welfare of the people. Endless talk had only worsened living conditions, and no end to the deterioration was in sight. The constant conflicts and the evident contradictions of government policy only increased the popular sense of the incompetence and venality of the officials. The regime's use of force in Lithuania and Georgia, and some unexplained military maneuvers in Russia itself, raised questions about its ultimate intent, especially since it was by no means clear which factions and organizations had power at any given time. The actions of the regime seemed inexplicable and unpredictable, and, as of old, beyond the control of the people. A measure of the alienation between state and society was the fact, painful for Gorbachev, that the most popular and admired leaders in the country were Sakharov and Yeltsin. For the Russian people, honesty and purity could still only be found away from the center of power.

Gorbachev's stake on the socialist consensus, which would unite the whole working people around his program, concealed a painful truth: in fact, his reforms had no fixed social base. (We recall that Stolypin had placed his hopes on a *future* class, a yeoman peasantry that did not yet exist. The tsarist government also acted largely in a social vacuum.) The masses who were called upon to participate actively in the creation of a shared socialist future displayed little such initiative. Rather, the important mass movements, whether in the form of labor protest in the coal mines of Siberia, nationalist movements for independence, or intelligentsia movements for the deepening of reform, almost uniformly acted in opposition to the regime, or at least to its concrete policies. Just as decisively, no strong social elite existed as a bulwark of social support (Nicholas II had faced the same dilemma).

The party and government apparatus was deeply split ideologically, and in terms of its practical activities officials were increasingly going in two separate directions. On the one hand, some officials whose only resource was their state or party position struggled against privatization and political reform. They formed the social base for the conservative party movements that became increasingly strident in their opposition to Gorbachev in the last period of his rule. On the other hand, other officials took advantage of the regime's powerlessness to act in their own interests, making use of formally state property for their own profit and participating in the burgeoning private economy, some of it criminalized. A new class of de facto private owners was emerging within the state sector, whatever the preference of Gorbachev and his strategists. The lawlessness and chaos of the late Gorbachev period suited such people more than a coherent program of economic reform, one that might have subjected them to fixed rules and curbed their appetite for the spoils of the socialist economy.

In other times, such an elite that threatened to become an organized class would have proved extremely useful to a regime bent on change from above. They combined the same enticing mixture of elite status and vulnerability that gave so much mileage for scapegoating during the Stalin period, and during Gorbachev's regime the same potential clearly existed. Indeed, they provided a ready target for both conservatives and radicals. In the "Word to the People" of late July 1991, a group of Russian nationalist and Communist leaders called them "greedy and rich moneygrubbers . . . [who] have seized power and are pilfering our wealth, taking homes, factories and land away from the people, carving the country up into the separate parts."[50] For the democratic reformers they were equally odious: a corrupt group of partocrats who were engaged in what would later be called "nomenklatura privatization." Everyone knew, too, that the activities of the new elites were intimately bound up with the blossoming criminal groups in the country. Connected to the old apparatus, but also the harbinger of a new social structure, they were the other side of Gorbachev's contradictory attempt to combine Communism and aspects of Western-style modernization.

They can also be regarded from another angle. Their role made clear the dilemmas that were bound to arise within the socialist system when the primary enemy was seen to be the "administrative command system," an allegedly tightly centralized entity that killed all initiative. But this ideological stereotype, especially beloved by the democrats, was wrong, and the weakening of party control did not lead to a flowering of creativity and initiative. Instead, another potential of Russian life, always latent within the interstices of the eternally inefficient dictatorships, whatever their form, returned to haunt the perestroika period: the flourishing of self-enclosed micro worlds, hierarchically ordered and based on personal ties rather than abstract relationships. These micro worlds were always highly nondemocratic and tended to withhold and monopolize resources under their disposal for their own purposes. Esoteric and relatively impenetrable to outside understanding and control, they testified to the weakness of general integrating ties, such as laws or markets, those aspects of abstract "society" that were always rejected by the Russian idea in favor of a more familial model of community.

The regime was well aware of the tendency of the new elites to take control of the resources allegedly in the public trust and make use of them through these dense networks of interpersonal connections. It was also clear that subordinates were co-opted into an implicit localized social contract, for they were often bought off, perhaps through the distribution of bartered items or special access to products. (Imported Japanese electronics, which could be resold for enormous profits, were particularly welcome to workers.) But as in everything else, the government was impotent to counteract this inevitable consequence of its own decomposition. It tried to mobilize the working class, passing a law authorizing "workers' control over the movement of consumer goods all the way from producer to consumer, in order to stop the concealment of goods, spoilage, theft and speculation."[51] But there is absolutely no reason to think that such populist measures, which reeked of past experiments of the dictatorship of the proletariat, had any effect whatsoever, especially since workers themselves were deeply involved.

It is with ulterior intent that I end this section with remarks on the emerging economic elite. We have seen that Gorbachev's contradictory strategy, with its back-and-forth movements and its increasingly incoherent mix of people and principles, inevitably weakened the party-state and so made real reform, especially of the economy, impossible. Either the "left" or the "right" had to break the stalemate that had paralyzed the society. When the right made its move, with its incompetent attempt to impose a military coup on the country, the way seemed open for the "democrats" to enact a consistent set of policies. Ironically, however, they were forced to rely upon this hybrid new economic elite, which was as much a part of the past as it was of the future. For this reason, the policies of the new regime were beset by troubling dilemmas from the beginning. Could a "normal society" be created through the activity of a semilegal or even criminal economic elite, closed in nature, that operated on the basis of monopolistic principles? If not, what other preconditions were present to promote the emergence of Western-style capitalist democracy?

CONCLUDING REMARKS

Toward the end of his rule, Gorbachev made the startling public declaration that his two grandfathers had suffered from Stalinist repression. "One was convicted for not having fulfilled the sowing plan in 1933, when half the family died of starvation. He was sent to Irkutsk to cut timber." His other grandfather was imprisoned and interrogated for fourteen months as a suspected enemy of the people. "He survived, thank goodness. But he lived in that 'plague house,' in the house of an 'enemy of the people.' "[52] Yet later in the same speech Gorbachev makes another kind of confession: he was a convinced and profoundly committed socialist. "And I don't merely believe in it. It is my knowledge, it is my thinking."

Whatever its defects, the socialist system clearly had the capacity to compel belief, even when that belief had to be sustained in apparent contradiction to the actual conditions of life and the oppressive actions of self-proclaimed socialist governments that constantly changed their policies. By an inverse logic, this claim on the heart was also often turned against socialist values and the socialist system—commitment to an alternative set of beliefs was held with fervor. In a sense, too, such counterbelief was a product of the system. By contrast, in Western societies beliefs about the meaning of life tend to be focused not on society and politics, but on religion and personal life.

In this analysis of Soviet Communism, I have examined the key source of this belief: the accommodation of socialist values to the Russian idea. Accommodation, and not synthesis: for we have seen at numerous points how the different elements of these very broad sets of ideas were in great tension with each other. Similarly, as has been discussed throughout, the imperatives of state-led modernization further undermined this already contradictory complex of ideas and practices.

A society whose integration depends on shared beliefs has a logic at variance with a society based on abstract mechanisms of interdependence. Inconsistencies among values or contradictions between the official belief and sociopolitical practice is of much greater consequence for social stability. Political leaders in the Soviet Union could therefore not avoid confronting the dilemmas that their own espousal of ideological truth created. Nonetheless, in their separate ways, the Stalin and Brezhnev regimes backed away from an attempt to make practice and doctrine more consistent with each other. Stalin appealed to the mysteries of dialectics and made use of repression and his own aura of leadership in order to cut short any direct confrontation between the real traits of the dictatorship of the proletariat and the promises of Marxist doctrine. The Brezhnev regime was more passive: it enforced an orthodoxy that almost no one believed in, and it responded to tensions between its teachings and social reality by stifling debate and co-opting broad sectors of the society. Hypocrisy and corruption created less suspicion than did real ideological belief, which was much more dangerous in its implications.

The Khrushchev and Gorbachev periods bore significant resemblances to each other, key among them the leadership's commitment to restore belief to the society. In both cases, leaders convinced of the superiority of the socialist system attempted to stimulate mass participation, to revitalize the party, and on these bases to create a stable socialist society with a dynamic economy. They were convinced that Soviet society was fundamentally harmonious, that antagonistic social relations had been eliminated, and that there was broad consensus on the virtues of the system.

In both cases their optimistic assessments proved wrong. The attempt to democratize the party weakened rather than strengthened it and thereby gave rise to centrifugal tendencies that ran counter to the overall desires for scientific planning and coordination. Communist modernization had not led to a consensus of belief but had reinforced schism, both within the party and between the party and important groups in society. The promise of reform polarized political life into those who opposed reform and those who were dissatisfied with its limited nature. The leaders, Khrushchev and Gorbachev, were left in the middle, with little party or societal support. Under Khrushchev the party-state's levers of power remained sufficiently intact in order to neutralize the threat of further disintegration of its position, whereas under Gorbachev the leader and the party fell victim to the contradictions that they had been unable to resolve.

These two periods of attempted reform, so different in their logics and outcomes, seem to have exhausted the alternatives. The belief in a separate Soviet path to modern society based on a cultural tradition antagonistic to modernization and an ideological doctrine that embraced a mythical and utopian version of modern society suffered a crisis. Correlatively, in losing faith in the regime that propounded this contradictory ideological blend, many people lost faith in the beliefs themselves: in the possibility of a deeper form of community; in the value of equality; in a political system based on shared values; in a vision of a more just and more prosperous future that would compensate for present deprivations.

As the example of Gorbachev himself shows, such a moral vision had always been a key source of dynamism in Soviet society, in this respect the inheritor of the Russian past. Will the new society find a substitute?

CHAPTER FIVE

The Failure of Yeltsin's Reforms

THE LATEST Russian experiment, the attempt to rejoin the "civilized world," marks another dramatic break with the immediate past. At the same time, it has striking parallels with other such Westernizing reforms in Russian history, from Peter the Great in the early eighteenth century to Alexander II in the 1860s. Just as Peter looked to Germany and Sweden to unlock the secret of combining social dynamism with political order, and Alexander II and his fellow reformers looked to France, England, or America to understand how to combine freedom, order, and efficiency, so the new Russian reformers have recognized the superiority of Western institutions and rationality.

Although it is too early to judge the larger historical significance of these changes, enough time has passed to draw some very pessimistic lessons. There was room for creative political initiative in the early years of the Yeltsin regime, a flexibility that now, with the sedimentation of an ugly new form of society, has largely been lost. Despite some achievements, which certainly include the avoidance of outright social and economic collapse, the Yeltsin regime has not been able to meet its historical responsibilities. It has misunderstood its task in the larger context of Russian history, and for this, at least, it will be judged harshly. At a time when the fundamental challenge was to restore a sense of hope, the government has done its part to increase despair. Hope depended upon a revival of the Russian people's sense that they have a future, which in turn is closely linked to a sense of connection to the past. For rejection of the past creates schism, reinforcing the gaps between state and society and among social groups. Early in the last century Pyotr Chaadaev argued that the lack of a sense of historical tradition and continuity, which gives meaning and purpose to action, was a root cause of Russia's historical tragedies. His diagnosis applies with equal force to the present.

The current threat to a sense of both the past and the future has created a crisis of national identity, described in the following way by a commentator in *Moscow News*. The author laments that the old spirituality, whose bearer was the Russian intelligentsia, is now in crisis. One of the fundamental traits of "spirituality" (*dukhovnost'*), he asserts, is an orientation toward the future. For the spirit the present world is not good enough. *Bytie*—being in its deep and authentic sense—always implies this reference to a purer future state. *Byt*—everyday life—this is only the inescapable present that real spirituality must transcend. Our tragedy now, he claims, is that the future has disappeared, and only life in the sense of an endless present remains for us.[1]

But the Russian government led by Yeltsin has been unable to see its role in this larger context. In its crucial early period it was completely absorbed in preaching to the public about inflation and the necessity for unemployment, as well as preoccupied by the apocalyptic battle with an anathematized opposition. At times Yeltsin was reminiscent of Avvakum, unleashing curses at the bearers of evil who were his opponents. (Clear proof, if any is needed, that total rupture with the past is impossible.)

Meanwhile, a strange alchemy has taken place. For two centuries the Russian tradition, from Slavophiles to pan-Slavists and from Eurasianists to Communists, has elaborated a nightmare vision of the West as the kingdom of Moloch. Capitalism, it was argued, was without moral foundation. Proponents of a superior Russian path did not understand that law and morality could stand behind contract and exchange. The pursuit of interest was seen to be selfish and pointless. They did not accept that there could be a hidden hand in society that might work to the general welfare. Nor was there any awareness that this-worldly activity, the world of *byt*, might also be laden with value. Similarly, adherents of the Russian idea attacked the heterogeneity and conflict of complex Western societies, failing to realize that they might be held together by such social adhesives as interdependence, abstract trust, law, and mutual tolerance. Finally, the state in Western societies was seen to be cut off from the people, responsive only to the will of the dominant elites. They did not understand that the provision of political rights to all social groups gave some degree of counterweight to the power of elites, for they undervalued political rights in favor of political truth.

Ironically, the best way to conceptualize the new Russia that has emerged in the past few years is precisely as this nightmare vision of the West. For reasons to be discussed at length, contemporary Russian economics, politics, and cultural life very much resemble a West manqué, in which institutions and practices have been stripped of their foundations in law and morality.

The clearest illustration of my point comes from the harsh new world of Russian capitalism, about which few illusions remain in the outside world. In Russia itself there never were such illusions, partly because of the traditional cultural hostility to elites and private interest. According to public perceptions in Russia, the new capitalist class feels no responsibility to the rest of society; it is parasitic, because it produces little; it has clawed its way to the top not through hard work, but through dishonesty or connections; and it is closely tied to organized criminality.[2]

Unfortunately, these public perceptions of the nascent capitalist system ring all too true. Instead of abstract relations based upon recognized rules and economic interdependence, the ideal of liberal society, Russian society has continued to be characterized by highly personalized, clanlike relations that monopolize resources and information. We recall that such closed relationships emerged in the Communist system as a means of self-defense against the relentless demands of the political leadership, and that they flourished whenever the Communist regime attempted to create an environment of social and political normalcy. With the attacks on the Communist Party during perestroika, but especially after the end of the former regime, the new fused economic- political elite that was emerging was not subject to controls from the state. In becoming private owners, they used their privileged access to information, their dense networks of ties, and their knowledge of how the system worked to consolidate a dominant position in the new capitalist economy. The new elite, with roots in the old Communist nomenklatura as well as in the private sector that began to prosper under Gorbachev, was immune to control from above and below. For just as the collapse of Communism weakened political and administrative controls from above, so it left the common people powerless. In part their impotence stemmed from their lack of knowledge about how to act in the new situation, but it was also connected to the absence of any authorities to whom they could appeal for redress.

The position of the new capitalist elite thus combines many of the worst features of the old and new systems. From the tradition of the Communist nomenklatura dictatorship, the new elite displays a sense of narrow self-interest and seeks to monopolize information and resources for itself.[3] When challenged about their lack of a sense of social responsibility, they have a ready response. We are now in the stage of the primitive accumulation of capital, they say. Concern about social justice, worker safety, environmental pollution, law, and other niceties of advanced capitalism must wait until the future. For now it is the survival of the fittest, and these fittest will create a great and prosperous capitalist country that will rival the United States. Along these lines, I well remember the speech of Mark Masarsky, one of Moscow's leading businessmen, which I heard at a conference for intellectuals, government officials, and businessmen that I attended in Moscow in late 1991. Our task now, he claimed, is to create a strong middle class through the development of entrepreneurship. We will be effective because we will not be worried about social justice. A market isn't a means of justice. We will only worry about results. I cannot help recalling Lev Kopelev's judgment about the early 1930s: we had now entered the "slaveholding period of primary socialist accumulation." During this period, "barbarian means of overcoming barbarism were unavoidable."[4]

Further, like the former party nomenklatura, this new capitalist elite has no regard for formal rules and laws in the exercise of personal authority. Typical is this comment about the boss of Northern Steel: "he does whatever he wants, he's the boss here, and there is no opposition to him, no force to counterbalance him. But stability in society comes when a balance of interests is maintained."[5] In the factories that I visited, in talking to the workers I always came away with the same impression: they felt that they had no power or rights whatsoever. Very often they did not even know if they had a trade union, but in their view trade unions would make little difference, because they too were manipulated by the bosses.

Finally, like its Communist predecessors, the new elite seeks to monopolize both economic and political power, thereby cutting off any potential challenges to its dominant position. Laws restricting the economic activities of political bosses are almost nonexistent. The Russian press has been replete with articles about how political leaders have turned themselves into wealthy capitalists and property owners with impunity. Here is a typical example of press reports of this type, this one from Lipetsk:

> So let us state the facts, and no more. Viktor Donskikh, former first secretary of the province Party committee, is the general director of a joint-stock company. Yevgeny Vasilchikov, former first secretary of the city Party committee, is vice-chairman of the board of a joint-stock bank. Anatoly Negrobov, former chief of the administrative office of the province Party committee, is co-owner of a private firm. Nikolai Naumov, former First Secretary of the Zadonsk District Party Committee, is the general director of a commodities and raw materials exchange.[6]

Given such a network of interconnections, it is understandable that workers will be hesitant to complain about abuses. Discontented workers are aware that their struggle against the bosses will almost certainly be in vain. As a group of workers who discovered some illegal activities of their boss were warned: Watch out! He's got connections everywhere.[7]

If it is not already clear enough what kind of entrepreneurship is involved here, let me give an example from my own experience. In Moscow I met a surgeon whose father-in-law was head of a collective farm that produced dairy products in an infamous region of Siberia. This was in 1992, and dairy products in Moscow were in short supply and expensive. The father-in-law's monopolistic control over his farm's production became the basis for the doctor's business initiative. The dairy products were never sold on the market but were "allocated" (as under the command economy) to the son-in-law, who received very high prices in the capital. This case had an unusual twist, however. To protect himself from the local mafia, which is ubiquitous in such affairs, the doctor treated their knife and gunshot wounds gratis. None of this was based on competition, markets, or laws. *Vse skhvacheno*, as Russians say. Everything's been taken care of (literally, has been grabbed).

The predominance of such clanlike monopolistic micro worlds underlies the current development of Russian capitalism. Such personalized networks have been impermeable to the penetration of abstract processes such as competition, generalized trust, or law. Typical are the comments of two government officials in charge of enforcing paper laws against monopoly. The new entrepreneurs neither know nor respect the law, and the officials admit that the law against monopolistic practices has had little effect.[8] It should come as little surprise, then, that to many Russians this new form of power is as burdensome as the Communist system.

A radical labor newspaper explains the problem in the following way. Under Communism property was controlled by the bureaucracy, but on the basis of a social contract that gave people meager but real guarantees of employment, stability of living standards, free education and medical care, and the like. Now the government, composed largely of the same nomenklatura, divests itself of the property, but the people receive no security or guarantees. There is no longer any reciprocity.[9] As I discovered through interviews with workers at factories, the situation is especially painful for older workers, who labored for a pittance for so many years in the expectation that they would receive a modicum of benefits and security after retirement. There is a very widespread sense among workers that no one defends or protects them now. The old hierarchical system, which did have the semblance of a social contract, is now dead. The logic of a balance of forces based upon worker organization and a sense of rights has not yet arisen to take its place. How long will the sense of injustice that this violation of the old social contract engenders be accepted as part of the necessary pain of a transitional period?

The clanlike and monopolistic character of the new capitalist elite is linked to a whole series of other malfunctions of the new capitalism, all of them flowing from the ability of these closed micro worlds to pursue their own interests almost without regard to the interests of others, countervailing power, or law. Perhaps of greatest significance is the interconnection of this new elite with the now infamous Russian mafia. Indeed, the emergence of criminal organizations that use the threat of force illegally to create and maintain a monopoly of resources is but an extreme version of the overall logic of the new Russian capitalism. It is well known that to do business in Russia requires paying "taxes" to criminal organizations. I was even told that the beggars on the street are required to pay criminal groups for the right to occupy their spaces.

But this system of extortion is not the most disturbing element of the new organized criminality in Russia. Reliable reports have described how criminal groups are acquiring privatized property for extremely low prices through intimidating potential rival bidders. According to information in *Izvestiia*, some 70 percent of the privatizations through auctions in St. Petersburg followed something like the following scenario:

> Before a public auction begins, the information is conveyed to everyone that an "authority" is interested in this piece of property, and that if anyone takes the risk of competing for it, he shouldn't complain later that he wasn't warned. Then a representative of the "authority" appears in the hall, escorted by 10 to 20 thugs. They behave in a demonstratively aggressive manner, making it clear who is the boss here.

As the same article makes clear, corrupt local officials are also involved in such maneuvers. Recently the deputy general director of the St. Petersburg Property Fund (the local government body in charge of organizing privatization) was arrested for corruption, and authorities have noted that "corrupt bureaucrats are themselves extending their hands to criminal 'authorities.'"[10]

Thus has the traditional Russian disregard for abstract relations culminated in the predominance of closed, clanlike groups based on personal ties, often of a criminalized nature; the mistrust of markets has led to the emergence of a capitalist system based on suspicion and the monopolization of resources, including information; the promise of a higher form of community than that of abstract civilization has culminated in the attenuation of broad ties of interdependence at all levels; and the belief that justice transcends law has generated unpredictable and lawless behavior. None of the practices and institutions of civil society were strong enough to restrain the rapid transformation of the promises of the Russian idea into their opposite.

For the majority, then, capitalism has not brought freedom, but the rule of the strong. It is therefore not buttressed by any moral foundation that might replace the Russian idea. The following account from a newspaper epitomizes what capitalism means to many Russians. The author describes the privatization of a Leningrad firm that occurred before the passage of the law on privatization. The new owners (undoubtedly the old managers) did not feel obligated to obey the law and decided to rid themselves of their financial obligations to the firm's pensioners. "And so what? Whoever was bold enough could simply grab what he wanted. And in general, capitalism and competition mean that everyone is for himself."[11]

This predatory understanding of the nature of capitalism finds everyday support in Russia in a whole series of calamities that afflict the population. There has been a dramatic growth in the rate of industrial accidents, especially among private firms, who do not regard the protection of their workers as cost-effective. Contaminated food is flooding the marketplace. Suppliers of produce, wrote one commentator, have understood privatization in their own peculiar way: elimination of any control over the quality of products. Maybe, concludes the author wryly, people should not get too upset about the high prices of vegetables after all![12] Rarely is any concern shown for ecological issues. Contracts mean little, unless they are backed up by the threat of force. Immense inequalities have emerged, more often based on connections, fraud, or violence than on merit. There is a widespread sense that honest work will get you nowhere, and surveys have shown that prostitution and organized crime have little stigma attached to them among the young. In this brave new world, no one is surprised when newspapers print alarmist articles that human organs will soon be put up for sale for hard currency.[13]

Many apologists for the nascent Russian capitalism argue that such phenomena inevitably accompany the transition from totalitarianism to civilization. Nothing from the old society was of any conceivable use in the construction of the new, and a moral and political vacuum during the period of the primitive accumulation of capital is the heavy price that the present must pay to the future in penance for the past. Ironically, however, such a rejection of the past based on a binary vision of the world is itself a part of the Russian tradition. In attempting to reject the past, the Yeltsin reformers unwittingly reinforced some of its worst elements, at the same time stripping away some of the political controls on exploitation and corruption that did exist in the previous system.

The Legacy of the Past

I believe that the Yeltsin government in the earliest period did have a degree of leverage over the future course of events. Of course, it would be foolish to argue, as Peter the Great or Chaadaev or the Bolsheviks believed, that the very weakness and decay of the old society made it possible to embark on a program of utter transformation. Russian history has amply demonstrated the tragic consequence of such views. Nor do I wish to suggest that the state should have reasserted its traditional role as the catalyst of change, dragging behind it a hesitant and uncomprehending society. Nonetheless, I do maintain that a more honest and perceptive analysis of the fundamental problems of the transition might have led to policies with less painful consequences. Even if, following the "inevitable" logic of the West, Russia does eventually reach some approximation of capitalist democracy, it will remain true that the route to this endpoint was unnecessarily harsh.

What could have been concluded from a careful analysis of the Russian past? What kind of future made sense on the basis of the concrete conditions of Russia after the collapse of Communism? Although the impediments to social change were of great weight, as will be argued shortly, there were also reasonable grounds for optimism. Contemporary Westernizers could point to a broad range of favorable circumstances and underlying conditions. Perhaps reform could truly be successful for the first time in Russian history.

First, the country was at peace and faced no immediate threat from more powerful foreign enemies. Therefore, the pace of change did not have to be artificially accelerated, at least on this basis. (The Gaidar government did, however, raise the specter of complete social and economic collapse in the final months of 1991, thus arguing in favor of immediate "shock therapy.")

Of equally great significance, many of the old illusions of the past are largely dead. The Russian people could not be tempted by a new utopian vision of complete transformation based upon an apocalyptic idea. The interweaving of the Russian idea and Communist modernization had, as we have seen, largely stripped away such illusions. The following assessment will have a real ring of truth to anyone who has spent much time in contemporary Russia. "Today there is no more bourgeois people on earth," wrote Leonid Radzikovski in the magazine *Ogonyok*. "After seventy-four years of collectivization, egalitarianism, great power patriotism and much else there emerged the figure of the hungry petit bourgeois as the main historical type." He also asserted, with more questionable accuracy, that the broad masses want a peaceful transition to a Western-type society and that they are ready to make temporary sacrifices for this goal.[14] With respect to this last point, it is probably more accurate to say that, although there are polar extremes of committed democrats and staunch Communists, the painful transition period has created an overall mood of skepticism and uncertainty about all political ideologies, institutions, and leaders.[15]

Optimists could also ground their hopes in the broad changes that had transformed the human landscape of Russia. Russia was no longer a patriarchal culture based on agriculture, and both its social structure and its political culture bore little resemblance to the kind of society that facilitated Stalinism. There had emerged a large social group roughly equivalent to a middle class in Western societies, an educated group with knowledge about the rest of the world. Many of these people had participated as experts in many arenas of social and political life and so could not be seduced by the alluring simplicities of some new political vision.

Further, even though there had not been a full-fledged market system, in fact the elite of socialist managers in the Brezhnev period were part of a large-scale bargaining system that required initiative. In this system of decentralized bargaining over resources, ties of trust and even a kind of customary law had developed that might provide a social infrastructure for a market economy. In reality, it could have been argued, the Communist system had not been nearly as top-heavy as many had claimed, and it had allowed many shoots of the new society to emerge without official recognition. In the late Gorbachev period, ministers Nikolai Ryzhkov and Valentin Pavlov had permitted the de facto privatization of much of the economy. Could it not have been argued that an incipient capitalist class structure already existed? And if some kind of market system, even if distorted, already existed, the tasks of the government would look very different: not to create capitalism out of nothing, but to encourage and develop social and economic practices that already existed. With the expected help of foreign governments and capital, was there not a real hope for success?

Such a hopeful diagnosis of the prospects for social change in Russia rested upon perceptions of phenomena that could be looked at from a much more negative point of view. The "bourgeois" essence of the Russian public might be interpreted more properly as a vacuum of deeper cultural values rather than as a commitment to the moral foundations of Western society. In this regard, countless Russian analysts have given us gloomy portraits of the contemporary Russian soul disfigured by socialism: a "total alienation of man from social ties, from the means and conditions of his existence, the final transformation of man into a thing, into an object of development." The human person, continues this author, has been driven to the very border of extinction, a tragedy that is just as much a catastrophe as nuclear war.[16]

The political legacy inherited by the Yeltsin regime also posed innumerable barriers to the project of Western "normalization." Not just under the Communists, but for centuries Russians had felt an immense gap between themselves and the state, always devising strategies for survival in the face of this hostile power. Although Peter the Great and Alexander II had wanted to connect their governments to society in a deeper way, to this purpose seeking to encourage some forms of local self-government, even by the time of the demise of Communism there was no real public sphere in Russia. The "interest groups" identified by some political scientists in the Brezhnev period were nothing of the sort, having no connection to any larger public and defining themselves almost wholly in relation to the state apparatus. This orientation toward the state, a more general characteristic of social groups under Communism, prevented the development of ties of trust and interdependence among different sectors of the society. Workers and intelligentsia, city and countryside, capital and provinces, service-sector workers versus workers in production: all saw state action on their behalf rather than organized political life as the solution to their problems. Differential access and privilege created widespread mutual resentments among different social categories. Since they sought favors and not rights, they did not know how to define or struggle for their interests.

Finally, although in many ways "private," the new economic elite that had begun to assert itself in the late Gorbachev period was not, as we have seen, really a capitalist class in the classic sense. Its rights were still defined as much by its political power as by its ownership of property. It did not have to act by market principles but could continue the closed monopolistic practices inherent in the Communist system. Although there were superficial resemblances to a modern capitalist class, in fact what looked like similarities were really distortions. These distortions probably posed more dilemmas for the creation of "civilized" capitalism than did the total absence of such a distorted economic elite. In his reflections on his period as head of the government, Yegor Gaidar argued that his major political challenge in the early period was to fight against this all-encompassing nomenklatura greed and lawlessness (*bespredel*), which sought to monopolize both economic and political power. He believed that the introduction of market mechanisms into the economy would separate economics and politics, at least to some degree, and would force the new economic elite to act in terms of an economic logic.[17]

These peculiarities of the Russian Communist legacy did not escape commentators and scholars at the time. Indeed, endless lists of the impediments to "normalization" were drawn up and given wide publicity. To the cultural, political, and socioeconomic dilemmas just listed, some other "peculiarities" of Russia should be added, among them the enormous size and diversity of the country, which made the enactment of a coherent reform program more difficult; the historically weak rural sector, which was never fully integrated with urban society; the continuing weight of localism and the strength of centrifugal tendencies in a formally highly centralized society; the legacy of egalitarian and anti-elitist sentiments; the much longer experience of Communism than in Eastern Europe or China; and the militarization of the economy. Major reports, such as the Shatalin study in mid-1992, thoroughly analyzed such factors and urged the Russian government to be less abstract in its policies and more attuned to the special features of Russian history and society.[18]

But already by the time of Shatalin's report, not quite two years after the end of Communism, it may have been too late. The Russian people had been subject throughout this time to what I shall call "surgical dictatorship," a novel form of government in Russian history. And, as usual in Russian history, they had made their own accommodation to the reforms. Fearful of both government action and abandonment by the government, they had responded as they always had: by working out their own arrangements, which bore little relationship to the expressed goals of the government. Further, their improvisations, which often followed the logic of personal ties, closed associations, and lawlessness, will impede any further progress along the path of "civilized society." Just as the parody of a capitalist class may be worse than no private elite at all, so the present-day parody of capitalist democracy may be farther from the goal than ever before.

In using the term "surgical dictatorship," I am not adopting a phrase in use at the time, as is the case with "the Russian idea." Indeed, I am not aware that this concept has been elaborated as part of a typology of modern dictatorships at all. Although much of the inspiration for these practices came from Pinochet's Chile, the object of widespread admiration among "democratic forces" in Russia, it also has a specifically Russian lineage. Nonetheless, despite some historical continuities, it is absolutely novel in Russian history. The many forms of political dictatorship in modern Russia have always before followed an identifiable logic. If the dictatorship was more "traditional," as in the case of Nicholas I's or Nicholas II's Russia, autocracy was always connected to the promise to protect the population—the obvious fact that such commitments were often unrealistic is beside the point. Building on this logic, the modernizing Communist dictatorship added to these promises of protection a new form of political practice: it penetrated, shaped, and mobilized social groups in service to broader political goals.

The iconoclasm of the Yeltsin regime can be appreciated through contrast. Like the tsars or Communists, Yeltsin made claims to dictatorial power, even repeating many of the same practices and appealing to similar cultural traditions as had his predecessors. However, other people in the government made it painfully clear that the government was renouncing its responsibility to protect people. We're building capitalism and democracy, they said; it's time to take care of yourself. The government as repository of skilled knowledge (akin to the surgeon) can conduct the painful operation, but the patient must heal himself.

Here are some reflections on this theme of "the government as surgeon" from Yeltsin himself. "I remember that morning in Spain, in the hospital, where they operated on me. Right after the operation they suggested that I get up. And I got up, without crutches, even though sweating from fear and stress, and I took several steps." Gaidar, continued Yeltsin, had the same role as his surgeons: to quickly lift up "our paralyzed economy." His policy was tough and cruel, but necessary. "While other doctors argued about the methods of cure, he dragged the sick patient up from the bed." And the patient has stood up and started to move, Yeltsin assures us. Why the optimism? Not on the basis of any economic indicators, which are objectively very poor, Yeltsin admits. His grounds for hope are the following: in the country there have appeared people with a completely new psychology, a psychology of real men, who don't expect help from anyone else. They curse everyone and stubbornly get down to business.[19] No more than Nicholas II, Stalin, or Khrushchev could Yeltsin understand the logic of a complex and interdependent modern society. Just like advocates of the Russian idea, he believed that the key to change was to let heroes perform miracles.

A strange combination of the Russian idea's traditional emphasis on the prowess of the ruler and technocratic ideas of social engineering, this conception of the state's role, so crudely sketched by Yeltsin, is quite different from alternative models such as the nightwatchman state, the welfare state, or the paternalistic state. It is more one-sided than any of these, a further exemplification of the attenuation of reciprocity in contemporary Russia. For this state curses and demonizes opposition and rules in an often lawless fashion, since it sees itself as the fount of progress; yet it also proclaims that it has a reduced role in society. Basing itself upon such a fundamental contradiction, this surgeon state has undermined public confidence in both its competence and its concern for the welfare of the patient. Through its own conception of itself, it has undermined both capitalism and democracy, already extremely fragile models of economic and political behavior in Russia. Just as people became disillusioned with Communism because it broke its own promises, so the words democracy and reform have become unbearable to large sectors of the public. And all of this was achieved in less than three years—a record for speed that would be the envy of any Bolshevik enthusiast.

A GOVERNMENT OF DEMOCRATIC REFORMS

From the beginning the new government of Russia rested only upon one man, Boris Yeltsin. For with the temporary outlawing of the Communist Party, and its complete destruction as a ruling body, the entire state apparatus was left without foundations. The apparatus of government of course continued to exist, but without any firm leadership, principles of action, or legitimacy. Nor were there any other political institutions to fill up some of the vacuum of authority, for no strong alternative political parties existed. To add to the government's weakness, its social base was ill-defined and inchoate. Whatever public support there was for the new government, it existed only as an amalgam of vague and often conflicting ideological currents.

Only Yeltsin had authority in the country. In the weeks after the defeat of the coup Gorbachev was still nominally head of the Soviet Union, but the whole world watched on television when Yeltsin deeply humiliated him. It was now apparent that Yeltsin would make the fundamental decisions about the new political regime. His initial legitimacy was based on a very Russian combination of factors. First, he had been the hero of the August events, showing undeniable courage in defying the putschists and rallying the opposition around himself. He thus exemplifies Max Weber's concept of charismatic authority: his mandate to lead was based on the perception that he could perform miracles. As an additional Russian overtone, it also seemed that this hero acquired such powers only through suffering and overcoming the malice of those around him—we recall the campaigns of slander against Yeltsin for his alcoholism and womanizing, his humiliation by Gorbachev before the party. Such charismatic authority, as analyzed by Weber, is extremely transitory and must eventually be supplemented by other institutional and ideological supports.

In this regard, Yeltsin had a couple more roles in his repertory, both of them deeply rooted in Russian political culture. Indeed, it is this very groundedness in the culture, this connection with underlying cultural presuppositions, that makes Yeltsin's evident appeal to many Russians so difficult for foreigners to appreciate. One role that Yeltsin played to great effect, particularly before his great victory in August 1991, was that of the real Russian *muzhik*, the embodiment of the good and bad traits of the national character. Courageous, passionate, unpredictable, a good drinker, a man of the people hostile to elites: these were some of the images that Yeltsin transmitted to broad sectors of the population. He was "ours," and not "theirs," not part of the "foreign" ruling partocrats. Throughout his presidency he has used this image of the good ruler allied with the people against the elites to discredit and demonize his opposition.

A sense of the appeal of this folk image of the hero-leader can be gleaned from these edited excerpts from a graffiti-poem that I copied down in the late summer of 1990, when the battle between Gorbachev and Yeltsin was in full swing. In Russian, this language will bring to mind a famous poem written by Gorky in the revolutionary period.

> Gorby is gathering the masses for the victory of perestroika. Between the masses and Gorby, Borya the herald soars proudly. . . . In his roar the masses hear the thirst for power, the force of anger, the flame of passion, and the

assurance of victory. . . . The masses yearn for Borya, they don't want to struggle with drunkenness and alcoholism. And the regional party committees also moan, hiding themselves from the masses in their congresses. Only proud Borya the herald soars boldly and freely, and soon he will noisily burst apart the Soviet house of fools.

As the preceding passage shows, this real Russian *muzhik* attacked the authorities and thus came to represent good over evil. This was the third aspect of Yeltsin's populist image: the representative of truth against the oppressor. As in his role of mass folk hero, this archetype was difficult to reconcile with Yeltsin's own past as a top party official in Sverdlovsk and then in Moscow. How was it possible for him to support demands for the removal of all the former party nomenklatura from leadership positions in his government when he himself was one of their number? Because, replicating the ancient pre-Petrine model of tsarist rule, the suffering tsar had repented for his people. Here is an extraordinary set of remarks from Yeltsin's press secretary about the president's conversation with Solzhenitsyn in the summer of 1992.

> In the President's words one could sense repentance, the authorities' repentance before the great writer. Yeltsin understands that a great moral injury was done to Solzhenitsyn. But his work opened the way for the truth, on the basis of which the President of Russia is building his relations with the people today.[20]

Many observers wondered how these rather vulgar versions of traditional Russian political imagery were consistent with the ruler's sponsorship of Westernizing reforms.[21] How, asked the commentator Vladimir Kosmynin, could the people so warmly embrace Yeltsin and at the same time react very cooly to the reforms announced by his government? He gave the following answer to his own question. We Russians have our deep emotional inclinations similar to the Aquarian electrical charge of Yeltsin. "And dry Western reasoning and mercantilism has never prospered among us. Russia is Russia. It always responded only to warm, emotional relations, finding in this new powers and truly accomplishing miracles."[22] Clearly, for some people Yeltsin represented a kind of purified version of deeply felt elements of the Russian idea and became a kind of symbolic guarantor that the country would not lose its soul during the changes.

The fragility of a government based purely upon personal charisma and a deep emotional tie with a mythically defined people is obvious. In the first weeks after the coup a variety of reformers suggested political innovations that might create a more solid foundation for the bumpy changes to come. There were appeals for a *zemskii sobor*, the ancient assembly of the land, and for a constituent assembly that would legislate a new institutional structure. Some democrats urged the democratic movement to unify itself in order to provide a political base for the regime, and others called for the creation of an organized party of reform. But none of these appeals was heeded. As a result, a president elected as an opposition candidate to Communist domination has continued in office in an entirely new political context, without a party, without a real administrative structure, without a new set of laws, and perhaps most importantly, with only an extremely vague popular mandate for a program that did not yet exist.

For several years before August 1991, debates on the desirability of a "democratic" dictatorship had been appearing in the reformist press and journals. In Russian conditions, it was said, truly democratic methods would inevitably lead to stalemate. The people would not accept the pain necessary for the birth of a new economic and political system. Even more importantly, the egoistic bureaucracy, far from cleansed of Communist values, would struggle against reform with every weapon at its disposal. Even the democratic activists, so effective in mobilizing popular support against the Communist regime, often saw themselves as anarchistic utopians, true representatives of the maximalist intelligentsia, who would undermine the new political system.[23]

Such considerations underlay one of the crucial decisions of the Yeltsin government: the political system must be based on dictatorial executive power. An administrative apparatus directly subordinate to the executive must be created throughout the expanses of Russia. For this purpose special presidential representatives were sent around the country to oversee the enforcement of the president's decrees—a policy that bore uncanny resemblances to the tsars' use of personal emissaries and representatives. Such a political strategy inevitably set the executive branch on a course of head-on confrontation with the parliament, which was politically marginalized from the very beginnings of the Yeltsin regime. Officials in the executive branch (75 percent of them of nomenklatura lineage according to a recent sociological study)[24] dismissed the parliamentary deputies as relics of the old regime whose main function was to shout irrelevancies at each other.

The decisions to rule by decree and through a new administrative apparatus appointed solely by the chief executive lacked political wisdom. By cutting itself off from the country's surviving political apparatus, the Yeltsin leadership lost control over its only potentially effective political lever. The marginalized local political leaders, often still occupying their positions, proceeded to connect themselves to the new economic elite and to pillage the country in unprecedented ways. Scandal after scandal rocked cities and regions, as the old party nomenklatura divided up the spoils of the defunct regime. Moscow in particular witnessed the sorry spectacle of a mad scramble for property in the center of the city. Bribery, financial scandals, and other forms of corruption reached unprecedented new heights. As contrasted with the Soviet period, these abuses were widely publicized in the media.

In this atmosphere of political decay, the population understood that the central government had little control over the nerves of society. According to a June 1992 survey taken in Moscow, St. Petersburg, and Vladimir, only 6 percent of Russian citizens considered that power in fact belonged to the visible official organs of government. Almost 30 percent believed that the mafia was the most powerful political force in the country, while 15 percent were convinced that the old party elite was still dominant.[25]

In the best traditions of tsarist administration, this officially highly centralized system proved itself to be rather impotent. The new presidential envoys could do little in the face of the growing political disintegration of the country. Even in those cases when regions did not formally announce their sovereignty, the main tendency was toward local autonomy. In this new system, the population at large was deprived of those few rights that they had under the Communists. No one was accountable to the public, for there was no centralized administration to bring a modicum of discipline to local affairs.

Further, the new rulers made it quite plain that they were not interested in public participation. Fundamentally, they wanted an anesthetized population upon which they could perform their new experiment. As Gennady Burbulis, in the early period Yeltsin's main political adviser, candidly admitted: "Most people have stopped needing the authorities and the government. No one listens to the opposition anymore. The indifference of the masses is useful; it is even stabilizing. This indifference is a protection against rebellion, as it were."[26] This same Burbulis, a self-confessed avid reader of thinkers such as Berdyaev, Solovyev, and Florovsky, a true adherent of the Russian idea, was fond of the following kind of public reflection. "And despite all smiles, I insist on a certain romantic formula. And it's like this: the tasks which lie before us today can only be resolved in a regime of inspired power." To the interviewer he confessed that if at their next meeting classic Russian works had been replaced on his shelves by such trifles as statutes, laws, orders, and the like, it could be concluded that Burbulis had spiritually perished.[27] Mr. Burbulis had previously been a teacher of scientific Communism at Sverdlovsk University. I cite such passages in the text in order to give the distant reader a certain taste of what the Russian public has been treated to during the birth pangs of civilized society.

So far I have discussed the more traditional elements of the regime of "surgical dictatorship"—those time-honored images of rule that legitimate arbitrary authority in the hands of a single government. But, committed to the Westernization of Russia, this "regime of inspired power" came to see as its main immediate task the administration of economic "shock therapy" to the long-suffering Russian population. Although for Yeltsin himself such a conclusion was more a matter of faith than of expertise (we already examined his reasoning), he chose a team of political leaders deeply imbued with a technocratic ethos that saw professional expertise as more important than political vision for the reconstruction of society. Then political architect Gaidar's book *State and Evolution* fully reflects this technocratic mentality, as he devotes far more attention to economic policy than to other pressing issues facing his government, such as the restoration of confidence in the future.

Especially telling, in this regard, are the following remarks from then Minister of Foreign Economic Relations Pyotr Aven:

> And in order to bring this subject—what the Gaidar team is like—to a close, I would like to say just one more thing. It so happens that this team is drawn from our first generation of economists who read English. It just so happens that that's the case. Few people in this country have read Okun. We'd be lucky to find anyone at all who has read Coase's work on privatization, for which he received a Nobel Prize. But these people [the Gaidar team] read Samuelson as a first-year textbook.[28]

Undoubtedly they had also read Francis Fukuyama on the end of history, which taught them that all social development will culminate in the one true path of liberal capitalist democracy. But nowhere in these works did they read an equally important lesson: such a full-scale rejection of national experience and culture will only deprive leaders of a wealth of historical experience, deepen the cleavages of society, and exacerbate the crisis of morality that, in Russia, has turned out to be one of the main impediments to the creation of Western-style capitalism. Worldwide experience, to which reference was constantly made, teaches a lesson very different from the one they drew. Reform programs require synthesis and creative adaptation, and they are deeply moral and political, not just technical, in nature. It would have been far more fruitful to study the history of Meiji Japan, when Japanese leaders sought to assimilate Western technology and learning into their own society, rather than economic teachings that treat the economy as a self-enclosed and manipulable autonomous sphere. It is impossible to disagree with the nationalist intellectual and politician Sergei Kurginyan: "The rejection of the people's moral and historical self-definition and choice is the road to nowhere."[29]

Preparations were made for the new policy throughout the fall of

1991, accompanied by mounting public anxiety, exacerbated by the rapid disappearance of food from the stores. All sorts of amazing statements by local and national government officials appeared in the press, the main message of which to the Russian people was that the government did not care at all about the people's welfare. A. Chubais, later destined to lead the government's privatization, proudly compared the government's policy with the actions of a surgeon who operates on a patient without anesthesia.[30] Making use of the same metaphor, Yeltsin's adviser Rakitov explained that the government was able to take these strong measures without any anesthesia because, unlike Gorbachev's team, the cabinet was composed of experts and not professional politicians.[31]

Other officials sounded similar notes. Evgenii Yasin, the key government adviser cited earlier, explained to the public that the country was experiencing difficult, revolutionary times. The key thing was that people must understand that they are responsible for themselves, that they should not rely on others.[32] The Petersburg official Alfred Kokh was even blunter in the interview he gave to one of the most popular newspapers in the city. This is a time of Social Darwinism, he said, during which a process of natural selection must take place.[33]

I will never forget the anguished remark of an acquaintance of mine with a young family: how our government must hate us to abandon us like this! This relatively young man, who always impressed me by his kindness, drew his own conclusions. He is now in hiding from the police for mafia-related activities. I also remember the fear among a group of schoolteachers to whom I spoke in a rural area a few hours outside St. Petersburg. They had been led to fear that the government would now no longer provide free public education or childcare. They were at a loss to know how they could possibly cope with these changes. Whether these rumors about government intentions were true or false is not at issue. The key point is that it was the style of the government's interaction with the public that created fertile soil for such rumors. They expressed the uncomfortable truth that in the eyes of the population a fundamental violation of the implicit contract between government and society had taken place.

In many ways the government's style in the early period was more radical than the content of its programs. Indeed, it has been heatedly debated whether there really was any policy of shock therapy in early 1992, and Gaidar has explicitly denied that he was really the radical economic reformer that he was made out to be. I would put it this way: there was certainly shock, but there was little real reform. The shock came in the following form: the government allowed prices to increase dramatically, at the same time trying to curb a growth of the money supply and increases in wages. The implications of this new policy were soon felt in the streets of St. Petersburg and Moscow. Tens of thousands of people, including pensioners who had been utterly ruined by the huge price increases, brought their personal possessions out to sell for a pittance so they could survive. Equally painful, in both an economic and a psychological sense, was the near collapse of the ruble. Gaidar later defended his policy by claiming that if these tough measures had not been taken, the monetary system might have collapsed altogether.

This economic policy of early 1992 was criticized from all directions. Many reform economists scored Gaidar for his lack of attention to basic structural reforms, particularly the privatization of industry and encouragement of individual farming to replace the collective farms. Other analysts and leaders, both on the right and more to the center, accused the government of artificially creating the huge decline of industrial production and paying no attention to the welfare of the population, all in the name of a foreign ideological vision. Critics also attacked the government for its unwillingness publicly to present and defend a consistent overall program of reform, and they claimed that it violated the democratic norms that it was itself espousing. In America and Europe, wrote Igor Zakharov in the newspaper of St. Petersburg University, democracy means freedom of speech, rights, and even social protection. With our "democrats" it is reduced to a series of "objective laws" of the market and civilization, which only the democratic elite know. Our authorities do not respect us.[34]

Throughout the spring of 1992, opposition to the policies of Gaidar's government mounted, and the political temperature of the country heated up. Two fundamental forces of opposition can be identified: a moderate opposition exemplified by Arkadii Volskii and his Civic Union, and a more militant and uncompromising combination of Communist and nationalist groups. The first group favored the general direction of the reforms but felt that the period of the "demolition experts" was now over. It was time to rely on more sensible, moderate people who would pay more attention to the decline of industry [read: would distribute state monies to failing industries to save them from bankruptcy], would make greater attempts to regulate the market, and would proclaim a broader conception of the meaning of reform in Russia. Some of their leaders proposed that this new political program, a break from the narrow economism of the Gaidar team, should be centered around the idea of the resurrection of the country as a great power. This moderate movement denied that it was an opposition in the strict sense of the word, and indeed it included many members of the government. They tended to work, not through mass mobilization, but through elite channels of influence.

The second oppositional current was more confrontational and more intransigent in its attacks. It was also incoherent, embracing strange bedfellows that had a very difficult time coming together for joint political action. But whatever the differences among the Communists and the assortment of right-wing nationalist groups, they agreed that the new government was destroying Russia in the name of foreign values and with the help of foreign powers. They hammered away at a set of potent themes: the government did not care about the people; it acted in a dictatorial way; and it had ruined the life prospects of young and old alike. Story after story appeared in *Pravda* and *Sovetskaia Rossiia* about the plight of the poor in Russia, with particular attention given to the aged. Perhaps if *Pravda* and the groups that it represented had shown such compassion in the past, the Communist regime would never have collapsed.

Like Yeltsin himself, this intransigent opposition calls forth echoes from deep in Russian history. For example, the film director Stanislav Govorukhin, creator of the movie "The Russia We Have Lost," analyzed the nature of Yeltsin's democratic regime in the following way. It is composed of ex-Communists who have led a criminal revolution bringing the mafia to power. The mafia has not been happy with the parliament because the latter institution has put a brake on its own power. Consequently, the criminal groups have demanded new elections, which they will dominate because of their money and control over the mass media.[35] For such people, as for Archpriest Avvakum, the regime is an unalloyed evil force betraying the nation. Vladimir Osipov, a pensioner who formerly served a sentence in the Gulag for fifteen years, declared in a letter to *Moscow News* that it is the moral duty of every righteous person to speak out against the anti-Russian regime of Boris Yeltsin. He added: I evaluate Yeltsin's actions as the conduct of a complete mason and hater of Christ, for his declaration suspending Parliament was made on the holy day of the Birth of the Virgin.[36]

Yeltsin could deal with critics such as Volskii. In fact, his own statements sometimes echoed the positions of the moderate opposition. For example, in the fall of 1992, Yeltsin confessed that "tough measures, painful measures for the population, were frequently conducted callously and created additional difficulties for people." He then proceeded to attack some of his own ministers by name![37] In fact, already by this time fundamental changes had been made in the directions of the reform that gave members of the Civic Union much cause for cheer. The good tsar was still protecting truth and justice against the evil bureaucracy that was somehow separate from his own power.

By contrast, the other opposition—the enragés—were not at all appeased. But ironically, they were in many ways useful to Yeltsin. Nothing could give him more legitimacy than to call forth the specter of the Communist-fascist alliance. If these are the enemies, my government must be on the right track after all—this was the conclusion that people were expected to draw from the violent confrontation between these two absolutely polarized forces. Further, following the classic Stalinist logic, all deficiencies and shortcomings could be blamed on the enemies of reform.

Concessions to the moderates, outright war with the "red-brown" alliance: this was the essence of Yeltsin's political strategy from the spring of 1992 to the end of 1993. In theory, it made sense. Despite the fact that the government was now moving away from its shock therapy program, replacing the demolition experts by respectable and experienced economic managers and shoveling money to industrial enterprises, it could still present itself as the party of reform—for look, the enemies of civilization and democracy are still against us.

In real political life, this strategy has backfired. The attempt to depart from the previous narrow and technocratic approach to politics through making concessions to economic and political elites deprived government policy of any coherence. Just as Nicholas II's half-hearted efforts to stimulate capitalism within the framework of political autocracy had led to a divided and amorphous government, so Yeltsin's designation of Viktor Chernomyrdin to lead a new, more conciliatory course in the name of political compromise has undermined the logic of reform. Since late summer 1992, sarcastically called by one commentator the time of the "great breakthrough," the retreat from the previous economic policy has become clear. Yet this change, in some ways so sensible, has had an enormous cost. The regime can no longer even claim that it is the engine of progress, as it tried to do under Gaidar.

The political war against the red-brown opposition had a tragic outcome, both because of the bloodshed of October 1993 and for the impetus that it has given for Yeltsin's increasing use of dictatorial methods. To those us of who watched the episodes of this increasingly polarized and violent confrontation in Russia played out on television screens every day, the whole drama had something of a comic opera character. It is also important to understand that the Russian people were paying very little attention to the escalating campaigns of charges and counter-charges. The speaker of the parliament, Ruslan Khasbulatov, a rallying point for these opposition forces, became one of the most hated figures in the country, making Yeltsin look good by comparison. If words were to be believed, the country was ripe for civil war, but the reality was somewhat different. The level of public cynicism and apathy had become so great that the government knew that widespread active support for its opponents would not be forthcoming. Taking advantage of the political weakness of his enemies, in the spring of 1993 and then in early fall Yeltsin made dramatic announcements giving himself virtually dictatorial powers (at least on paper—in fact the country had become not too far from ungovernable). The latter decrees, dissolving the parliament, provoked the rebellion of early October 1993, which culminated in the government's attack on the parliament, considerable loss of life, and the arrest of the key political leaders of the rebellion, including Yeltsin's own vice president, Alexander Rutskoi.

Simply to describe this complicated sequence of events fully would require an excessive amount of space. Such a description would soon become tedious, for we would soon find that the same general logic kept repeating itself: the logic of schism, of binary opposition, of intransigent polarization, culminating in violence. Also constant, and traditional in Russian politics, was the deepening of another split, that between the political system and the people. For in the final accounting, neither side has won these conflicts. Yeltsin's prestige has suffered tremendously, for this surgeon now has blood upon his hands, even though the operation has not gone at all as planned. As Boris Fyodorov, previously Yeltsin's minister of economics, declared, "the very word 'democrat' has become a swearword."[38] The "familiar aroma of falsehood" (in the words of a friend of mine) has once again become pervasive.

Everything became clear in the parliamentary elections of December 1993, when Vladimir Zhirinovsky astonished the world by his quasi-fascist party's strong showing in the election. It would be easy to interpret this stunning defeat for Yeltsin's team by reference to the difficult economic situation, the pain of the transitional period, and the like. But something more profound has happened: people have become disillusioned with "democracy," for it has come in the guise of a dictatorship that shields corruption and allows arbitrariness.

The government is well aware of this crisis of legitimacy, and various remedies, some of them verging on the absurd, have been proposed. Perhaps the choicest desperate remedy was the urgent call for the creation of a constitutional monarchy, to be headed by an adolescent boy, Count Georgii Romanov, who at the time lived in Madrid. Apart from such piquant proposals, once again reminiscent of Saltykov-Shchedrin, little of real interest is occurring in Russian politics. The decisive time has passed; the surgical dictatorship has failed; the time-honored logic of schism is at work. This parody of Western democratic capitalism may drag on for a long time, at times threatening to career into crisis. But it will not inspire either the Russian people or the rest of the world. Even worse, since the failure of the Russian idea has taught us to be skeptical of inspiration, it does not function efficiently or justly even in the most petit bourgeois way. For this reason, Russia will continue to be a world apart, not in the sense of forging a new path to the future, but as testimony to broken dreams and lost possibilities.

LOST POSSIBILITIES

Chaadaev had hoped that Russia's lack of fixed tradition would permit its leaders to synthesize, learning from the experiences of other countries in order to resolve the general problems facing modern society. And it is undeniably true that too fixed a sense of historical tradition engenders its own kind of tyranny, hampering people in their ability to confront contemporary problems. Thus, a scholar of China has recently written that the country "has not yet had a clean enough break with the past to be able to escape from its [the past's] tyranny."[39]

As the decisive early period of the Yeltsin regime shows, Russia has also not been able to break from the past, but that past was not one of a sense of timelessness and continuity, as China's was imagined to be, but of ruptures and explosions. In a certain sense, it seems that Yeltsin, Gaidar, and their colleagues were simply acting according to the classical script of Russian history, repeating the binary logic so criticized by Lotman. They defined a mythological West, which was primarily understood in terms of everything that was opposed to the Soviet Union. In this West, economics meant everything, "spirituality" nothing. And the economic idea that was promoted, a primitive version of capitalism, was utterly disconnected from traditional Russian morality and culture.

This idea of "civilization" as the antipode to Russia generated a whole series of other oppositions. The young and the old were seen to belong to different worlds, and only the young could construct the future, which had no real place for other generations. The new heroes that Yeltsin perceived emerging in Russia were young, he felt.[40] In the same way, the old society was completely opposed to the new, just as state was disjoined from society. Only the new capitalist class was composed of real men, for all the other groups were stained by the old culture of mental slavery. Workers and educated groups who had the misfortune to be state employees suffered from the reforms, no matter how talented or productive they were. Any sharp young person with questionable scruples could easily earn in the private sphere many times what famous scientists received from their government employment.

Based on this binary logic, the tone and style of the reforms alienated people as much as their content. Broad sectors of the Russian people came to understand that no one now valued either their former lives or their present work. Thus, while the demise of Communism gave new opportunities for some people to prosper, often dishonestly, the new society created resentment and fear among wide sectors of the public. For if their own past lives, like the country's history as a whole, had no meaning, how could they act on the basis of a vision of the future?

People responded to their fear in different ways. Just as in feudal times, some people joined closed groups for self-protection. Uncertainty about the future is one of the sources of the mafia's strength in contemporary Russia. Confronted by the prospect of a hostile new society unwilling to protect them, many young people surrendered themselves to these groups that gave some sense of belonging and provided immediate material benefits. Unable to think about long-term goals for their lives, they pursued their immediate goals with no moral constraints. But almost no one, after all, was communicating to people that action in the new Russia should be based on morality. Isn't capitalism a struggle for the survival of the fittest? Since, as people were told constantly, they could not count on the government, wasn't it logical, as Yeltsin's senior adviser Sergei Shakrai stated, that above all people must think of themselves and their families?[41]

A small but noisy minority of people responded in a more political way, creating the intransigent opposition to the regime. Convinced, as right-wing novelist Vasily Belov declared, that the democrats are "quite deliberately trying to destroy our thousand-year-old state,"[42] they used inflamed rhetoric against the government and organized numerous marches and demonstrations, some of them culminating in violence. For Yeltsin this opposition justified his dictatorial practices, but did not their intransigence have some basis in the practices of the surgical dictatorship, which performed painful operations but did not heal? If the reforms had not been promoted in such binary fashion, would the opposition have taken the same form? If there had been some concern with historical continuity, thus assuring the population that they did not have to fear the new Russia and its bold young men, perhaps skeptics unhappy with the government might not have seen their adversaries as demons.

The extreme polarization of society and politics in the early post-Communist period was not inevitable, though serious conflicts could not have been avoided. However, the Yeltsin government acted in such a way as to maximize, not minimize, fear. Effective reform would have required a rhetoric and logic, not of revolutionary break with the past, but of well-conceived changes based on compromise. Yeltsin was surely right that "the misfortune of Russia was not in the lack or overabundance of reformers, but in the inability to carry through a consistent policy."[43] But this failure was rooted not simply in weak nerves or lack of commitment, but also in the policy of the reformers themselves. Identifying themselves with the truth, and unable to understand the real nature of the society around them, they provoked opposition and created divisions. The expressed goals of the reformers were never reached, although, as with Nicholas II after 1905, the language of reform (Russia was allegedly a "constitutional monarchy") was still used. The government therefore appeared hypocritical in the eyes of the population, who were aware of the lack of correspondence between words and things. The hope for change dissolved.

Yeltsin's government could have attempted to break with this classical logic of the failure of reform in Russia. To do so, they would have had to have presented a vision of Russia's future that provided a bridge to the past. From the Russian idea they might have taken modified ideals of equality, belief, community, and the responsibility of government for social welfare. Paradoxically, such a modified image of capitalism and democracy would have been a better approximation to Western practices than was the traditional image of Western society inherited from the Russian idea. On the basis of such a modified set of goals, they might have attempted to ensure that the painful transition to civilized society would not culminate in new barbarism. Further, such a synthesis, of the kind that Lotman advocated, would have made plain to the people that their collective past had value and their present lives might once again have meaning.

But such a vision would have required a government that itself had an appreciation of the past and trust in the future. The current Russian leadership has been graced with neither. At the time of writing, the current prime minister, Viktor Chernomyrdin, reportedly has his private plane ready, prepared to abandon the country immediately if it should become necessary. Like too many of his countrymen, both inside and outside the government, he too seems to be thinking only about himself, and then only in the short term. This is the real misfortune of contemporary Russia, and it is far from clear that there is a way out of the inevitable consequences.

Notes

INTRODUCTION
CYCLES OF BREAKDOWN IN RUSSIA

1. *Komsomolskaia pravda*, 2 March 1993.

2. B. P. Kurashvili, *Kuda idet Rossiia?* (Moscow: Prometei, 1994), 6.

3. Nikolai Gogol, *Dead Souls* (New York: Holt, Rinehart, and Winston, 1963), 304.

4. Quoted in A. S. Akhiezer, *Rossiia: Kritika istoricheskogo opyta* (Moscow: Izdatel'stvo FO SSSR, 1991), 1:141.

5. Fyodor Dostoyevsky, *The Diary of a Writer* (New York: George Braziller, 1954), 296–97.

6. I. Il'in, "Russkaia revoliutsiia byla katastrofoi," in *Russkaia ideia*, ed. V. M. Piskunov (Moscow: Iskusstvo, 1994), 2:288.

7. A. S. Khomiakov, "O starom i novom," in *Russkaia ideia*, ed. M. A. Maslin (Moscow: Respublika, 1992), 58.

8. Nicolas Berdyaev, *The Russian Idea* (New York: Macmillan, 1948), 255.

9. Arsenii Gulyga, *Russkaia ideia i ee tvortsy* (Moscow: Soratnik, 1995).

10. Vissarion Belinsky, "Letter to N. V. Gogol," in *A Documentary History of Russian Thought*, ed. W. J. Leatherbarrow and D. C. Offord (Ann Arbor: Ardis, 1987), 131.

11. Lev Kopelev, "The Lie Can Be Defeated Only by Truth," in *The Political, Social and Religious Thought of Russian "Samizdat"—an Anthology*, ed. Michael Meerson-Aksenov and Boris Shragin (Belmont, Mass.: Nordland, 1977), 327.

12. Boris Shragin, *The Challenge of the Spirit* (New York: Alfred A. Knopf, 1978), 67.

13. Quoted in Akhiezer, *Kritika*, 1:195.

14. See, for example, Sergei Kurginian, *Sed'moi stsenarii*, 3 vols. (Moscow: Eksperimental'nyi tvorcheskii tsentr, 1992).

15. Iu. M. Lotman, *Kul'tura i vzryv* (Moscow: Gnozis, 1992).

16. *Nezavisimaia gazeta*, 12 September 1991.

17. *Nevskoe vremia*, 5 March 1993.

18. Quotation from Alexander Herzen in *Russkie o russkikh. Mneniia russkikh o samikh sebe* (St. Petersburg: Petro-Rif, 1992 [reprinted from 1905 edition]), 49.

19. Marc Raeff, *The Well-Ordered Police State* (New Haven: Yale University Press, 1983).

CHAPTER ONE
THE RUSSIAN IDEA

1. Ivan Kireevski, "On the Nature of European Culture and Its Relation to the Culture of Russia," in *Russian Intellectual History: An Anthology*, ed. Marc Raeff (New Jersey: Humanities Press, 1978), 180.

2. G. Florovskii, "Puti russkogo bogosloviia," in *Russkaia ideia*, ed. Piskunov, 2:159.

3. G. P. Fedotov, *Sud'ba i grekhi Rossii* (St. Petersburg: Sofiia, 1991), 1:79.

4. Alexander Herzen, *My Past and Thoughts* (Berkeley: University of California Press, 1982), 302.

5. Dostoyevsky, *Diary*, 76.

6. Ibid., 104.

7. P. Ia. Chaadaev, "Apologiia sumasshedshego," in *Russkaia ideia*, ed. Maslin, 41–42.

8. Moshe Lewin, *Political Undercurrents in Soviet Economic Debates* (Princeton: Princeton University Press, 1974).

9. Fedotov, *Sud'ba*, 2:201.

10. Ibid., 202.

11. M. Osorgin, "Vremena. Avtobiograficheskoe povestvovanie," in *Russkaia ideia*, ed. Piskunov, 1:420–21.

12. Dostoyevsky, *Diary*, 36.

13. K. Kas'ianova, *O russkom natsional'nom kharaktere* (Moscow: Institut natsional'noi modeli ekonomiki, 1994), 110–11.

14. I. Gessen, "Gody izgnaniia. Zhiznennyi otchet," in *Russkaia ideia*, ed. Piskunov, 1:342.

15. A. F. Losev, *Strast' k dialektike* (Moscow: Sovetskii pisatel', 1990), 68.

16. *Sevodnia*, 23 February 1993.

17. Quoted in Abbott Gleason, "Republic of Humbug: The Russian Nativist Critique of the United States 1830–1930," *American Quarterly* 44 (March 1992): 6.

18. *Nezavisimaia gazeta*, 1 October 1992.

19. Kas'ianova, *O russkom*, 71–73.

20. Statement by V. M. Mezhuev, round-table discussion, "Russia and the West," *Voprosy filosofii* 6 (1992).

21. S. Platonov, *Posle kommunizma* (Moscow: Molodaia gvardiia, 1991), 512.

22. B. Tarasov, "Chto s nami proiskhodit," *Chto s nami proiskhodit*, ed. Vladimir Lazarev (Moscow: Sovremennik, 1989), 174.

23. Kazakevich, *Novyi mir* (January 1959): 6.

24. Ilya Ehrenburg, *People and Life 1891–1921* (New York: Alfred A. Knopf, 1962), 412.

25. A. Batalov, "A vse-taki ono vertitsia," *Svobodnaia mysl'* 2 (1993): 92.

26. *Nezavisimaia gazeta*, 22 May 1992.

27. Osorgin, "Vremena," 400–403.

28. Platonov, *Posle kommunizma*, 524.

29. Herzen, *My Past*, 285.

30. Berdyaev, *Russian Idea*, 253.

31. G. P. Fedotov, *The Russian Religious Mind* (Cambridge: Harvard University Press, 1966), 1:15.

32. Luba Brezhneva, *The World I Left Behind* (New York: Random House, 1995), 295–96.

33. Yuri Borodai, "Krest'ianskii trud i sel'skaia obshchnost'," in Lazarev, *Chto s nami*, 136. Another excellent source for such views is Kurginian's three-volume *Sed'moi stsenarii*. See, for example, 1:238.

34. Osorgin, "Vremena," 418.

35. Paul Miliukov, *The Origins of Ideology* (Gulf Breeze, Fla.: Academic International 1974), 133. Krizhanich's statement was written in the 1660s.

36. Boris Mironov, "The Russian Peasant Commune after the Reforms of the 1860s," in *The World of the Russian Peasant*, ed. Ben Eklof and Stephen Frank (Boston: Unwin Hyman, 1990), 25.

37. Valerii Blagovo, "Nikolai Ogarev. Russkie voprosy" *Svobodnaia mysl'* 2 (1993): 110.

38. V. Rasputin, "Esli po sovesti," in Lazarev, *Chto s nami*, 158.

39. Quoted in P. S. Squire, *The Third Department* (Cambridge: Cambridge University Press, 1968), 78.

40. I. A. Isaeva, ed. *Puti evrazii* (Moscow: Russkaia kniga, 1992).

41. P. Chaadaev, in *Russian Intellectual History*, ed. Raeff, 167.

42. P. Chaadaev, "Apologiia sumasshedshego," 45.

CHAPTER TWO
THE DILEMMAS OF TSARIST MODERNIZATION

1. Alexander Blok, "The People and the Intelligentsia," in *Russian Intellectual History*, ed. Raeff, 360.

2. Tim McDaniel, *Autocracy, Modernization, and Revolution in Russia and Iran* (Princeton: Princeton University Press, 1991).

3. See, for example, Michael Cherniavsky, *Tsar and People: Studies in Russian Myths* (New Haven: Yale University Press, 1961).

4. Raeff, *Well-Ordered Police State*.

5. Aleksandr Gertsen, "Prolegomena," in *Russkaia ideia*, ed. Maslin, 124.

6. Alexander Herzen, *My Past*, 289.

7. Andrew Verner, *The Crisis of Russian Autocracy: Nicholas II and the 1905 Revolution* (Princeton: Princeton University Press, 1990), 196. Verner provides a brilliant analysis of the role of the autocracy in the late imperial period.

8. Ibid., 260.

9. Tim McDaniel, *Autocracy, Capitalism, and Revolution in Russia* (Berkeley: University of California Press, 1988), 59.

10. Ibid., 68.

11. Ibid., 61.

12. Ibid., 111–12.

13. Franco Venturi, *Roots of Revolution: A History of the Populist and Socialist Movements in Nineteenth-Century Russia* (New York: Alfred A. Knopf, 1960), 212.

14. Gertsen, "Prolegomena," 122.

15. Ibid.

16. McDaniel, *Autocracy, Capitalism, and Revolution*, 210.

CHAPTER THREE
THE LOGIC OF SOVIET COMMUNISM

1. Quoted in V. A. Kozlov, ed., *Perestroika i istoricheskii opyt* (Moscow: Mysl', 1989), 21.

2. Alexander Tsipko, *Is Stalinism Really Dead?* (San Francisco: Harper & Row, 1990), 16.

3. For a highly overstated version, see Theodore Von Laue, *Why Lenin? Why Stalin?* (New York: Lippincott, 1971).

4. For example, Moshe Lewin's books, *Political Undercurrents in Soviet Economic Debates* and *The Making of the Soviet System* (New York: Pantheon, 1985). Robert Tucker has emphasized the political archaism of Stalinism, its reversion to ancient Russian patterns of rule. Robert Tucker, "Stalinism as Revolution from Above," in *Stalinism: Essays in Historical Interpretation*, ed. Robert Tucker (New York: Norton, 1977), 98.

5. For further discussion of the concept of modernization, see McDaniel, *Autocracy, Modernization, and Revolution*, 70–88.

6. Lev Kopelev, *Ease My Sorrows* (New York: Random House, 1983), 185.

7. Tucker, "Stalinism as Revolution from Above" and *Stalin in Power* (New York: Norton, 1990).

8. William Henry Chamberlin, *Soviet Russia: A Living Record and a History* (Boston: Little, Brown, 1933), 335.

9. Raisa Orlova, *Memoirs* (New York: Random House, 1983), 39.

10. Chamberlin, *Soviet Russia*, 308.

11. Tucker, *Stalin in Power*, 50–58.

12. There is a brilliant analysis in V. A. Kozlov, "Donosy v sisteme NKVD-MVD v 1944–1953 gg," ms.

13. Andrei Sinyavsky, *Soviet Civilization: A Cultural History* (New York: Little, Brown, 1990), 107.

14. Kopelev, *Ease My Sorrows*, 148.

15. Lev Kopelev, *To Be Preserved Forever* (Philadelphia: Lippincott, 1977), 110–11.

16. Ehrenburg, *People and Life 1891–1921*, 413.

17. Kozlov, *Istoricheskii opyt*, 188.

18. Kopelev, *To Be Preserved*, 12.

19. See Moshe Lewin, *Political Undercurrents*.

20. Kopelev, *To Be Preserved*, 92.

21. M. Ilin, *New Russia's Primer* (Boston: Houghton Mifflin, 1931), 28.

22. Ibid., 16.

23. Quoted in Sinyavsky, *Soviet Civilization*, 115.

24. Tucker, *Stalin in Power*, 104.

25. Nicholas S. Timasheff, *The Great Retreat: The Growth and Decline of Communism in Russia* (New York: E.P. Dutton, 1946), 120.

26. Hiroaki Kuromiya, *Stalin's Industrial Revolution: Politics and Workers, 1928–1932* (Cambridge: Cambridge University Press, 1988), 141.

27. Shragin, *Challenge of the Spirit*, 141.

28. V. P. Danilov, *Rural Russia under the New Regime* (Bloomington: Indiana University Press, 1988), 205.

29. For a recent summary of some of the huge literature on this topic, see Walter Laquer, *Stalin: The Glasnost Revelations* (London: Unwin Hyman, 1990), 19–45; for a judicious Russian account of the debates, see Gennadi Bordiugov and Vladimir Kozlov, *Istoriia i kon"iunktura* (Moscow: Politizdat, 1992), 51–136.

30. Sheila Fitzpatrick, *Stalin's Peasants: Resistance and Survival in the Russian Village after Collectivization* (New York: Oxford University Press, 1994), 39.

31. Lev Kopelev, *The Education of a True Believer* (New York: Harper & Row, 1980), 235.

32. Ibid., 185.

33. Fitzpatrick, *Stalin's Peasants*, 288.

34. John Scott, *Behind the Urals* (Bloomington: Indiana University Press, 1989 [originally published 1942]), 18.

35. Kopelev, *Education*, 197.

36. *Molotov Remembers* (Chicago: Ivan Dee, 1993), 265.

37. David J. Dallin, *The Real Soviet Russia* (New Haven: Yale University Press, 1947), 62.

38. Kopelev, *Education*, 266–67

CHAPTER FOUR
A VIABLE FORM OF MODERN SOCIETY?

1. Alexander Solzhenitsyn, *The Gulag Archipelago* (New York: Harper & Row, 1978), 3:421–22.

2. Ilya Ehrenburg, *Post-War Years: 1945–54* (Cleveland: World, 1967), 243.

3. See, for example, George Fischer, *The Soviet System and Modern Society* (New York: Atherton Press, 1968), 148–53.

4. Ehrenburg, *People and Life 1891–1921*, 265.

5. Amy Knight, *Beria: Stalin's First Lieutenant* (Princeton: Princeton University Press, 1993), 185. For a fascinating description of Beria's initiatives, see pp. 183–94.

6. Quoted in V. A. Kozlov and O. V. Klebniuk, *Nachinaetsia s cheloveka* (Moscow: Izdatel'stvo politicheskoi literatury, 1988), 214–15.

7. Akhiezer, *Kritika*, 2:127.

8. Kopelev, *Education*, 212.

9. Timasheff, *The Great Retreat*.

10. Ehrenburg, *Post-War Years*, 321.

11. Shragin, *Challenge of the Spirit*, 18.

12. Particularly valuable are Iu. V. Aksiutin, ed., *Nikita Sergeevich Khrushchev. Materialy k biografii* (Moscow: Politizdat, 1989), and L. A. Kirshner and S. A. Prokhvatilova, eds., *Svet i teni "velikogo desiatiletiia." N. S. Khrushchev i ego vremia*, (Leningrad: Lenizdat, 1989).

13. *XXII S"ezd kommunisticheskoi partii sovetskogo soiuza. Stenograficheskii otchet* (Moscow: Politizdat, 1961) 1:151.

14. Ibid., 1: 210.

15. Kirshner and Prokhvatilova, *Svet i teni*, 259.

16. V. A. Kozlov, ed., *Neizvestnaia Rossiia. XX vek* (Moscow: Istoricheskoe nasledie, 1992) 1:275–76.

17. Ibid., 276.

18. Kirshner and Prokhvatilova, *Svet i teni*, 240.

19. Aksiutin, *Materialy k biografii*, 139.

20. Ibid., 150, 140.

21. Kirshner and Prokhavtilova, *Svet i teni*, 256.

22. Brezhneva, *The World I Left Behind*, 184.

23. Ibid., 315.

24. Ibid., 288.

25. Ibid., 162.

26. Letter of Mikhail Puchkov to his parents.

27. Brezhneva, *The World I Left Behind*, 245.

28. Yegor Ligachev, *Inside Gorbachev's Kremlin* (New York: Pantheon, 1993), 15–16.

29. Shragin, *Challenge of the Spirit*, 44.

30. See N. V. Vitruk, "Prava cheloveka: sostoianie i perspektivy razvitiia," in *Pravo i vlast'*, ed. M. P. Vyshinsky (Moscow: Progress, 1990), 157.

31. A. N. Alekseev, ed., *Ozhidali li peremeny?* (Moscow: Institut sotsiologii AN SSSR, 1991), 1:33.

32. Ibid., 2:241.

33. Platonov, *Posle kommunizma*, 299–300.

34. Stephen Cohen, ed., *An End to Silence: Uncensored Opinion in the Soviet Union* (New York: Norton, 1982), 158.

35. Vladimir Voinovich, *The Anti-Soviet Soviet Union* (San Diego: Harcourt Brace Jovanovich, 1986), 68.

36. Quoted in Stephen Baehr, *The Paradise Myth in Eighteenth-Century Russia* (Stanford: Stanford University Press, 1991), 269.

37. Boris Yeltsin, *Against the Grain* (New York: Summit Books, 1990), 139.

38. *Nezavisimaia gazeta*, 21 November 1991.

39. Otto Latsis, "The Deep Roots of Our Problems," in *Chronicle of a Revolution*, ed. Abraham Brumberg (New York: Pantheon, 1990), 177–78.

40. Padma Desai, *Perestroika in Perspective* (Princeton: Princeton University Press, 1989), 106.

41. *Current Digest of the Soviet Press*, 7 August 1991, 7.

42. Ibid., 28 August 1991, 3.

43. Ibid., 5.

44. Robert Kaiser, *Why Gorbachev Happened* (New York: Simon and Shuster, 1992), 383.

45. Ibid.

46. *Current Digest*, 24 July 1991, 4.

47. N. Popov, "Narod i vlast,'" in *Cherez ternii*, ed. A. A. Protashchik (Moscow: Progress, 1991), 775–77.

48. G. Vodolazov, "Formuly konsolidatsiia," in ibid., 720.

49. *Current Digest*, 2 January 1991, 3.

50. Ibid., 28 August 1991, 9.

51. Law signed by Gorbachev on 30 November 1990. Ibid., 2 January 1991, 14.

52. Ibid., 2.

CHAPTER FIVE
THE FAILURE OF YELTSIN'S REFORMS

1. *Moskovskie novosti*, 21 February 1993.

2. Nikolai Popov, *The Russian People Speak: Democracy at the Crossroads* (Syracuse: Syracuse University Press, 1995), 103–107.

3. V. P. Pastukov, "Ot nomenklatury k burzhuazii: 'novye russkie,'" *Polis* 2 (1993): 54.

4. Kopelev, *Ease My Sorrows*, 165–66.

5. *Current Digest*, 8 June 1994, 5.

6. Ibid., 6 April 1994, 11.

7. *Sankt Petersburgskie Vedemosti*, 5 March 1993.

8. *Vesti*, 9 October 1992.

9. *Solidarnost'*, special issue devoted to privatization, November 1992.

10. *Current Digest*, 19 January 1994, 14–15, 28.

11. *Chas pik*, 28 April 1993.

12. *Nezavisimaia gazeta*, 10 June 1992.

13. *Trud*, 27 April 1993.

14. *Ogonyok*, 13 June—4 July 1992, 2.

15. Popov, *The Russian People Speak*, 74.

16. G. S. Kiselev, *Tragediia obshchestva i cheloveka* (Moscow: Nauka, 1992), 34.

17. Egor Gaidar, *Gosudarstvo i evoliutsiia* (Moscow: Evraziia, 1995), 152–56.

18. See the long summary of this report in *Nezavisimaia gazeta*, 1 July 1992.

19. Boris Yeltsin, *Zapiski prezidenta* (Moscow: Ogonyok, 1994), 235–36.

20. *Current Digest*, 15 July 1992, 31.

21. *Chas pik*, 3 February 1992.

22. *Nezavisimaia gazeta*, 22 May 1992.

23. *Demokraticheskaia Rossiia*, 12–19 October 1991.

24. *Current Digest*, 15 June 1994, 8–9.

25. *Sotsiologicheskie issledovaniia* 11 (1992): 66–67.

26. *Current Digest*, 10 August 1994, 7.

27. *Literaturnaia gazeta*, 13 November 1991.

28. *Current Digest*, 8 April 1992, 12.

29. Kurginian, *Sed'moi stsenarii*, 1:237.

30. *Rossiiskaia gazeta*, 1 September 1992.

31. Ibid., 5 March 1992.

32. *Rossiiskie vesti*, 1 September 1992.

33. *Chas pik*, 12 October 1992.

34. *Slovo i delo*, 22–28 April 1993.

35. *Izvestiia*, 9 October 1993.

36. *Moskovskie novosti*, 3 October 1993.

37. *Current Digest*, 4 November 1992, 1–2.

38. Ibid., 10 August 1994, 7.

39. W.J.F. Jenner, *The Tyranny of History: The Roots of China's Crisis* (London: Allen Lane, 1992), 244.

40. Yeltsin, *Zapiski*, 236.

41. *Chas pik*, 26 October 1992.

42. *Current Digest*, 16 December 1992, 27.

43. Yeltsin, *Zapiski*, 236.

Select Bibliography

Akhiezer, A. S. *Rossiia: Kritika istoricheskogo opyta.* 3 vols. Moscow: Izdatel'stvo FO SSSR, 1991.

Aksiutin, Iu. V., ed. *Nikita Sergeevich Khrushchev. Materialy k biografii.* Moscow: Politizdat, 1989.

Alekseev, A. N., ed. *Ozhidali li peremeny?* 2 vols. Moscow: Institut sotsiologii AN SSSR, 1991.

Askol'dova, C. A., et al. *Iz glubiny.* Moscow: Izdatel'stvo moskovskogo universiteta, 1990 [originally published 1918].

Berdyaev, Nicholas. *The Russian Idea.* New York: Macmillan, 1948.

Berdiaev, N., et al. *Vekhi. Sbornik statei o russkoi intelligentsii.* Moscow: Novoe vremia, 1990 [originally published 1909].

Bordiugov, Gennady, and Vladimir Kozlov. *Istoriia i kon"iunktura.* Moscow: Politizdat, 1992.

Brezhneva, Luba. *The World I Left Behind.* New York: Random House, 1995.

Brumberg, Abraham, ed. *Chronicle of a Revolution.* New York: Pantheon, 1990.

Chamberlin, William Henry. *Soviet Russia: A Living Record and a History.* Boston: Little, Brown, 1933.

Cherniavsky, Michael. *Tsar and People: Studies in Russian Myth.* New Haven: Yale University Press, 1961.

Cohen, Stephen, ed. *An End to Silence: Uncensored Opinion in the Soviet Union.* New York: Norton, 1982.

Dallin, David J. *The Real Soviet Russia.* New Haven: Yale University Press, 1947.

Danilov, V. P. *Rural Russia under the New Regime.* Bloomington: Indiana University Press, 1988.

Desai, Padma. *Perestroika in Perspective.* Princeton: Princeton University Press, 1989.

Dostoyevsky, Fyodor. *The Diary of a Writer.* New York: George Braziller, 1954.

Ehrenburg, Ilya. *People and Life 1891–1921.* New York: Alfred A. Knopf, 1962.

––––––. *Memoirs: 1921–1941.* Cleveland: World, 1963.

––––––. *Post-War Years: 1945–54.* Cleveland: World, 1967.

Eklof, Ben, and Stephen Frank, eds. *The World of the Russian Peasant.* Boston: Unwin Hyman, 1990.

Fedotov, G. P. *The Russian Religious Mind.* Vol. 1. Cambridge: Harvard University Press, 1966.

––––––. *Sud'ba i grekhi Rossii.* 2 vols. St. Petersburg: Sofiia, 1991.

Fitzpatrick, Sheila. *Stalin's Peasants: Resistance and Survival in the Russian Village after Collectivization.* New York: Oxford University Press, 1994.

Gaidar, Egor. *Gosudarstvo i evoliutsiia.* Moscow: Evraziia, 1995.

Gulyga, Arsenii. *Russkaia ideia i ee tvortsy.* Moscow: Soratnik, 1995.

Herzen, Alexander. *My Past and Thoughts.* Berkeley: University of California Press, 1982.

Ilin, M. *New Russia's Primer.* Boston: Houghton Mifflin, 1931.

Isaeva, I. A., ed. *Puti evrazii.* Moscow: Russkaia kniga, 1992.

Kaiser, Robert. *Why Gorbachev Happened.* New York: Simon and Shuster, 1992.

Kas'ianova, K. *O russkom natsional'nom kharaktere.* Moscow: Institut natsional'noi modeli ekonomiki, 1994.

Kirshner, L. A. and S. A. Prokhvatilova, eds. *Svet i teni "velikogo desiatiletiia." N.S. Khrushchev i ego vremia.* Leningrad: Lenizdat, 1989.

Kiselev, G. S. *Tragediia obshchestva i cheloveka.* Moscow: Nauka, 1992.

Knight, Amy. *Beria: Stalin's First Lieutenant.* Princeton: Princeton University Press, 1993.

Kopelev, Lev. *To Be Preserved Forever.* Philadelphia: Lippincott, 1977.

———. *The Education of a True Believer.* New York: Harper & Row, 1980.

———. *Ease My Sorrows.* New York: Random House, 1983.

Kozlov, V. A., ed. *Perestroika i istoricheskii opyt.* Moscow: Mysl', 1989.

———, ed. *Neizvestnaia Rossiia. XX vek.* Moscow: Istoricheskoe nasledie, vol. 1: 1992; vol. 2: 1992; vol. 3: 1993; vol. 4: 1993.

Kurginian, Sergei. *Sed'moi stsenarii.* 3 vols. Moscow: Eksperimental'nyi tvorcheskii tsentr, 1992.

Kuromiya, Hiroaki. *Stalin's Industrial Revolution: Politics and Workers, 1928–1932.* Cambridge: Cambridge University Press, 1988.

Lazarev, Vladimir, ed. *Chto s nami proiskhodit.* Moscow: Sovremennik, 1989.

Leatherbarrow, W. J., and D. C. Offord, eds. *A Documentary History of Russian Thought.* Ann Arbor: Ardis, 1987.

Lewin, Moshe. *Political Undercurrents in Soviet Economic Debates.* Princeton: Princeton University Press, 1974.

———. *The Making of the Soviet System.* New York: Pantheon, 1985.

———. *The Gorbachev Phenomenon.* Berkeley: University of California Press, 1988.

Ligachev, Yegor. *Inside Gorbachev's Kremlin.* New York: Pantheon, 1993.

Lotman, Iu. M. *Kul'tura i vzryv.* Moscow: Gnozis, 1992.

McDaniel, Tim. *Autocracy, Capitalism, and Revolution in Russia.* Berkeley: University of California Press, 1988.

———. *Autocracy, Modernization, and Revolution in Russia and Iran.* Princeton: Princeton University Press, 1991.

Maslin, M. A., ed. *Russkaia ideia.* Moscow: Respublika, 1992.

Meerson-Aksenov, Michael, and Boris Shragin, eds. *The Political, Social and Religious Thought of Russian "Samizdat"—an Anthology.* Belmont, Mass.: Nordland, 1977.

Molotov Remembers. Chicago: Ivan Dee, 1993.

Piskunov, V. M., ed. *Russkaia ideia.* 2 vols. Moscow: Iskusstvo, 1994.

Platonov, S. *Posle kommunizma.* Moscow: Molodaia gvardiia, 1991.

Popov, Nikolai. *The Russian People Speak: Democracy at the Crossroads.* Syracuse: Syracuse University Press, 1995.

Protashchik, A. A., ed. *Cherez ternii.* Moscow: Progress, 1991.

Raeff, Marc. *The Well-Ordered Police State.* New Haven: Yale University Press, 1983.

———. *Understanding Imperial Russia.* New York: Columbia University Press, 1984.

———, ed. *Russian Intellectual History: An Anthology.* New Jersey: Humanities Press, 1978.

Scott, John. *Behind the Urals.* Bloomington: Indiana University Press, 1989 [originally published 1942].

Shragin, Boris. *The Challenge of the Spirit.* New York: Alfred A. Knopf, 1978.

Sinyavsky, Andrei. *Soviet Civilization: A Cultural History.* New York: Little, Brown, 1990.

Solzhenitsyn, Aleksander. *The Gulag Archipelago.* New York: Harper & Row, vol. 1: 1973; vol. 2: 1974; vol. 3: 1978.

————, ed. *From Under the Rubble.* Chicago: Regnery Gateway, 1981.

Timasheff, Nicholas S. *The Great Retreat: The Growth and Decline of Communism in Russia.* New York: E.P. Dutton, 1946.

Tsipko, Alexander. *Is Stalinism Really Dead?* San Francisco: Harper & Row, 1990.

Tucker, Robert. *Stalin in Power.* New York: Norton, 1990.

————, ed. *Stalinism: Essays in Historical Interpretation.* New York: Norton, 1977.

Venturi, Franco. *Roots of Revolution: A History of the Populist and Socialist Movements in Nineteenth-Century Russia.* New York: Alfred A. Knopf, 1960.

Verner, Andrew. *The Crisis of Russian Autocracy: Nicholas II and the 1905 Revolution.* Princeton: Princeton University Press, 1990.

Voinovich, Vladimir. *The Anti-Soviet Soviet Union.* San Diego: Harcourt Brace Jovanovich, 1986.

Vyshinsky, M. P., ed. *Pravo i vlast'.* Moscow: Progress, 1990.

Yeltsin, Boris. *Against the Grain.* New York: Summit Books, 1990.

————. *Zapiski prezidenta.* Moscow: Ogonyok, 1994.

Index